Georg Lukács

Georg Lukács

by

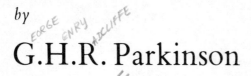

G.H.R. Parkinson

Professor of Philosophy
University of Reading

Routledge & Kegan Paul
London, Henley and Boston

First published in 1977
by Routledge & Kegan Paul Ltd
39 Store Street,
London WC1E 7DD,
Broadway House,
Newtown Road,
Henley-on-Thames,
Oxon RG9 1EN and
9 Park Street,
Boston, Mass. 02108, USA
Set in Bembo by Computacomp (UK) Ltd
Fort William
and printed in Great Britain by
Lowe & Brydone Printers Ltd
Thetford, Norfolk

British Library Cataloguing in Publication Data

Parkinson, George Henry Radcliffe,

George Lukács.
1. Lukács György
199'.439   B4815.L84   77-30010

ISBN 0-7100-8678-4

Contents

Preface

This book is an expository and not a critical study. It tries to give an outline of Lukács' views and to say how they are related to the relevant cultural traditions of his epoch; it does not comment on the rightness or wrongness of those views. This absence of criticism may be seen as a defect, but I believe that there is a place for a purely expository book about Lukács. It is a commonplace maxim (though one that is not always followed with any determination) that one should try to understand what a writer's views are before one criticises them. In some cases, and Lukács' is one of them, the achievement of such understanding is not easy, and the expositor performs a useful task. Second, Lukács was a systematic writer, and it may be that once a writer's system is set out, with its assumptions made explicit and the links between propositions made clear, defects in the system can be seen more easily.

I have said that to understand Lukács' work is not easy. The reader is faced with difficulties of two kinds. The works of Lukács' earlier years are often obscure in style; some of his earliest writings are almost prose poems, and his most famous book, *History and Class Consciousness*, is heavily impregnated with the language and thought of one of the most difficult of philosophers, Hegel. Lukács' later works are written in a plainer and clearer style, but even here the reader is faced with difficulties. These spring from the sheer bulk and detail of Lukács' writings, which are such as often to obscure the overall structure of his thought. Any attempt at a concise account of this structure must omit a great deal, and it may sometimes be thought that what has been omitted is of major importance, or that what has been included is comparatively unimportant. But it is hoped that, whatever its defects, the book will give some idea of the range of Lukács' thought, and that it will make the reader want to explore Lukács for himself.

To help those readers who will want to use this book as an aid to the further study of Lukács, I have supplied extensive notes, most of which consist of textual references. Readers who are concerned only to get to know the main lines of Lukács' thought may safely ignore them. Translations of the passages from Lukács quoted in the course of the book are my own. This is primarily to secure consistency in the rendering of Lukács' technical terms; it does not necessarily imply dissatisfaction with existing English translations, many of which are good and some of which are excellent.

G.H.R.P.

I

Lukács' Life and Times

I

There is general agreement that Georg Lukács is one of the most important Marxist critics and philosophers of this century. His views have been energetically defended, and as energetically — and perhaps more often — attacked. The aim of this book is neither to attack Lukács nor to defend him, but to contribute to an understanding of him by stating clearly what his ideas were and how they developed.

Lukács would have said that if any writer is to be understood he must be placed within his historical and social context, and any general study of Lukács must take this as its first task. He was born in Budapest on 13 April 1885, the second son of József Lukács, a wealthy banker. His parents named him 'György', but it is now more usual to refer to him by the German name 'Georg'. This practice has more to recommend it than mere convenience. The fact is that Lukács was permeated with the German language and with German culture. His father had changed his name from the German Löwinger to the Hungarian Lukács; his mother, whose maiden name was Wertheimer, was brought up in Vienna and had to learn Hungarian after her marriage.[1] The family language, then, was German, and most of Lukács' books were originally written in German — indeed, he is reported as saying that he could not write philosophy in Hungarian.[2] Yet when all this has been said, it has to be considered that Lukács regarded himself as a Hungarian,[3] and that he was, after all, born and brought up in the capital of Hungary. If he is to be understood, then, he must first of all be placed within the context of the Hungary of his time.

The Hungary in which Lukács grew up was still part of the dual monarchy of Austria and Hungary, with a king who resided in Vienna and a Parliament situated in Budapest. Liberal ideals were widely professed, but the franchise was very restricted and the government looked to the interests of relatively few. The few consisted of aristocrats, who owned enormous estates, and a class of lesser nobility known as 'gentry', who constituted a bureaucracy. The government also looked after the interests of a growing, and largely Jewish, middle class. One of these middle-class Jews was Lukács' father, who rose from humble origins to be Managing Director of the Hungarian General Credit Bank, and who was ennobled by the government for his services. As might be expected, the rise of a middle class was accompanied by a rapid growth of industry. In 1900, there were in Hungary about 300,000 industrial workers out of a total population of some 20 million; by 1910, the number of industrial workers had risen to over 500,000. But the economy of the country was still predominantly agrarian, with about 3,800,000 agricultural workers at the turn of the century.

Aristocracy and gentry were intensely nationalist, and their attitudes were shared by many of the middle class. His father's business activities brought the young Lukács into contact with attitudes of this kind; he rejected them entirely and (as he said later) from an early age felt strongly opposed to 'the whole of official Hungary'.[4] In this, of course, he was not alone. Aristocratic and middle-class values were challenged by, among others, the Hungarian Social Democratic Party. This small party — before 1914 its membership did not exceed 50,000 — disseminated the ideas of Marx and Engels, but it was reformist rather than revolutionary, concentrating on demands for higher wages and for the reform of the suffrage. Much more important in the history of the young Lukács, however, were some of the intellectual journals of the period, which were tied to no political party. One such journal was *Nyugat* (*West*), a literary periodical founded in 1908. Lukács contributed regularly to this journal between 1908 and 1917, and several of the articles which were later to be collected in his book *The Soul and the Forms* were first published here. As its title suggests, *Nyugat* was opposed to Hungarian chauvinism and was in favour of an outward-looking, European Hungary. It attacked everything that was old-fashioned in art, but not all its contributors had radical political views; some, indeed, inclined to liberal conservatism. But two at least were radicals, and they were two of the greatest figures in modern Hungarian literature — the novelist Zsigmond Móricz and the poet Endre Ady. Lukács said later that the poems of Ady — poems, not of reconciliation with reality, but of protest against it — had a decisive effect on him.[5] Another important journal in the life of the young Lukács was *Huszadik Század* (*Twentieth Century*), founded in 1900 and soon adopted as its periodical by the Social Sciences Society, a group which included both liberals and socialists. Many of Lukács' early papers were to appear in *Huszadik Század* between 1906 and 1918.

Such was the Hungarian milieu within which Lukács grew up. He studied jurisprudence at the University of Budapest between 1902 and 1906; whilst an undergraduate he became deeply involved with the stage, writing plays (which he later destroyed) and helping to found a theatre group, the Thalia, whose aim was to bring modern drama to the working class.[6] But Hungary was not wide enough to satisfy Lukács, and from 1906 onwards he began to spend a good deal of time in study abroad. Though his first degree was in jurisprudence, the course was not of his own choice, but had been followed in accordance with his father's wishes; his real interests were in sociology and philosophy, particularly aesthetics. The two chief figures in German sociology in the first decade of this century were Georg Simmel and Max Weber. Simmel taught in Berlin, and it was in Berlin, during 1906-7, that Lukács wrote in Hungarian a draft of his first book, *A History of the Development of Modern Drama*.[7] The book places modern drama within the context of a sociological theory, and although Lukács had not yet attended Simmel's lectures and seminars — that was to happen in 1909-10 — the theory is that of Simmel. Though not a Marxist, Simmel adapted some of Marx's ideas to his own system,[8] and it will be seen later (chapter 3) that his influence can be found in Lukács' first important Marxist work.

Lukács met the other great German sociologist of the time, Max Weber, in Heidelberg, where he stayed from 1912 to 1915. But it was not primarily his interest in sociology that took him there, but his interest in philosophy. At this period, the dominant school in German philosophy was the neo-Kantian school, a number of philosophers who tried to adapt the ideas of Kant (1724-1804) to the solution of philosophical problems posed by the rapid expansion of the natural sciences and the rise of the social sciences during the nineteenth century. Lukács had already felt the influence of their ideas, which can be traced in his first important book, *Die Seele und die Formen* (*The Soul and the Forms*), published in Hungarian in 1910 and in an enlarged German version in 1911.[9] The neo-Kantian school had two main centres, one in Marburg and the other in Heidelberg. The Marburg school, whose main representatives were Natorp and Cohen, concentrated on the philosophy of the natural sciences; the Heidelberg or 'South-Western' school, whose leaders were Windelband and Rickert, concentrated on the philosophy of history. In view of Lukács' interest in the social sciences, it is not surprising that he should have chosen to study in Heidelberg. Here, he attended the lectures of Windelband and Rickert, and also formed a friendship with a young neo-Kantian philosopher, Emil Lask, whose ideas were to have an influence on his Marxism.

In Heidelberg, Lukács worked on problems of aesthetics, and completed in 1914 a draft of *The Philosophy of Art*, which he had begun three years previously. But his views on philosophy were changing, and he abandoned *The Philosophy of Art* and began in 1915 a draft of a completely new work, which he referred to as the *Aesthetics*. What had occurred between the two drafts was the writing, in the winter of 1914-15, of *Die Theorie des Romans* (*The Theory of the Novel*). In this work, which was first published in 1916, Lukács began to move away from the philosophy of Kant and towards that of Hegel.[10] A revival of interest in the philosophy of Hegel had been stimulated by Wilhelm Dilthey, whose book on Hegel's youth had been published in 1906. Dilthey himself was no Hegelian but, like Hegel, he was deeply concerned with history, and the ideas of the school of thought with which he is associated[11] can also be traced in *The Theory of the Novel*.

The book was written in a mood of acute depression, occasioned by the First World War. Lukács regarded the prospect of ultimate victory by Germany as a nightmare; but, as he said later, if Germany were defeated, 'then the question arose: who would save us from Western civilisation?'[12] News of the Russian October Revolution of 1917 did something to rouse Lukács from his despair,[13] but he did not immediately take the decisive step of becoming a Communist.

II

Lukács' conversion to communism occurred soon after the end of the war.[14] The collapse of the Habsburg regime after the defeat of the

Central powers was followed on 16 November 1918 by the establishment of a republic in Hungary, with the former opposition leader Mihály Károlyi at its head. On the next day the Communist Béla Kun and some of his comrades arrived in Budapest after captivity in Russia, with the aim of organising a Communist Party. On 24 November 1918, the Communist Party of Hungary was established; Lukács joined it on 2 December. His conversion appeared to be sudden, and surprised his friends; as one of them[15] put it, 'Between one Sunday and the next, Saul became Paul.' But although sudden, the decision had not been an easy one. Shortly before joining the Communist Party Lukács wrote an article entitled 'Bolshevism as a moral problem',[16] in which he said that a choice had to be made between Communism and Social Democracy, and that this constituted a moral dilemma. To work with the Social Democrats meant working with classes and parties which did not sympathise with the Social Democratic aim of the end of class oppression. The Communists shared the aims of the Social Democrats, and were free from the need to compromise in this way. But to join them meant an acceptance of the view that the end justifies the means, it meant opting for terrorism rather than for true democracy. Such were the two horns of the dilemma, and Lukács said that the choice between them was entirely a matter of faith. When he wrote this article, Lukács believed that good could not come from evil; that a man could not (as Dostoevsky put it in *Crime and Punishment*) lie his way through to the truth, and for this reason he rejected communism. Soon afterwards, rejection was followed by acceptance, but it would be wrong to say that Lukács the Communist came to believe that the end justifies the means. In 'Tactics and Ethics' (a pamphlet written after December 1918, but before the establishment of the Hungarian Soviet Republic in March 1919) Lukács argued that situations arise in which it is impossible to act without incurring guilt, and that the revolutionary finds himself in just such situations.[17]

The reasons for Lukács' conversion to Communism were complex. There was the intellectual conviction that Marxism (which he had studied intermittently since 1902) was true; but this was not all. Lukács said later[18] that his motives were ethical, and this is borne out by the titles of many of his earliest works as a Marxist — titles such as 'The Moral Basis of Communism' (1919), 'Tactics and Ethics' (1919), 'The Role of Morality in Communist Production'

5

(1919) and 'The Moral Mission of the Communist Party' (1920). The last of these gives a clear indication of some of Lukács' motives for becoming a Communist; in it,[19] he speaks of the Party's self-discipline, of its ideals of brotherhood, true solidarity, and self-sacrifice. To these motives may be added what Lukács later called[20] the 'disdainful hatred' which he had felt since his youth for capitalist life.

The Károlyi government tried to follow a pro-Entente policy, but the Entente took the view that Hungary should pay for having sided with Germany, and insisted on a drastic contraction of its frontiers. After what was in effect an ultimatum delivered to Hungary on 20 March 1919 — the so-called 'Vyx note' — the Károlyi government, its pro-Entente policy in ruins, resigned. The Social Democrats were not strong enough to form a new government, and found themselves compelled to negotiate with the Communists. An agreement between them was signed on 21 March; a new government was formed, and a Hungarian Soviet Republic was proclaimed.

In the new government, Communists were often given posts which were nominally inferior to those held by Social Democrats. Lukács, for example, was made Deputy Commissar for Public Education, the Commissar being Zsigmond Kunfi, previously the editor of the Social Democratic Party's theoretical journal *Socialism*. But it was generally believed that, whatever their official position might be, the Communists were in control; this was certainly the view of Kunfi, who said that the Social Democrats' agreement of 21 March was a capitulation to the Communists.[21] The next few months were a period of frenzied activity for Lukács. He embarked on an extensive programme of educational re-organisation, and he also saw service on the Eastern front as Political Commissar of the 5th Division, which was facing an invading Rumanian force. But the Hungarian Soviet Republic lasted only 133 days. Its armies had some successes on the Northern front against the Czechs, but they were unable to halt an advance on Budapest by the Rumanians. On 1 August, the Hungarian Soviet Republic came to an end, shortly to be followed by a right-wing regime under Admiral Horthy. Lukács stayed in Hungary during August and September, carrying out illegal work for the Communists, but had to be smuggled out of the country at the end of September.

He moved to Vienna, where many other Hungarian Communists

had taken refuge, and stayed there until 1929. During this period, he seems to have been isolated from the mainstream of Viennese cultural life. As a condition of staying in Vienna, the Hungarian refugees were obliged not to enter too closely into Austrian affairs, and in any case Lukács was very much concerned at this time with the internal politics of the Hungarian Communist Party.[22] Though defeated, the Hungarian Communists were by no means in despair. They believed that the great revolutionary wave had not been broken by recent events in Hungary, and that it would soon sweep the whole world, or at any rate the whole of Europe, to Socialism. This mood of 'messianic utopianism', as Lukács called it later,[23] was expressed by the journal *Kommunismus* (*Communism*), of which Lukács was an editor. The journal, which lasted only from 1920 to 1921, followed the line of the extreme left wing, and proclaimed a total break with all institutions which stemmed from the bourgeois world. So, in his essay 'Zur Frage des Parlamentarismus'[24] ('On the question of Parliamentarism': *Kommunismus*, 1920), Lukács said that Communists should not participate in bourgeois parliaments — a thesis which Lenin criticised severely in the same year in his 'Left-Wing Communism: an infantile disorder'. According to Lukács, the same messianic utopianism was expressed by his book *Geschichte und Klassenbewusstsein* (*History and Class Consciousness*), which was published in Berlin in 1923, and which he later regarded as summing up and concluding that period of his development that began with the last years of the war.[25]

III

The book had a great impact on Communist circles, though hardly of the kind that Lukács would have wished.[26] It met with some support from Lukács' friends and acquaintances, in particular from the philosopher Ernst Bloch, whom Lukács had first met when a student in Germany, and József Révai, one of the first members of the Hungarian Communist Party.[27] But much more powerful figures spoke against it, among them the influential Russian philosopher Deborin and, most important, Zinoviev. At that time, Zinoviev was head of the Communist International and one of the group of three who controlled the USSR immediately after the death of Lenin. At the 5th World Congress of the International, June-July 1924, he launched an attack on 'ultra-leftism', and in the course of it condemned *History and Class Consciousness* as 'revisionist', offering a watered-down Marxism of a kind damaging to the Communist cause.[28] But although Zinoviev was a formidable adversary he did not have the power that Stalin later possessed, and there was no immediate and overwhelming pressure on Lukács to recant. Lukács did not reply to the attacks on the book, but occasional references to the work in essays published in 1925 and 1926[29] indicate that he did not immediately repudiate it; repudiation was to come later.

Between the publication of *History and Class Consciousness* in 1923 and the end of his stay in Vienna in 1929 Lukács published relatively few works, and these were largely *pièces d'occasion*. The most important are a study of Lenin which appeared in 1924, and two substantial reviews of new editions of works by contemporaries of Marx — the Social Democrat Ferdinand Lassalle (1925) and the philosopher Moses Hess (1926). The explanation of the uncharacteristic sparseness of Lukács' productions during this period is that he was very much occupied with party politics. The exiled Hungarian Communists had formed two groups. One of these was based on Moscow and was led by Béla Kun, who had become a high official of the Comintern in 1921 and who had Zinoviev's support. The other group was based on Vienna and Berlin and was led by Jenö Landler, a member of the Hungarian Communist government of 1919 and a former trade-union leader. Lukács saw Kun as trying to impose bureaucratic rule on the Party and, together with Révai and others, joined the Landler group in opposing this.

Much of the struggle between the Kun and Landler groups is of no great importance for the student of Lukács' thought; however, in the year 1928 events took a critical turn for Lukács. A Congress of the Hungarian Communist Party was to be held in 1929, and in 1928 Lukács began to prepare the political theses for it. These — known as the 'Blum theses', after the pseudonym that Lukács used at the time[30] — followed the ideas of Landler, who died in the same year. They concerned the form of government towards which the Party should work. Lukács argued that conditions in Hungary made it impossible to move directly from the Horthy regime to a soviet republic, based on the dictatorship of the proletariat; instead, the Party should aim at a democratic dictatorship of workers and peasants. These proposals seemed wildly paradoxical to Lukács' fellow-Communists. The Kun group denounced them as 'opportunist', and Lukács' own group gave only lukewarm support. Learning that Kun was

8

planning to have him expelled from the Party, Lukács took back what he had said, making a public self-criticism in 1929. He also underwent a private self-criticism, of a different kind. He came to the conclusion that if he was clearly in the right, as he believed, and yet was unable to persuade others of the rightness of his policy, there must be something seriously lacking in his capacity for practical politics. He therefore decided to retire from the political scene and concentrate again on theoretical matters.

Lukács said later that a fundamental change in his outlook underlay the Blum theses, and because of this he came to regard 1928 as marking the end of his *Lehrjahre*, his years of apprenticeship in Marxism. The change in outlook is not obvious from the theses themselves, but Lukács later described it as follows. First, he was beginning to overcome the dualism that had characterised his thought since the last years of the war, by which he seems to mean a dualism between revolutionary good and bourgeois evil.[31] Second, he was beginning to overcome the abstractness of his earlier views, and 'for the first time took his cue from reality itself'.[32]

IV

The three phases distinguished so far within Lukács' intellectual life — the pre-Marxist phase, ending in 1919; the 'messianic' phase, ending in 1923; and the transitional phase, ending in 1928 — are those recognised by Lukács himself. It is unlikely that Lukács would have recognised any further divisions within the remainder of his intellectual life; he clearly believed that after 1928 his approach was the right one and that what remained was a matter of following this approach. However, the years between the Blum theses and his death can conveniently be divided into three further phases, the criteria used being political rather than intellectual. Viewed in this way, the fourth phase of Lukács' life may be taken to be the period between 1929 and his return to Hungary from exile in 1945. A fifth phase may be recognised between 1945 and 1956, which saw Lukács' participation in the revolution of 1956 and a further exile from Hungary; the sixth and last phase covers the period from his return from exile in 1957 until his death in 1971.

Lukács left Vienna in 1929[33] and next year went to the Marx-Engels Institute in Moscow, where he was able to study the recently edited text of Marx's *Economic and Philosophic Manuscripts of 1844*. He

9

said later that the reading of this work — now famous for its views about alienation — enabled him to sweep aside the 'idealist prejudices' of *History Class Consciousness*. He also made the acquaintance of Mikhail Lifschitz, a student of the aesthetics and literary criticism of Marx and Engels, and began to turn his attention again to problems of aesthetics. He had abandoned the Heidelberg *Aesthetics* in 1918; now he began to consider the subject from a new, Marxist angle.

In the summer of 1931 Lukács went to Berlin, where he wrote some of his first articles as a Marxist literary critic. There had been established in Germany in 1928 a 'League of Proletarian Revolutionary Writers', whose organ was the journal *Die Linkskurve* (*Left Curve*), founded in 1929. In the pages of this journal, Lukács said what proletarian literature should be, and criticised the proletarian novelists Willi Bredel and Ernst Ottwalt. Though never the editor of *Die Linkskurve*, Lukács gradually came to dominate the journal, and in the second half of 1932 he used its pages to elaborate his literary theory in a number of important articles, 'Tendenz oder Parteilichkeit?' ('Tendentiousness or spirit of party?'), 'Reportage oder Gestaltung?' ('Reportage or creative shaping?') and 'Aus der Not eine Tugend' ('A virtue from necessity').

When Hitler became Chancellor of Germany in January 1933 *Die Linkskurve* ceased publication and Lukács returned to Moscow, where he was to stay until the end of the Second World War. In 1933 he published in Moscow, in a German language journal, an autobiographical sketch entitled 'Mein Weg zu Marx' ('My road to Marx'). In this, he sharply criticised *History and Class Consciousness*. He said that the book's approach to its problems was that of philosophical idealism, not of materialism; it was also tainted with 'subjectivist activism', which means roughly that it assumed that revolutionary fervour could achieve anything, irrespective of social conditions. In 1934, in the Russian language journal *Under the Banner of Marxism*, he criticised the work still more severely, saying[34] that the work's idealism was not only theoretically false but also practically dangerous. Any concession to idealism, he said, was a concession to Fascism. He ascribed his new insight into his errors to his practical party work and to his study of the works of Lenin and Stalin, and he said that 'with the help of the Comintern, of the All-Union Communist Party and of its leader, Comrade Stalin', all sections of the Communist International would henceforth struggle against deviations from true Marxism-Leninism.

From what Lukács said later, it is now clear that his motives in making this recantation were complex. First, he felt that it was all-important that socialism should continue to exist, and this, in conditions that had become much more difficult for socialism, meant making concessions to the Communist Party of the Soviet Union and to its leader, Stalin. Even if opposition to Stalin had been possible at this time it would have been wrong, as giving moral support to Fascism. Second, Lukács thought that his condemnation of the views of *History and Class Consciousness* — views which, in any case, he had ceased to hold — was a small price to pay for the ability to write and publish his literary criticism. On the whole he avoided direct confrontation with Russian critics — the controversies in which he was involved during his Moscow stay were mainly with fellow emigrants, such as his old friend Ernst Bloch and the novelist Anna Seghers[35] — but he claimed later that he was able to wage a kind of guerilla warfare on behalf of his own ideas. He did this by producing works which contained the requisite quotations from Stalin but which, at the same time, put forward views which were by no means those of Stalinist orthodoxy.

These views were expressed in articles which appeared in a number of journals published in Moscow,[36] and which formed the basis of many of the books of literary criticism which Lukács published in the years immediately following the end of the war — books such as *Goethe und seine Zeit* (*Goethe and his Age*: 1947), *Essays über Realismus* (*Essays on Realism*: 1948), *Schicksalswende* (*The Turning-Point of Destiny*: 1948), *Der russische Realismus in der Weltliteratur* (*Russian Realism in World Literature*: 1949), *Deutsche Realisten des 19. Jahrhunderts* (*German Realists of the 19th Century*: 1951), *Balzac und der französische Realismus* (*Balzac and French Realism*: 1952) and *Der historische Roman* (*The Historical Novel*: 1955). Besides writing literary criticism during his years in Moscow Lukács was also working on the history of philosophy, and in 1938 he completed his book *Der junge Hegel* (*The Young Hegel*). The book, however, could not be published during the war because it differed from what was then the official Soviet view about Hegel, namely that he was the ideologist of feudal reaction against the French Revolution. After the war this view was abandoned, and Lukács was able to publish his book in 1948.

In the first half of the 1930s the accepted view among

Communists was that Social Democrats were (in Stalin's phrase) the twin brothers of the Fascists. This view changed with the adoption of a policy of co-operation with anti-Fascist parties, the so-called 'Popular Front', given formal approval at the 1935 Congress of the International. The new policy led to an improvement in Lukács' situation, and it was during the Popular Front period that Brecht, who disagreed sharply with Lukács' views as a critic, described his position in Moscow as 'very strong'.[37] But the Popular Front was brought to an end by the Hitler-Stalin pact of 1939, and soon after this the situation worsened for Lukács. *Literary Critic*, the journal through which he was able to reach a Russian audience, ceased publication in 1940, and in 1941 Lukács was put in prison, accused of being a Trotskyite. He spent several months there, and was released only as a result of the personal intervention of Dimitrov, the head of the International at that time.

With the entry of Russia into the war in June 1941 and the considerable initial successes of the invading German armies, opportunities for publication became much more restricted, and Lukács produced very little between 1942 and 1944. At the end of the war he returned to Hungary, arriving in Budapest on 1 August 1945.

V

The Hungarian Communist Party was now under the leadership of Mátyás Rákosi; Kun had been executed in Moscow in November 1939, a victim of a Stalinist purge.[38] The Communists fared badly in the 1945 elections in Hungary, obtaining only 17 per cent of the votes, but they had two major factors in their favour: they had the support of the Soviet occupation forces and they had control of the secret police. As Rákosi declared,[39] 'We held this bureau [the secret police] in our hands since its first day of existence and saw to it that it remained a reliable sharp weapon in the fight for a people's democracy.' So Rákosi was soon able, as he put it, to 'slice off like salami' all parties other than his own. By May 1949 the Communists were able to hold elections on a single-list basis, and a new constitution, dedicated to the building of socialism, was adopted in August.

Rákosi's regime, like that of Stalin in the USSR, was accompanied by political trials and mass arrests. The Roman Catholic leader Cardinal Mindszenty was put on trial early in 1949 and sentenced to life imprisonment; in June of the same year the veteran Communist László Rajk, at that time Minister of Foreign Affairs, was arrested and charged with treason, and after a show trial was sentenced to death on 24 September. It was later admitted that the charges against Rajk were fabricated.[40] Widespread arrests were made throughout Hungary, and it is now known that between 1952 and 1955 (i.e. within four years) 1,136,434 people were denounced and investigated; of these, 516,708 were charged and condemned.[41] To put these figures in their proper perspective, it should be realised that the total population of Hungary during this period did not exceed 10 million in any year.

It is against this background that the first years of Lukács' return to Hungary have to be set. He was made Professor of Aesthetics and the Philosophy of Culture at the University of Budapest; he also became a member of the Hungarian Parliament, the National Assembly, but he did not hold any important post within the Communist Party. In the years immediately following his return his literary activity was intense. He published many articles in the Hungarian press and, as mentioned earlier, began the process of publishing in book form much of the literary criticism that he had published in journals in the USSR; he also published his book on the young Hegel. Besides this, the work known later as *Skizze einer Geschichte der neueren deutschen Literatur* (*Sketch of a History of Modern German Literature*) appeared in two parts in 1945, and in 1947 Lukács published in Hungarian a work on existentialism. This appeared in French in 1948, in which year Lukács also published in Hungarian the first version of his book on Thomas Mann.

In 1949 attacks on Lukács began in the Communist press, the attacks being concentrated on his *Literature and Democracy*, a work in Hungarian which had gone through two editions in 1947 and 1948. The book was first condemned by Lázló Rudas, who had been one of the critics of *History and Class Consciousness* in 1924; he was then joined by Révai, at that time Minister of Culture, and by his deputy Márton Horváth. In the USSR, the novelist and important Party functionary Fadeyev joined in the condemnation of Lukács. There seems to be no reason to connect these attacks with the Rajk trial; rather, they seem connected with the beginning of one-party rule in Hungary in 1949, and the Communist Party's resolve that Hungarian literature should henceforth be in its service. Lukács himself saw the attacks as aimed at his view that the transition to socialism could, and should, be made in a gradual way, founded on persuasion.[42] Lukács escaped lightly; he was not imprisoned, and he was still able to publish in Hungary. However, he decided to withdraw from public life and concentrate on his theoretical work. The first major result of this was the completion in November 1952 of *Die Zerstörung der Vernuft* (*The Destruction of Reason*), a long attack on 'irrationalism' in philosophy in the nineteenth and twentieth centuries; this was first published in 1954.

In March 1953, Stalin died. The new leaders of the Communist Party of the USSR emphasised the importance of collective leadership, and criticised the Hungarian Communist Party for its failures in this respect. As a result, Rákosi lost some of his powers, but he continued to hold the all-important post of First Secretary of the Party. However, the general 'thaw' in the Communist world which followed Stalin's death clearly benefited Lukács. In Hungary, he was honoured by the award of the Kossuth prize in 1955; in East Germany, a *Festschrift* was issued in his honour in the same year, and he became a corresponding member of the German Academy of Sciences in Berlin. He also published in East Germany between 1954 and 1956 a number of important articles on aesthetics, which first appeared in book form in Hungarian in 1957 as *On Speciality as a Category of Aesthetics*. (The book did not appear in its German version, *Über die Besonderheit als Kategorie der Ästhetik*, until 1967.) He also began in 1955 a new work of literary criticism, *Wider den missverstandenen Realismus* (translated into English as *The Meaning of Contemporary Realism*), a book which he did not complete until April 1957, after the Hungarian revolution.

At the 20th Congress of the Communist Party of the Soviet Union, in February 1956, Khrushchev delivered his now famous attack on Stalin, and stressed the damage done by his 'cult of personality'. Rákosi could be, and later was, accused of fostering a similar cult,[43] but for the moment he retained his position. But open opposition to his regime was soon widespread. There was opposition from writers such as the poet Zoltán Zelk, the playwright Gyula Háy and the novelist Tibor Déry, and there was opposition from the young. In March 1954 the Communist Party had set up the 'Petöfi Circle', a discussion forum for young people named after the great Hungarian poet who died fighting for his country in 1849. Discussions in the circle, however, did not go as the Party would have liked, many speakers attacking the regime. Lukács spoke in a

debate organised by the circle on 15 June,[44] at which he condemned
the dogmatism of the Stalin era. The circle was suppressed at the end
of June, but next month the Central Committee of the Party relieved
Rákosi of his post as First Secretary.

This did not end the opposition to the Party's rule, and on 23
October 1956 the Hungarian revolution began. During the 13 days
that the revolution lasted, Lukács held important posts in both the
Party and the government, but he was not one of the real
protagonists of the revolution. He was, after all, over 70 years old,
and it seems fair to say that on the whole he lent his prestige to the
policies of others rather than took a decisive part in directing policy.
Consequently, his part in the revolution can be described briefly. He
was elected to the Central Committee of the Party on 24 October,
and on 27 October he was made Minister of Culture in Imre Nagy's
government. On 30 October he was elected to the Provisional
Executive Committee which was set up to organise a new
Hungarian Communist Party. He was not, however, included in the
new government set up by Nagy on 3 November, perhaps because of
his opposition to Nagy's withdrawal of Hungary from the Warsaw
Pact on 1 November. On the suppression of the revolution by Soviet
forces on 4 November he took refuge, with others who had been
leaders of the revolution, in the Yugoslav embassy. On leaving the
embassy he was arrested and deported to Rumania.

VI

Lukács was allowed to return to Budapest in April 1957.[45] Many
leading figures in the revolution — among them Déry, Háy and Zelk
— were punished by imprisonment; the execution of Nagy was
announced later, on 17 June 1958. Lukács was relatively fortunate;
he merely ceased to be a professor at the University of Budapest. He
was not expelled from the Party, but when the Party was re-formed
early in 1957, its name being changed from the Hungarian Working
People's Party to the Hungarian Socialist Workers' Party, Lukács
was one of the many who did not re-apply for membership.[46]

As part of a general counter-attack on the ideas that led up to the
events of 23 October 1956, Lukács was attacked repeatedly in the
Communist press.[47] In 1960 some of these attacks, together with
some earlier ones, were collected in a volume entitled *Georg Lukács
und der Revisionismus* (*Georg Lukács and Revisionism*), published in

East Berlin by the Aufbau Verlag, which had published Lukács' works in German since the war. From 1961 onwards, Lukács' German works have been issued by a West German publisher.

Pressure on the revolutionaries of 1956 gradually eased. An amnesty was granted to some of them on 4 April 1960 (the anniversary of the liberation of Hungary during the Second World War), and on 1 January 1962 János Kádár, First Secretary of the Communist Party, announced a more liberal policy with the slogan 'He who is not against us is with us'. There was a further amnesty on 4 April 1963. However, attacks on Lukács continued for a time. In December 1963 and again in March 1964 he was criticised for advocating a policy of universal democracy, as opposed to the official doctrines of class struggle and proletarian revolution. Only in 1965 was he taken back into favour, when the Hungarian Academy of Sciences compiled a bibliography of his works and a translation of a chapter from *The Young Hegel* was published in *The Hungarian Review of Philosophy*.[48] A few years later, Lukács rejoined the Communist Party.

In the years following 1957 Lukács concentrated on the writing of large-scale works which he had long planned. He published in 1963 *Die Eigenart des Ästhetischen* (*The Specific Nature of the Aesthetic*), a massive two-volume work which was intended as only the first part of his complete aesthetics, but which was in fact the only part that he wrote. Work on the remaining parts was put aside so that Lukács could proceed with another large-scale project that he had in mind, a book on Marxist ethics. However, it became clear to him[49] that before he could write this he must turn his attention to another branch of philosophy and write a Marxist work about ontology, or more exactly about the ontology of social existence. This project occupied Lukács for the rest of his life, and although the book on ethics was never written, Lukács completed (though he did not live to publish) two books on ontology. The first and much the longer of these was *Zur Ontologie des gesellschaftlichen Seins* (*The Ontology of Social Existence*). This was a two-part work, the first part being historical and the second theoretical, and Lukács came to think that the form of the book obscured what he wanted to say. So he began in 1969 the writing of another book, *Prolegomena zur Ontologie des gesellschaftlichen Seins* (*Prolegomena to an Ontology of Social Existence*), which he left complete at his death. Besides these major works, Lukács wrote many shorter works during this last period, among them two important articles on Solzhenitsyn, published in book form in 1970; he also wrote valuable prefaces to some of his books that were re-issued. One such preface, dated July 1962, was to *The Theory of the Novel*; still more important was a long preface, dated March 1967, to the second volume of his collected works, which contains *History and Class Consciousness*. In the last few years of his life Lukács gave a large number of interviews; of these, the most substantial was one granted to a number of West German writers, H. H. Holz, L. Kofler and W. Abendroth, published in 1967 as *Gespräche mit Georg Lukács* (*Conversations with Georg Lukács*), edited by T. Pinkus.

Lukács died on 4 June 1971; he was working on his books almost to the very end.

VII

It will be clear that Lukács' interests were wide and his publications very many. In an introduction to his work, it is simply not possible to consider all his writings; nor, indeed, is it desirable even to attempt it — to do so would involve the risk of not seeing the wood for the trees. Discussion, then, must be restricted to his most important works. In discussing these, a straightforwardly chronological sequence can be followed without difficulty as far as *History and Class Consciousness*. Chapter 2, then, will consider Lukács' pre-Marxist criticism, as contained in *The Soul and the Forms* and *The Theory of the Novel*, and chapter 3 will discuss *History and Class Consciousness*. After this, Lukács' work is best divided in accordance with the main topics that concerned him — the history of philosophy, Marxist criticism, aesthetics, and the ontology of social existence. As *History and Class Consciousness* contains an important discussion of the history of philosophy, it will be convenient to consider this topic in chapter 4, immediately after *History and Class Consciousness*. Lukács' Marxist criticism and his aesthetics are closely related, the latter being in effect the theory of the criticism. It will be best to discuss the criticism before its theory; chapters 5-6 will therefore be devoted to Lukács' Marxist criticism, and chapter 7 to his aesthetics. The ontology of social existence will be considered last in chapter 8.

Before going further, the reader without a knowledge of German may find it useful to know what help he may expect in the study of Lukács from translations. English translations of Lukács' works have been appearing since 1962 at an average rate of about one a year. Full details are given in the bibliography, but it may be said now that the translations available at present (1976) are heavily weighted towards Lukács' literary criticism. *Soul and Form*, *The Theory of the Novel*, *Goethe and his Age*, *The Historical Novel*, *Studies in European Realism* (which includes essays on Balzac, Tolstoy and Gorky), *The Meaning of Contemporary Realism*, *Essays on Thomas Mann*, *Solzhenitsyn* and *Writer and Critic* (a collection of critical essays, mainly from the 1920s and 1930s) provide the English reader with access to a large part of Lukács' critical work. Lukács' political writings are represented in English by his *Lenin* and by a volume entitled *Political Writings, 1919-29*. Some of Lukács' political writings are also included in a miscellaneous collection entitled *Marxism and Human Liberation*. The theory of politics also forms part of the extremely important *History and Class Consciousness*, of which there is an English translation. Lukács' philosophical writings, however, are still poorly represented in English. Parts of *History and Class Consciousness* are philosophical in nature, as are some of the essays in *Political Writings, 1919-29*; apart from these, however, the only major philosophical work of Lukács at present available in English is *The Young Hegel*.

2

Pre-Marxist Literary Criticism: *The Soul and the Forms* (1911) and *The Theory of the Novel* (1916)

I

Die Seele und die Formen (*The Soul and the Forms*)[1] consists of ten essays, most of which are works of literary criticism, dealing with writers such as Novalis, Theodor Storm, Stefan George and Lawrence Sterne. Seven of the ten had already been published in various journals, and in view of this it is natural to ask whether the book forms a unity. In an introductory essay which he wrote especially for the book, 'On the essence and form of the essay', Lukács poses this very question, and indeed takes the question further. He asks, not only whether these essays constitute a unity, but whether they *can* constitute a unity.

His doubts are connected with the very nature of the essay, as he understands it.[2] When he speaks of 'the essay' here he uses the term in a special sense, such that it covers, not only the essays of Montaigne, but also the writings of the mystics and the dialogues of Plato. What, then, is an essay, as Lukács understands the term? In *The Soul and the Forms*, Lukács tends to equate the essay with the work of criticism (*die Kritik*), and says that for the most part it speaks about pictures, books and ideas. So much is uncontroversial; the problem is, in what precise way it is related to them. There is, says Lukács, a commonly held view that the critic must speak the truth about things, whereas the creative writer (*der Dichter*) is not bound in this way. This contrast he finds too abstract, too sharp. Certainly, the essay is concerned with truth — but in the way that the portrait painter is concerned with truth. If we look at a painting of a landscape, we do not ask if the mountains and rivers are really as they are painted, but in the case of a portrait the question of a likeness always arises. We stand in front of a portrait by Velasquez, say, and we *feel* that it is a likeness. Truly significant portraits give us the life of a man who once really lived, and make us feel that his life really was as the colours and lines of the portrait show. Much the same can be said of the essay. The essay, too, is[3]

> a struggle for truth, for the embodiment of life, which someone has read out of a man, an age, a form; but it depends entirely on the intensity of the work and of the vision, whether we derive from what is written a suggestion of this life.

The difference between the essayist and the creative writer is that the latter gives us a mere illusion of life, and there is no reality against which his creations can be measured. The hero of the essay, on the other hand, was once alive, and his life has to be depicted in a certain way. This life, however, is within the work, just as it is in the case of creative writing.

It is now possible to approach the problem whether the essays that constitute *The Soul and the Forms* have, and can have, a unity. If the question is taken to mean whether they form a complete system, to be judged solely in terms of truth and falsity, the answer is clearly 'No'. On the other hand, Lukács also views the essayist as a kind of John the Baptist, a forerunner, and says that what is to follow him is a great aesthetic system.[4] So it might be said (though Lukács does not say so expressly) that the essays which constitute *The Soul and the Forms* at any rate *point towards* a unity, the unity of the system that is to come.

Lukács' views about the relations between the essay and life reflect a trend of thought, widespread when he wrote, which it is usual to call *Lebensphilosophie*. This 'life-philosophy' was not the doctrine of a specific philosophical school, but was more of a current or trend of thought. It was, Lukács said later,[5] the dominant view among German philosophers of many schools during the period of the German empire, and it also had representatives elsewhere, such as Bergson in France. It is perhaps in Bergson's *Creative Evolution* (1907) that the main features of life-philosophy can most easily be seen. Bergson argued that we conceive matter by intellect, and life by intuition. Life, however, is what is real; matter is only a fiction created by the intellect for the purposes of action. In other words, the thesis of *Lebensphilosophie* was that reality — that is, life — is to be grasped by intuition, not by reason. It was because of this that when

Lukács made a critical survey of German philosophy some fifty years later in *The Destruction of Reason*, he said that *Lebensphilosophie* was a manifestation of 'irrationalism'. It may seem that the charge of irrationalism could also be brought against *The Soul and the Forms*. But this would hardly be just. It is true that Lukács held that the essay is a valid literary form, that it incorporates life, and that it is closely connected with feeling or experience; nevertheless, he did not suggest that only life is real, or that feeling is superior to reason.

II

There is little that can be said about Lukács' essays from the standpoint of their success or failure in incorporating life; the reader either feels the life or he does not. However, the essays also express a number of views to which truth and falsity can be ascribed, and there is much to be said about these. The first and most obvious question is: what are the 'forms' of which Lukács speaks in his title? The superficial answer is that they are that which is the concern of the critic: e.g. literary forms such as the lyric, the idyll, or tragedy.[6] But this at once raises further questions: questions about the way in which the critic is related to these forms, and the forms' precise nature. The first question is answered in Lukács' first essay. The critic's function, he says there, is not just to explain books and pictures. Rather, the critic has experience of the soul-content (*Seelengehalt*) which the forms conceal, and his task is to express this experience.[7] But what, it may be asked, is a form? Lukács answers this question as he makes clearer the nature of the critic's activity. The decisive moment for the critic, he says, is the moment at which feelings and experience obtain a form; it is 'the mystical moment of the union of external and internal, the soul and the form'.[8] Feelings and form, then, are intimately connected, and this connexion is made more explicit in a later essay in the book, a dialogue on Sterne. Here, one of the characters says that 'the form is the raising of ultimate feelings, experienced with the greatest power, to independent significance'.[9] Every such feeling, even that aroused by tragedy, is a feeling of our power and of the richness of the world. The various art forms differ only in that the occasions on which they allow this power to become manifest are different.

It seems, then, to be Lukács' view that the critic gives expression to certain experiences, experiences of the unity that exists between feeling and artistic form. But it must not be supposed that the critic is concerned with pure art, as something isolated from the rest of life. Lukács quotes with approval Matthew Arnold's view that poetry is a 'criticism of life'. The forms with which the critic is concerned become a world-view, a standpoint, and so Lukács can say, when speaking of tragedy, that the form is the highest judge of life. The fact that the critic is concerned with world-views also accounts for another feature of the essay. In every great essayist, Lukács says, there is irony. This is because the essayist is talking about the ultimate questions of life, but in a tone that suggests that he is speaking only of pictures or books.[10]

Lukács adds that the essayist need not discuss works of art; it only happens that the experiences with which he is concerned come to most people through looking at pictures or reading literary works. Plato, however, was an essayist, and he wrote, not about books or pictures, but about a life — the life of Socrates. This was because he was able to use Socrates' fate as a vehicle for his own questions, to use it as 'a springboard to the ultimate'.[11] But not every expression of life can be a form, as is shown by the case of Kierkegaard. Lukács is concerned here, not with Kierkegaard's written works, but with a famous gesture that he made, namely his breaking off relations with his fiancée. Such a gesture, Lukács says, cannot be a form; that is, there is no art of life (*Lebenskunst*). This is because an art must be unambiguous, whereas life is highly ambiguous. Kierkegaard's tragedy was that he wanted to create forms out of life, to live what cannot be lived.[12]

When Lukács wrote *The Soul and the Forms*, he had not yet rejected the neo-Kantianism that was dominant in his intellectual milieu. Nevertheless, the influence of neo-Kantian ideas on the book does not seem great. Indeed, their influence seems to be restricted to the idea that the forms are *a priori*; that is, that they are not extracted from literary works by some process of abstraction, but are in a way prior to these works, eternal entities which are realised more or less adequately in concrete works of art. Looking back in 1962 at the aesthetic theories propounded at the time of *The Soul and the Forms*, Lukács noted how neo-Kantians such as Rickert and his school had created a gap between timeless values and the historical realisation of values.[13] Such a gap is present in *The Soul and the Forms*. It is expressed most clearly in the first essay, where Lukács draws a distinction between poetry and poems, and says that poetry is prior to and greater than individual poems. 'The idea', he says, 'is there before any of its manifestations', [14] and it is the business of the critic to bring to light its *a priori* character. The forms, then, are static and eternal; what vary are the temporal conditions in which they are manifested. These temporal conditions may be more or less favourable for the realisation of the forms — for example, Lukács argues that the soulless nature of the modern world is suitable for a rebirth of tragedy — but the forms themselves do not change.[15]

III

It was said just now that, for Lukács, the form is the highest judge of life. What this means is shown in 'The metaphysics of tragedy', which is the last essay in the book, and also one of the most important. Here, Lukács is not talking about criticism, but is practising it. He begins by observing that some have objected to the drama on the grounds that it creates a vacuum between the characters; its hard lines make rigid the flow of their relations to each other, and so deprive the characters of any real life. Lukács replies that what these critics count as failings are really the virtues of the drama. Life is a mere chaos, in which there are no clear boundaries, and in which nothing completely fulfilled. But into the banality of life of this kind there suddenly enters something disturbing: 'the accident, the great moment, the marvel'.[16] Such a marvel tears all deceptive coverings from the soul, which stands revealed in its naked essence. This unveiling is the work of tragedy, and is also its justification. 'Great moments', then, are fundamental to tragedy; indeed, in another essay in the book Lukács regards them as fundamental to all literary works.[17] What the tragedian has to do is to make such moments visible, immediately experienced.[18]

Lukács relates his views about tragedy to the traditional view that a drama should manifest the three unities of action, time and place. Tragedy, he says, must express time's becoming timeless, and to the extent that the traditional theory of the unity of time means that the tragic is essentially a moment, to that extent it is justifiable.[19] It is true that the moment, which by its nature has no duration that can be experienced, is given a temporal duration on the stage; but this springs from the inadequacy of every attempt at expressing a mystical experience in words. Not that mysticism and the tragic experience are the same. Mystical ecstasy provides an experience of the summit of being, of which tragedy is the form. But in mysticism the summit of being 'disappears in the cloudy heaven of the unity of the All';[20] mysticism destroys all distinctions, and must destroy all forms, since only behind the forms does reality exist for it. But the marvel that tragedy presents is form-creating; its essence is self-knowledge, whereas that of mysticism is the loss of self. The way of the mystic is that of surrender; that of the tragic hero is struggle.

Lukács sums up the difference between tragedy, mysticism and ordinary life by contrasting their attitudes to death.[21] Ordinary life, he says, regards death as something terrifying and senseless; mysticism treats it as something unreal. But for tragedy, death is ever present and ever real, bound up with every tragic event. Lukács adds that the tragic awareness of death is also the awakening of the soul to consciousness, consciousness of itself.

Some critics[22] see in *The Soul and the Forms* a forerunner of modern existentialism, and to support their view they refer in particular to the essay on tragedy. The claim is not easy to assess, because existentialism is more a current of thought than a definite philosophical school. However, one may safely take as typical of existentialism a concern with authentic, as opposed to inauthentic, existence; it is also a fact that at least one existentialist, Heidegger, has related authentic existence to a man's attitude to death. All this is reminiscent of Lukács' essay on tragedy; on the other hand, there is an important difference. For Heidegger,[23] the first step towards authentic existence is a man's recognition of his own mortality. Lukács' tragic hero, too, recognises his mortality, and does not try to hide the fact from himself. But here one must make the obvious point that the tragic hero does not exist; he is a mere fiction. If tragedy is to produce authenticity of life, what it must do is render authentic the lives of its audience. In effect, then, Lukács is preaching a doctrine of salvation through art, a doctrine which can hardly be called typical of existentialism.

IV

It was said in the last chapter that Lukács' next major work, *Die Theorie des Romans* (*The Theory of the Novel*), represents a move from Kant to Hegel. To be more specific, it represents the abandonment of the idea of timeless forms and a move towards what Lukács called 'a historicising of aesthetic categories'.[24] In this work, Lukács regards the novel as a form of what he calls 'the great epic' (*die grosse Epik*); it is, as he puts it, one 'objectification' of the great epic, the other being epic poetry,[25] the epic as distinct from the novel.

Lukács does not begin with a general account of the great epic; instead, he starts with the sub-form of the great epic which appeared first in history, namely the epic. When Lukács speaks of the epic he has in mind primarily the *Iliad* and the *Odyssey*; indeed, he says that strictly speaking, the poems of Homer are the only true epics. The historicisation of aesthetic categories that was mentioned just now is immediately evident in Lukács' treatment of the epic, which he puts in relation to its epoch. It is noteworthy, however, that Lukács does not discuss the social conditions under which the poems were written. Hegel had regarded the various stages of history as so many manifestations of mind, *Geist*; in much the same way, Lukács considers the general intellectual attitudes that are typical of the age of the epic.

The age of the epic, Lukács says,[26] is typified by the fact that it does not yet have any conception of an inner world, or any conception of the soul's search for itself. It is also an age in which the divinity is just as familiar and close to man, and just as incomprehensible, as a father is to a small child. Modern life, at the same time as it has immensely enlarged its world, has also established a gulf between the self and the world, which did not exist in the era of the epic. We have destroyed the meaning of Greek life, which was totality: a totality which was all-inclusive, there being nothing which pointed to a higher reality outside it.[27] In sum, modern man, unlike the man of Homer's epoch, is not at home in the universe; and the literary form which expresses this 'transcendental homelessness' is the novel.[28]

To clarify Lukács' views about the nature of the novel it is necessary to go further into the notion of totality, a notion which plays an important part, not only in *The Theory of the Novel*, but in Lukács' thought in general. In *The Theory of the Novel* a distinction is drawn between the 'extensive totality' of life and the 'intensive totality' of essence. The epic and the novel give form to the extensive totality, the drama gives form to the intensive totality. Here Lukács seems to have in mind some of the things that he said about tragedy in *The Soul and the Forms* — namely, that the chaotic nature of life is alien to the hard lines of the drama, which tries to portray the soul in its bare essence. This, according to Lukács, is why the drama (unlike the epic poem) continues to exist in the modern era. For although meaning is no long immanent in life, essence, which is alien to life, has survived. Needless to say, modern drama is different from that of the ancients; nevertheless, because of its concern with essence, modern drama can still find a world which is all-embracing and self-enclosed, a totality.[29]

After his account of intensive totality, Lukács considers that totality to which the epic and the novel give form; extensive totality. Since he was quoted earlier as saying that totality, once the meaning of Greek life, has been destroyed by the modern age, it may be asked what the novel, the distinctive literary form of the modern age, has to do with totality. The answer is that totality remains an aim, an ideal. The novel, Lukács says, is the epic of an age in which the extensive totality of life has ceased to be sensuously given, but which still has a 'disposition towards totality'.[30] Whereas the epic poem gives form to a totality which is self-enclosed, the novel seeks to discover and construct a totality of life that is now hidden. The basic intention of the novel is given objective form in the psychology of its heroes, who are *seekers*. The difference between epic poem and novel can be brought out in another, related way. Lukács, echoing Hegel,[31] says that the hero of the epic is the community. Now, the community is an organic totality, whereas the hero of the novel is an individual, and arises out of modern man's estrangement from the external world. As such, Lukács terms the novel's hero the 'problematic individual'.[32]

The problematic individual is a seeker, and what he seeks is himself; his journey is from captivity in a reality which has no meaning for him towards self-knowledge. But even when the hero has achieved self-knowledge, the distinction between things as they are and things as they ought to be still exists; 'the division between "is" and "ought" is not transcended'.[33] What the hero discovers is that the highest that life can offer is a mere glimpse of meaning. In other words, the novel expresses the insight that meaning can never wholly penetrate reality. This means that one of its typical features must be irony. The irony of the creative writer, Lukács says, is the 'negative mysticism of godless eras', a 'learned ignorance'[34] where meaning is concerned. But there is more to the novel's irony than this. There is in the novel what Lukács calls a 'self-transcendence' (*Selbstaufhebung*) of subjectivity. By this he means that the novelist sees that the distinction between subject and object is abstract and limited, and has a glimpse of a unified world. Lukács is in effect saying that the novelist has some kind of intimation of the Hegelian idea that subject and object are really one — an idea which was to play an important part in his first major work as a Marxist, *History and Class Consciousness* (cf. chapter 3, section IV).

V

This general account of the nature of the novel occupies the first part of *The Theory of the Novel*. In the second part, Lukács divides the novel-form into types, and allocates various novelists to these types. The principle of division that he uses is a simple one. In the modern age, the soul may find itself either narrower or wider than the external world, and these alternatives are expressed in two main types of novel.

The notion that the soul is narrower than the external world is not immediately comprehensible, and may give rise to misunderstanding. Lukács may be thought to mean that the world is too large for the soul in the sense that man feels alone and vulnerable in a vast and complex universe. But aloneness, in the sense of feeling abandoned by God, is typical of the novel-form in general, as Lukács understands it. What he has in mind when he speaks of the narrow soul is a certain manifestation of man's solitude. The narrowness in question is the narrowness of the fanatic, the man so obsessed with an idea that he takes it to be the only reality, the man who is 'maniacally imprisoned in himself'.[35] Such a man thinks that what ought to be, must be; and because reality does not correspond to his demands he thinks that it must be enchanted by evil demons. He feels no doubt or despair; he is an adventurer, who merely acts, and his life as portrayed in a novel is simply a series of adventures that he himself has chosen.

It is not surprising that Lukács should take *Don Quixote* to be the paradigm of this kind of novel. It will be worth while to go into his account of this novel[36] in some detail, both to see Lukács' critical method in action and because, at a time when he had rejected *The Theory of the Novel* as a whole, he regarded its account of *Don Quixote* as one of the better parts of the book. The historicisation of aesthetic categories that was mentioned earlier is at once evident, in that Lukács is not content (as he might have been when writing *The Soul and the Forms*) simply to relate Cervantes' novel to a psychological type; he also tries to place it within the history of the human mind. He begins by considering the novels of chivalry which Cervantes parodied, and the mediaeval epics of chivalry of which these novels were the poor descendants. The mediaeval epics were possible only as long as they could have roots in religion, in 'transcendent being', and the form withered away in the modern age. But the novels of chivalry which replaced the epics were at best mere fairy tales, and at worst were banal and superficial 'light reading'. Cervantes rediscovered the path to the true sources of this type of novel form. Don Quixote's ideal[37] is very clear to him, and he believes in it fanatically; at the same time, it is wholly lacking in any relation to reality. The world has been foresaken by providence, and has become meaningless; man has become a solitary individual, who can find meaning only within his own soul.

This must not be misunderstood. Lukács does not mean that Cervantes was an atheist, living in an atheistic age. On the contrary, he was a faithful Christian living in the epoch of the Counter-Reformation. But this was an age in which religion was already dying, an age of great confusion of values, and what Cervantes showed in his novel was that, in such an age, heroism must become grotesque and faith must become madness.

The adventure novels that followed *Don Quixote* became increasingly trivial, and the novel grew steadily closer to light reading. As the world grew more and more prosaic, the narrowed soul faced a new dilemma: either it must give up all relation to life, or it must cease to be directly rooted in the world of ideals. The first path was chosen by the German classical drama of the late eighteenth and early nineteenth centuries, but as his concern here is with the novel, Lukács ignores this and concentrates on the second path. In this, the narrowing of the soul has lost all visible relation to the world of ideals, and has become a purely psychological phenomenon. This means that the contact between the hero and the external world is now of merely marginal importance, and the hero himself becomes a secondary figure.

The central characters of the novel, then, become negative, and this negativity requires a positive counterpart. Lukács argues that in the case of the modern humorous novel, this counterpart could only be 'the objectification of bourgeois propriety'.[38] This is the artistic reason why the novels of Dickens, so infinitely rich in comic characters, seem ultimately to be flat and commonplace. Dickens had to make his heroes come to terms with bourgeois society and, for the sake of poetic effect, had to surround the qualities needed for this purpose with the lustre of poetry. Balzac followed a different path. In his case, the counterpart to negativity is an external world which is purely human, consisting of people who have a similar mental structure, though with quite different aims and contents. It was by this homogeneity of his material that Balzac was able to give his novels meaning.

In all these cases, a static psychology is a common feature, and Lukács finds it natural that the nineteenth-century novel, with its tendency towards psychological movement, should increasingly abandon this type. Lukács now turns to the other main type of novel that he recognises, that in which the soul is wider than the external world. This is the romantic novel; more exactly, the novel of romantic disillusion. In this type of novel the soul is more or less self-sufficient, and regards itself as the only true reality.[39] Since it is self-sufficient it does not (as in the case of the first type of novel) have to translate itself into action, and there is therefore a tendency towards passivity. A man becomes the hero of this type of novel, not by virtue of what he does, but because he is capable of certain sorts of experiences, experiences which resemble those of the creative writer. But as soon as a life of this kind is brought face to face with reality, it becomes evident that it must fail in its endeavours, and this is why the novel of the romantic sense of life is also the novel of disillusionment.

Lukács now gives an account of the part played by time in the novel, an account which he still thought worthy of mention long after he had abandoned most of the doctrines of *The Theory of the Novel*.[40] The relevance of this topic to his general theme is that time constitutes the greatest discrepancy between ideal and reality. The soul's most humiliating impotence, Lukács says, lies in the fact that it cannot check the slow but constant progress of time. Now, a certain type of novel takes account of this and (as Lukács puts it) makes time one of its constitutive principles, which is to say that the power of time is made into one of the elements of the novel itself. If it is asked why only the novel should do this, Lukács' answer is that the drama does not recognise the concept of time;[41] as to the epic poem, it is true that both the *Iliad* and the *Odyssey* cover a time span of many years. Nevertheless, their heroes are not affected by time within the poems. Nestor, for example, is simply *old*; he does not *age*. Time became a constitutive element of the literary work only when life had ceased to have meaning — that is, only with the modern age and its art form, the novel.

Lukács argues that novelists regard time in different ways when they treat it as a principle of construction in their works, and this gives rise to different types of novel. In many novels of romantic disillusion, time is merely the destroyer; youth and beauty must die, and time is ultimately responsible for their death. But it is also possible to have a feeling of resignation with regard to time, and from this feeling there spring the experiences of hope and memory. These experiences of time are victories over time, in the sense that they provide a vision of life as a temporal whole. As such, they convey the feeling of comprehending a meaning, a feeling which gives order or shape[42] to life. Such an experience of time, Lukács argues, is the basis of Flaubert's *L'Education sentimentale*. This is a novel of disillusion, but it differs from others of its type in that its attitude to time is not purely negative. At first sight, the novel may appear very loosely constructed; the hero's inner life is as fragmentary as his environment. Yet the novel is by no means formless; it is unified by the unbroken flow of time.

In novels of this type, everything that happens may be meaningless and fragmentary; nevertheless, it is always irradiated by hope or memory, with the result that the work attains a totality. As Lukács puts it:[43]

> The unity of the personality and the world — only dawning in the memory, and yet a lived experience — is ... the deepest and most genuine means of achieving the totality which the novel-form demands. It is the subject's return home to himself which is manifested in this experience, just as the anticipation of and demand for this return home is at the basis of the experiences of hope.

These lines are remarkably rich in anticipation. As Lukács noted later,[44] they were written some years before Proust became known in Germany, and before the publication of another great time-novel, Thomas Mann's *The Magic Mountain*. These novels were concerned primarily with memory and with the ways in which time is experienced; the theme of hope was to be taken up by a Marxist philosopher, Lukács' former fellow-student, Ernst Bloch.[45]

VI

Lukács has now completed his classification of the main types of novel, and the remainder of *The Theory of the Novel* — that is, the last two chapters — has the nature of a postscript, though an important one. Lukács begins by discussing the novels of two major writers, Goethe and Tolstoy. He sees Goethe's *Wilhelm Meister's Apprenticeship* as an attempt at a synthesis of the two main types of novel; that is, as an attempt to find a way of balancing activity and contemplation. He regards Tolstoy as occupying a dual position. If his work is viewed purely in respect of its form, Tolstoy is the conclusion of European romanticism. But such an approach does not touch on what is essential in his work. In the few great moments of his work — they usually involve death, or at any rate nearness to death, such as Andrei Bolkonsky lying wounded at Austerlitz — a reality is revealed to man. In such great moments, there is manifested a concrete and existent world which, if it could be extended to form a totality, would be wholly unsuited to the categories of the novel, and would demand a new art-form: a revived form of the epic poem.[46]

This new world is a world in which man exists as man, and not just as a social being, nor again as an isolated pure inwardness. If it existed, it would form a new totality, a new whole, leaving our divided reality far behind it. But such a transformation cannot be brought about by art. The novel is bound to a specific era; it is the art form of what Fichte, early in the nineteenth century, called 'the epoch of complete sinfulness',[47] and it must remain the dominant form as long as the world remains unchanged. Any attempt to portray utopia in the novel will only destroy the novel-form; it will not create the reality.

In Tolstoy, there are only intimations of a breakthrough into a new world-epoch; in the works of Dostoevsky, however, the new world is portrayed as a visible reality. From this, Lukács draws the conclusion that Dostoevsky did not write novels. Taken in isolation, this may appear to be a paradox, but it can now be seen to be a logical consequence of Lukács' views about the novel. It can also be seen that the assertion that Dostoevsky wrote no novels is not intended as a condemnation of Dostoevsky: quite the contrary. His works cannot be called novels, not because they are failures, would-be novels, but because they present a new world which is other than that which exists in 'the epoch of complete sinfulness'.

It will be clear from all this why Lukács should have said later[48] that *The Theory of the Novel* looked, not towards a new literary form, but towards a new world; a world in which, after the collapse of capitalism, there could emerge a life that is worthy of man. At this stage, however, Lukács' hopes for a new world were not yet linked to any political party; that was to occur just after the end of the world war during which *The Theory of the Novel* was written.

VII

Now that the framework of *The Theory of the Novel* has been described, it remains to say something about the methods of argument employed in it, and its relation to the thought of its own time and to Lukács' later views. A number of Hegelian ideas in the work have already been noted,[49] but in at least one important respect the book is not Hegelian. There will be occasion to speak about Hegel's philosophy in greater detail in the next chapter; for the moment, it must be sufficient to say that Hegel asserted, not only that thought is an historical process, but that it is also a process of development, in which the later stages are more rational than the earlier. To say this is also to say (in Hegel's language) that the later stages 'sublate' (*aufheben*) the earlier; that is, they do not merely negate or cancel the earlier stages, but also preserve what is rational in them. Hegel described the development of thought as a series of movements by three, usually termed 'triads', in which two opposing views are 'sublated' by a third, the 'synthesis'. In *The Theory of the Novel*, however, there is no suggestion of triadic development, indeed no suggestion that the history of literature is a rational development of any kind.[50] When Lukács has occasion to mention the relation between three literary genres — drama, lyric and epic — he is careful to say that they do not form one of Hegel's triads.[51]

In fact, as Lukács himself recognised, *The Theory of the Novel* is closely related to another trend in the German thought of its time, a trend which was not Hegelian. This was the so-called *Geisteswissenschaften* movement. The *Geisteswissenschaften* — the term is perhaps best rendered freely as 'the human studies'[52] — are the studies which have as their object history and society, and the movement is particularly associated with the philosopher Wilhelm Dilthey. In this connexion, it is significant that Lukács later[53] made special mention of the impact made on him by the publication of Dilthey's book *Das Erlebnis und die Dichtung* (*Lived Experience and Imaginative Literature*: 1905), a series of studies of Lessing, Goethe, Novalis and Hölderlin. Dilthey was also one of the representatives of the *Lebensphilosophie* movement which was mentioned in section I, but in the present context it is another aspect of his work that is important. Dilthey argued that the human studies must become clearer about their aims and methods, and in the course of his discussions he made a classification of fundamental ways of looking at the world, which he related to three basic psychological types. He did not seem to suggest that any of these three ways of looking at the world is superior to any of the others; he simply related each to its appropriate psychological type or types.[54] Lukács did not accept Dilthey's three basic psychological types, but in the way in which he relates the different types of novel to different types of soul, and in the absence of any suggestion of a hierarchical order among the types, he is strongly reminiscent of Dilthey.

Lukács came to reject *The Theory of the Novel* because of defects which he found in the ideas of the *Geisteswissenschaften* school. Adherents of the school, he said in his 1962 preface to the book, tended to generalise on the basis of just a few traits of a movement or school, which for the most part were grasped only intuitively, and they then proceeded to explain individual phenomena by means of these generalisations. This was the method of *The Theory of the Novel*, and this, Lukács said, was how he came to construct a theory of the types of the novel which proved to be too abstract and general — distorting Balzac, Flaubert, Tolstoy and Dostoevsky, and having no place at all for novelists such as Defoe, Fielding and Stendhal.[55]

3

Marxism and Hegelianism: *History and Class Consciousness* (1923)

I

In 1923 Lukács published his first major work as a Marxist, *Geschichte und Klassenbewusstsein* (*History and Class Consciousness*). The book consists of eight essays, most of which are occasional pieces, written at various times between 1919 and 1921, though two of them — 'Methodological remarks on the problem of organisation' and 'Reification and proletarian consciousness' — were written especially for the volume. The book is a difficult one. Its style is complex and loaded with abstractions, and because of the occasional nature of the essays the logical structure of Lukács' thought is often hard to grasp. Again, Lukács took for granted much that is no longer familiar; for example, he assumed a wide knowledge of recent Marxist discussion. In what follows, there will be no attempt to discuss the work piece by piece; the aim will be to give an account of the leading ideas of the work in their historical context and in their logical interconnexion.

It has already been seen (chapter 1, section III) that soon after its publication the work was accused by leading Communists of being 'revisionist'; that is, of arguing that important Marxist doctrines must be abandoned and replaced by others in order to keep abreast of modern knowledge. Lukács himself did not see the work in this light. He said that he was proclaiming orthodox Marxism; though, as is suggested by the title of the first essay, 'What is orthodox Marxism?', he thought that not everyone was clear about what orthodox Marxism really was. This claim to orthodoxy, to be putting forward the right opinions about the nature of genuine Marxism, may seem paradoxical to someone who merely reads the work and compares it with the recognised Marxist classics. Lukács' critics, it may seem, were right; there is much in the book that is not in the writings of Marx and Engels, and is not obviously derivable from them. But if one puts the book in its historical context then Lukács' claim becomes, if not justifiable, at any rate comprehensible.

There are certain similarities between the intellectual climates in which Marx wrote the first volume of *Capital* and Lukács wrote *History and Class Consciousness*. In each case, the generally held opinion was that Hegel's philosophy was obsolete; that, as Marx put it, Hegel was 'a dead dog'.[1] In roughly the first two decades of this century, the neo-Kantians who dominated German philosophy (cf. chapter 1, section I) had influenced Marxists and socialists generally; the slogan was 'Back to Kant!'[2] In particular, the leading revisionist, Eduard Bernstein, argued that Marxism should be purged of Hegel, and he appealed instead to the authority of Kant.[3] Marx had reacted to the general opposition to Hegel by proclaiming himself 'a disciple of that great thinker'.[4] In a corresponding way, Lukács argued in the 1920s that revisionism must be met and orthodoxy re-established by emphasising the Hegelian aspects of Marxism.

II

Our concern here is with the nature of Lukács' Marxism, and his reasons for adopting it; we are not concerned with the question whether or not it was really orthodox. Nevertheless it is important, and indeed essential, to establish as clearly as possible the relation of his ideas to those that can be found in the established classics, the writings of Marx and Engels. The point is that, whether Lukács was really orthodox or not, he saw himself as an orthodox Marxist, upholding a tradition of genuine as opposed to spurious Marxism. Yet he found that he had to say that Engels himself had seriously misunderstood Marx's ideas. In other words, Lukács defined his own position by rejecting some of what would usually be regarded as Marxist classics and accepting others. To understand Lukács, then, it is necessary to know something about the doctrines propounded in these classics.

It was said earlier that Lukács argued that orthodoxy was to be re-established by giving due weight to the Hegelian aspects of Marxism. To speak of such aspects is to speak of 'dialectics'; and indeed, *History and Class Consciousness* is sub-titled *Studies in Marxist*

Dialectics. First, therefore, it is necessary to establish the framework within which, and sometimes against which Lukács operated, by sketching the views on dialectics to be found in the Marxist classics that were available when he wrote the book.

The writings of Marx on the subject are few and unsystematic;[5] a reader in 1923, like the modern reader, would have found the classical exposition of Marxist dialectics in the writings of Engels. He would not have had access to *The Dialectics of Nature*, the book on dialectics which Engels left unfinished and which was first published in 1925, but he could have read the essay *Ludwig Feuerbach and the End of Classical German Philosophy*, published in 1886, in which Engels discussed the relations between Marxism and Hegelianism. More important, he could have read the book *Herr Eugen Dühring's Revolution in Science* (usually abbreviated to *Anti-Dühring*), which first appeared in book form in 1878. In the course of this critique of the writings of a German socialist, Engels devoted three chapters (1, 12 and 13) to an account of dialectics. This was the most comprehensive and systematic account of the subject given by either Marx or Engels which was available when *History and Class Consciousness* was written, and it will be useful to give a brief account of its contents.

In his first chapter,[6] Engels sketches the essential nature of dialectics, which he calls the highest form of thinking. This thinking has two main features. First, it grasps things and the thoughts that represent them, not in isolation but in their interconnexion, indeed as part of 'the whole vast interconnexion of things'. Second, it views things as moving rather than as fixed, and so Engels can say later[7] that dialectics is 'the science of the general laws of motion and development of nature, human society and thought'. With this way of thinking Engels contrasts what he calls the 'metaphysical' mode of thought, which regards things and concepts as rigid and fixed objects of investigation, given once and for all. The metaphysician thinks in terms of stark opposites, in terms of 'Yes' and 'No'. For him, a thing either exists or it does not, and it cannot at the same time be itself and something else. The metaphysician's way of thinking may seem a plausible and indeed a common-sense one, but Engels argues that it soon reaches a limit beyond which it becomes one-sided, abstract, and loses its way among insoluble contradictions. This is because, unlike dialectics, it does not see beyond individual things to their connexions, beyond their existence to their coming into being and passing away, beyond their rest to their motion.

Mention was made above of dialectics as a science of general laws. Chapters 12 and 13 of *Anti-Dühring* discuss two such laws, the transformation of quantity into quality, and the negation of the negation. In *The Dialectics of Nature* a third law is mentioned, that of the interpenetration of opposites.[8] This is not stated expressly as a law in *Anti-Dühring*, though it is suggested by a remark in the first chapter, to the effect that the two poles of an antithesis 'mutually penetrate each other'. The nature of these laws is best explained by some of Engels' examples. These examples, it is important to note, are taken both from the natural sciences and from what may be called the human studies. Among the illustrations of the transformation of quantity into quality is the transformation of water into ice at 0°C and into steam at 100°C, and the fact that if a certain sum of money is to be transformed into capital it must reach a certain minimum. Such a transformation is often called a 'qualitative leap', or simply a 'leap'. The negation of the negation is illustrated by the germination of a grain of barley (the grain becomes a plant, which is the negation of the grain, and the plant in turn produces grains of barley) and by an example from the history of philosophy — primitive materialism is negated by idealism, which in turn is negated by modern materialism. The interpenetration of opposites seems to be the principle used in rejecting the 'metaphysical' way of thinking, and states that one is not to think that a thing always either exists or not, and that it can never at the same time be itself and something else. The examples given in *Anti-Dühring* which may be regarded as illustrating this principle belong to the natural sciences; Engels notes that one cannot always say whether a thing is alive or not, or whether it is a gas or a liquid.

In *The Dialectics of Nature* Engels makes no secret of the fact that all three laws were developed by Hegel, but 'in his idealistic fashion'.[9] This introduces another aspect of Engels' exposition of dialectics. Dialectics is not only a form of thinking, a science of general laws, but also involves a view of the nature of reality. For Hegel, the laws of thought *were* the laws of reality, since reality is thought; for Marxists, on the other hand, reality is material. This is brought out clearly by Engels in *Ludwig Feuerbach and the End of Classical German Philosophy*. Philosophers, he says, fall into the two classes of idealists and materialists, the former asserting the primacy of mind over matter, and the latter asserting that nature is primary. In Engels' view, nature has the primacy, which he explains as meaning that matter precedes mind; matter is not a product of mind, as idealists assert, but mind is merely the highest product of matter.[10]

III

Such, in outline, is the classical account of Marxist dialectics. What is striking about Lukács' theory of dialectics is first, that even where he agrees with Engels his emphasis is very different, and second, that he goes beyond what Engels said, disagreeing with him on at least one important matter. To begin with the first point. There is no reason to suppose that Lukács would have rejected any of Engels' laws of dialectics; however, they do not constitute the core of his theory. The law of the transformation of quantity into quality, to which Engels devotes a whole chapter of *Anti-Dühring*, is discussed by Lukács in only a few pages, and there is only a glancing reference to the unity of opposites[11]; the negation of the negation is not mentioned as such. What, then, is Lukács' view of dialectics?

Marxism, Lukács says, is a method. It does not mean the uncritical acceptance of the results of Marx's inquiries; it does not mean the exposition of a sacred text. Rather, it is 'the scientific conviction that in dialectical Marxism, the correct method of inquiry has been found'.[12] In laying stress on method, Lukács was doing nothing new. In *Ludwig Feuerbach*, Engels contrasted Hegel's method with his system, and said that the former was much the more valuable of the two, whilst the neo-Kantians, for their part, claimed to follow Kant's method while rejecting his system. Again, Lenin had already said in *Materialism and Empirio-Criticism* (1908) that by following the *path* of Marxist theory one will draw steadily closer to objective truth, which implies that Marxism is not a complete and closed system.[13] However, Lukács' view that Marxism is a method is taken to great lengths, such that he asserts that even if modern research had shown that all Marx's statements are factually unsound, every orthodox Marxist could accept this and still remain a Marxist.

This is a paradoxical statement. It is hard to see, for example, how anyone could consistently call himself a Marxist and not accept the truth of the assertion, with which the first part of the *Communist Manifesto* begins, that 'The history of all hitherto existing society is the history of class struggles.' But although Lukács came to abandon much of *History and Class Consciousness*, he did not abandon the view that Marxism is essentially a method,[14] and it is important to be clear about his exact meaning. Faced with the thesis that Marxism is a method, it is natural to ask, 'A method of *what*? Is it a method of seeking for truth, or a method by which to transform society?' Lukács' answer would be 'Both'; but to see what he meant and why he said it, a long inquiry is necessary.

Lukács says that the essence of the method which Marx took over from Hegel — that is, the essence of dialectics — is the category of concrete totality, which he declares to be *the* category that governs reality.[15] What he has in mind here is Hegel's thesis that the most perfect form of thought is systematic in the highest degree. By this Hegel meant, not just that it is internally coherent, but also that it is complete and concrete. That is to say, it covers everything, but not in the way that (for example) physics may be said to cover everything, namely by abstracting from many of the features of its subject matter. The highest form of thinking leads to a system in which individuality is not obliterated, but is preserved, and this is what is meant by calling it 'concrete'. In short, every advance in knowledge is an advance from the less complete to the more complete, from the abstract to the relatively concrete, a view which Hegel crystallised in his famous assertion in the Preface to *The Phenomenology of Mind*, that 'The true is the whole.' This, broadly, is what Lukács had in mind when he spoke of 'concrete totality'. As will be seen later, he did not agree with all that Hegel said about this totality, but he did agree that if we are to understand some particular historical event or process we must see it as an aspect of a concrete whole, a whole which, as he said, is a unity of thought and history.[16]

What has been said so far about Lukács' concept of concrete totality has an obvious parallel in classical Marxism. In the first chapter of *Anti-Dühring* Engels said that dialectics grasps things as part of 'the whole vast interconnexion of things', and although he does not expressly mention a *concrete* totality, this is implicit when he rejects the metaphysical way of thinking because of its abstractness. But despite this resemblance between Lukács and classical Marxism there is also a fundamental difference. This lies in their views about the nature of the concrete totality. Lukács declares that this totality is a *subject*,[17] and in this connexion he quotes Hegel's remark (also from the Preface to *The Phenomenology of Mind*) that 'The all-important thing is to grasp and express the true, not as substance, but equally as subject.' He adds that Hegel was right in saying this, and only went

39

wrong in so far as he failed to live up to his own precept. There is no hint of this in classical Marxism, and indeed it may seem strange that a Marxist of any kind should approve of Hegel's remark. Hegel is in effect saying that what there is, is a thinking subject; that is, he is expounding a form of what is commonly called philosophical idealism. It has already been seen, however, that Engels declared Marxist dialectics to be materialist, and Lukács, who called himself a dialectical materialist,[18] would have agreed. He also believed, however, that Hegel's view expressed an important truth, although in a confused and misleading way.

What this truth was — what Lukács meant by saying that the concrete totality is a subject — can most easily be seen by following his attempt to establish it. Although the conclusion that he reaches is not one that Hegel would have accepted, the line of argument itself is Hegelian. Hegel had viewed philosophy as being essentially historical, in the sense that it is constituted by a developing process of thought, the latter stages of which correct the earlier, and are not comprehensible without reference to them. Lukács' argument is, in brief, that the proposition that reality is both a concrete totality and a subject is the culmination of a line of thought that began in the seventeenth century, and has to be seen in the light of the history of that line of thought. His argument is to be found in two sections of the essay 'Reification and Proletarian Consciousness', which are essential to an understanding of the concept of dialectics contained in *History and Class Consciousness*. These are section II, 'The Antinomies of Bourgeois Thought', and section III, 'The Standpoint of the Proletariat'.

IV

In the section on 'The Antinomies of Bourgeois Thought' Lukács is concerned with what he calls 'modern rationalism', and more especially with 'classical German philosophy'. By the latter he means (as Engels did) the period of German philosophy that runs from Kant to Hegel;[19] 'modern rationalism', in Lukács' sense, means more than what is now usually meant by 'rationalism' — that is, that trend of seventeenth- and early eighteenth-century philosophical thought whose main representatives were Descartes, Spinoza and Leibniz. For Lukács the term covers, not only these philosophers, but philosophers such as Kant and Hegel also. His point is that all these philosophers, despite their differences, had something in common: namely, they all aimed at the construction of a system of knowledge which was to be total, embracing all phenomena.[20]

Lukács is not concerned simply to chronicle the development of modern rationalism; his concern is to set out the logic that is displayed by that development, to present its various phases as stages in an argument. As the title of the section suggests, his thesis is that such rationalism issued, and had to issue, in antinomies: that is, contradictory propositions, each of which seems justifiable by argument. These contradictions, he believes, are reconcilable by taking the argument one stage further, by moving from the dialectics of Hegel to Marxist dialectics.

He begins by saying that the distinguishing feature of modern philosophy is its view that the world is not independent of the knowing subject, but has to be considered as the product of that subject. This was what Kant called his 'Copernican revolution' in philosophy, but it is to be found long before him, in philosophers such as Descartes, Hobbes, Spinoza, Leibniz and Vico.[21] Since it is in mathematics that it is most obvious that what we know has been created by us, mathematics becomes the paradigm of knowledge, and mathematical, formal knowledge is equated with knowledge in general. This is how philosophers came to have that aim which, for Lukács, is typical of modern rationalism — namely, the construction of one all-embracing system of knowledge, the connexions between whose components are necessary connexions.[22]

This is an important (and controversial) thesis. Lukács is saying that what is fundamental to modern rationalism is not its belief that human knowledge forms a total system, analogous to the systems of mathematics. This view is indeed a defining characteristic of rationalism, but it is derived from a view which is still more basic; the view, expressed most clearly by Vico, that what we know is what we ourselves have made.[23] It is important to realise that Lukács is not opposed to the view that knowledge is a making, nor to the idea of a total system that went with it. His argument will be that non-Marxist philosophy failed to give a satisfactory account of this activity, and more particularly of the subject of the activity; further, although the attempt to construct a total system was not mistaken, non-Marxist philosophy failed (and could not but fail) to do so.

The main problem that modern rationalism had to face was intimately connected with its own ideal of knowledge, that of an all-inclusive system. The problem was how to accommodate within such a system the irrational, the merely given. This problem can be seen most clearly, Lukács says, in the case of Kant's concept of the 'thing in itself'.[24] The essence of Kant's 'Copernican revolution' was the view that objects must conform to our knowledge. Any object which is knowable by us, Kant said, *must* display certain features, such as being a substance and being capable of entering into causal relations with other objects. These features are contributed by what Kant called the 'understanding', and to this extent the object that we know may be called our creation. But Kant insisted that the object known is not entirely the creation of the understanding. The understanding provides only the form or structure of our knowledge of objects; the material on which it works is provided by our sensations. This sensual content of our knowledge of objects is to be referred, not to the understanding, but to the unknowable 'thing in itself', which is independent of the operations of the understanding. In sum, Kant has to treat the existence and nature of the sensual content on which the understanding works as a mere datum, which cannot be explained rationally. This difficulty, Lukács says, is not peculiar to Kant, but attaches to rationalism in general. Rationalism demands a system, demands total explicability; but it cannot satisfy its own demands.[25]

Rationalism, then, seems to be faced with an insoluble dilemma. On the one hand, it cannot flatly deny the existence of an irrational content in our knowledge of objects; the problem that met Kant cannot be solved by naive dogmatism of this kind. Yet the only alternative seems to be to abandon the idea of a system entirely, and turn philosophy into a mere register of facts without any rational connexion — and this would mean the end of rationalism.[26] Lukács notes that many philosophers, including the entire neo-Kantian school, accepted the latter alternative; they rejected every 'metaphysics', every attempt at grasping reality as a whole.[27] They were, however, following a wrong path, for the dilemma just stated is not a real one. The right path, Lukács says, was pointed out by those classical German philosophers who laid the foundations of the dialectical method.

Their problem was to find a subject which produces what appears to be merely given.[28] Kant had already given a hint of the answer in his *Critique of Practical Reason*, where he argued that certain problems which are insoluble by the pure, theoretical reason have practical solutions. For example, the problem of free will, which leads the pure reason into insoluble antinomies, can be solved when it is realised that freedom is one of the demands of the *practical* reason. Fichte took this idea further, and put activity at the very centre of his philosophical system. Yet, according to Lukács, the demands of rationalism were still not met, as can again be seen clearly in the case of Kant. Rationalism demanded a unified and complete system, and Kant's system is neither. It is not unified, in that it sharply opposes freedom to necessity, the one as belonging to the intelligible world and the other to the world of appearances; indeed, the thinking subject itself is divided by Kant into reality and appearance. It is not a complete system, in that Kantian ethics remains at the level of formal, abstract law, from which no concrete rules of conduct can be derived.

Lukács now turns to the philosophy of Hegel. Hegel came closer to a solution of the problem of rationalism, in that his philosophy recognises the importance of history.[29] As Vico had already pointed out, we have made our own history, and by regarding the whole of reality as history — our history — Hegel was able to regard the whole of reality as our own creation. Now, the importance of history in this connexion is that in history, what we create does not stand in sharp opposition to us; we are both producer and product of the historical process. In this way, Hegel was able to remove the antithesis between subject and object, denying that the object is rigidly separate from the subject, and affirming instead that there is an identical subject-object. At the same time as he removed the problem of the thing in itself, Hegel did justice to rationalism's demand for a total system, by saying that the historical process can only be grasped as a concrete totality. To understand historical development, one must give due weight to what is unique in phenomena; that is to say, one must pay attention to their content and must not rest content with abstractions. But one must not treat phenomena simply as unique, but must place them within the context of a concrete totality, that is, of the concrete and total historical process.

But despite the great advances that Hegel made, he too was faced with a problem he could not solve: the problem of the nature of the subject of the historical process. He was unable to find the identical subject-object within history, and so was led to look for it outside history, in the timeless realm of what he called 'Absolute Mind' —

that is, art, religion and philosophy.[30] This, Lukács argues, was mere myth-making. In the end, then, Hegel's attempt at a philosophical system breaks down; not because it postulates an identical subject-object, but because it cannot locate this subject-object within history.

Lukács asserts that Marxist dialectics puts right this defect. It finds the identical subject-object within history; it finds it in a social class, the proletariat, which becomes an identical subject-object in so far as it becomes self-aware, class-conscious.[31] It will naturally be asked why the identical subject-object has to be a social class, and why this social class is the proletariat. Lukács' answers to these questions are closely linked. Most of what he says on the topic is to be found in section III of 'Reification and Proletarian Consciousness', entitled 'The Standpoint of the Proletariat', but other essays in *History and Class Consciousness* also throw light on the problems involved.

Before going further, it will be useful to review Lukács' views about knowledge, as these have so far been expounded. He has said that:

(1) What we know is what we have made.
(2) What we know must be, not only a totality, but a concrete totality, involving both form and content.
(3) These conditions are satisfied only if knower and known are one, i.e. if subject and object are identical.

Lukács insists that knowledge is not mere contemplation; for him, to know is to *do*, it is not to be a passive reflector of reality. As he noted, this brought him into conflict with Engels, who had said that concepts are images (*Abbilder*) of real things; Lukács might also have pointed out that he was contradicting views expressed repeatedly by Lenin in *Materialism and Empirio-Criticism*. He is quite firm on this issue. To treat thought as mere contemplation, he says, is to draw a sharp line between the subject which contemplates and the object which is contemplated, and leads one into difficulties of the type which met Kant.[32] The first question which faces Lukács, then, is this: given that knowledge is action, why should it also be the action of a social class? The answer involves his view that knowledge has to grasp a totality. Only a class, he says,[33] can 'entirely penetrate social reality and change it in its totality'. In other words, the action that Lukács has in mind is revolutionary action, action that changes the whole of society. Given this, the answer to a second question is clear.

The question is, 'Why must the action be that of the proletariat?', and the answer is 'Because, in contemporary society, the proletariat is the only revolutionary class.' The revolutionary character of the proletariat is no merely contingent feature, one which it just happens to have; rather, it springs from its very nature. In this connexion, Lukács quotes a passage from an early work of Marx, his *Introduction to a Critique of Hegel's 'Philosophy of Right'*: 'When the proletariat proclaims the dissolution of the existing world-order, it only expresses the secret of its own existence: for it is the factual dissolution of this world-order.'[34]

This may seem a long way from all the Hegelian language about totality and the self-awareness of the identical subject-object which has gone before it, but for Lukács the connexions are clear. Consider first the self-awareness of a class, its class-consciousness. If any class is to know itself, if it is to understand its own position in society, then (by virtue of what has been said about concrete totality) it must understand society as a whole. It might be thought that any class can have such knowledge: that the bourgeoisie, for example, can grasp its own nature as a class. Lukács would reply that this is not so. The bourgeoisie, the dominant class in capitalist society, is a minority which looks to its own interests, but which has to pretend that its rule is in the interest of all. It cannot, therefore, see its own true nature, whereas the proletariat is 'capable of seeing society from the centre, as a connected whole'.[35]

It may seem that Lukács, with this reference to what the proletariat 'sees', is here treating knowledge as contemplation, despite his own express warning against this. Lukács, however, would deny that this is what he is doing. Proletarian consciousness, like any correct consciousness, means a change in its objects, and primarily in itself. The worker's self-consciousness is not just consciousness 'of' an object; it is *practical*, in that it produces an alteration in the object of knowledge.[36] This appears to be what Lukács means when he talks about the 'unity of theory and practice' which exists in the case of the proletariat.[37] The notion of the unity of theory and practice has been part of orthodox Soviet Marxism for many years. An authoritative formulation of the doctrine may be found in Stalin's assertion (made a year after the publication of *History and Class Consciousness*) that 'theory becomes purposeless if it is not connected with revolutionary practice, just as practice gropes in the dark if its path is not illuminated by revolutionary theory'.[38]

This, however, does not seem to be Lukács' point. He is saying that in so far as the proletariat knows itself it changes itself; and not only does it change itself, it radically transforms society as a whole. Lukács would stress, however, that this radical transformation, this revolutionary activity, does not as it were turn history aside from its proper course. On the contrary — and here the Hegelian element in his thought re-appears — the revolutionary activity of the proletariat is a part of what may be called the logic of history. As Lukács puts it, the superiority of the proletariat over the bourgeoisie lies in the fact that it can bring to consciousness and transform into practice the 'immanent meaning' of historical development.[39]

Such, in outline, are Lukács' view about the identical subject-object. It is clear that they contain no hint of philosophical idealism; no hint, that is, of the view that physical objects are only disguised forms of mind. The proletariat is the identical subject-object in that it, and it alone, can know itself. There are still questions to be answered about this concept of dialectics; in particular, one wants to know more about the nature of that 'immanent meaning' of historical development of which Lukács speaks. This must be deferred until the next section, when Lukács' views about historical materialism will be discussed; however, what has been said about dialectics already is sufficient to throw light on a problem raised in section III, and also to enable a connexion between certain aspects of *History and Class Consciousness* and *The Theory of the Novel* to be pointed out.

The problem raised in section III was whether Lukács' view that Marxist dialectics is a method means that he was really prepared to abandon, if necessary, all the propositions that Marx had stated to be true. It is now clear that this is unlikely. Lukács' Marxism is dependent on the truth of at least one such proposition — that in modern society, the proletariat is the revolutionary class — and he could not cease to believe in its truth without ceasing to be a Marxist. If he is to be consistent, his assertion that Marxism is a method must be taken to mean merely that Marxist dialectics is not a formula that can be applied ready-made to any situation; that the correct course of action for the proletariat cannot be predicted on the basis of a cut and dried theory. This is an assertion which most, and perhaps all Marxists would accept; Lukács may have been led to over-emphasise the point because he thought that in the case of many Marxists, here at any rate theory and practice did not coincide.

The aspects of *History and Class Consciousness* and *Theory of the Novel* referred to above are the views about totality that they present. *The Theory of the Novel* was described earlier as belonging to a phase of Lukács' thought that preceded *History and Class Consciousness*, as indeed it did. But it must not be supposed that the phases in a man's thought are always sharply separated; on the contrary, ideas that belong to a later phase are often to be found in an earlier one in a more or less undeveloped form. This is the case with Lukács' concept of totality. In *The Theory of the Novel* (cf. chapter 2, section IV) he had argued that the novel tries to discover an extensive totality, and he had said that such an attempt must fail, for modern life has ceased to be a totality. For it to be a totality, then — by some means or other — the world must be made to change radically. The art-form to discover or construct this totality could not be the novel, which is tied to a fragmented world, but would have to be a new type of epic. In *History and Class Consciousness*, it is not so much art as human thinking in general that is said to try to grasp a totality, a concrete whole.[40] The chief difference, however, is this. The Lukács of *History and Class Consciousness* would agree that a totality can be grasped only through a revolution. But whereas in *The Theory of the Novel* there is no indication of the means by which the world is to be radically transformed, there is no such vagueness in *History and Class Consciousness*. Lukács now thinks that there is a class, the proletariat, that can grasp totality; this class is the means to the transformation of the world.

V

For Lukács, the theory of the class-conscious proletariat, the identical subject-object of history, was not just a peripheral part of dialectics but was central to it, was of its essence. So he was led to contradict Engels' views about dialectics. For if dialectics necessarily involves the idea of a conscious agent, then it follows that there can be no place for a dialectics of nature, understanding by this a dialectics which applies to what is purely physical. But, as was pointed out in section II, Engels believed that there is such a dialectics; his examples of the laws of dialectics in *Anti-Dühring* are taken both from inanimate nature and from society. Lukács argued that Engels was mistaken, but denied that this made his own views 'revisionist'. On the contrary, he claimed to be defending orthodox

47

Marxism against Engels. Marx, Lukács said, applied the dialectical method only to historico-social reality; it was Engels, mistakenly following Hegel's example, who extended the method to the whole of reality.[41]

The truth or falsity of this view, which Lukács later abandoned,[42] is not our concern here. There is, however, an important terminological point that must be noted. It is now customary to distinguish between dialectical and historical materialism. The laws of dialectics stated by Engels apply to each, but whereas dialectical materialism applies to all nature, animate and inanimate, historical materialism applies to society alone, and has special laws of its own. In *History and Class Consciousness*, Lukács refers both to dialectical and historical materialism, but it follows from what was said in the last paragraph that when he defends 'dialectical materialism'[43] he cannot have in mind the sense of the term just explained. 'Dialectical materialism' is for him merely a synonym for Marxist dialectics, as he understands the term, and so applies only to society.

Some of the most important pages of *History and Class Consciousness* are devoted to the topic of historical materialism. Before discussing Lukács' views on this topic, it will be useful to sketch the classical exposition of historical materialism that is provided by Marx in the Preface to the *Critique of Political Economy*.[44] Marx distinguishes within society between a 'basis' and a 'superstructure'. The basis consists of material productive forces and relations of production; the superstructure consists of (e.g.) law, politics, religion, art and philosophy, and is 'conditioned' by the basis, by the 'mode of production of material life'. As Marx put it in a famous sentence, 'It is not men's consciousness that determines their existence, but their social existence that determines their consciousness.' Marx explains social change as due to a conflict between the material productive forces and the relations of production. 'From forms of development of the productive forces these relations turn into their fetters. Then begins an era of social revolution. The changes in the economic basis lead sooner or later to the transformation of the whole immense superstructure.'

There is no space here to discuss all the problems connected with this celebrated passage, which was quoted simply to introduce a discussion of questions about Lukács' views. The first of these questions concerns the relation between historical materialism and Lukács' dialectics. Since both are concerned with society, it might seem that the two can simply be identified. However, the matter is not quite so simple. It is true that Lukács regards the assertion that social existence determines consciousness as 'the fundamental proposition of the dialectical method',[45] and says also that the proletariat, in its struggle to attain class consciousness, makes use of the doctrines of historical materialism.[46] Nevertheless, he does not think that historical materialism will always be applicable to society. Historical materialism presupposes that the economic factor is basic. So indeed, says Lukács, it is, for long periods of human history; but once the proletarian revolution has led to an epoch in which the economy is no longer the master, but rather is the servant of society, and mankind has entered what Marx and Engels called the 'realm of freedom', then historical materialism will cease to be applicable.[47] This does not mean that the dialectical method cannot be applied to the new society, but it may be assumed that Lukács thinks that it will take new forms.

However, Lukács was certain that the proletariat would have a use for historical materialism for many years to come.[48] It was therefore important for him to answer attacks on it, by finding solutions to two well-known problems generated by historical materialism. The first is the question, whether or not historical materialism is self-refuting. The second is the question whether it leaves any room for human freedom; that is, whether it is consistent with the view that at least some important historical events or processes are the outcome of free human decisions. The first problem arises as follows.

Law, politics, religion and philosophy have already been described as constituting a 'superstructure' which is raised upon the basis of the 'mode of production of material life'; Marxists also refer to them as 'ideologies'. The ideologist — a politician or philosopher, say — is unaware of the real forces that move him. He is a conscious agent, indeed, but his consciousness is what Engels called a 'false consciousness'.[49] The difficulty that this creates for the historical materialist is stated by Lukács as follows.[50] An ideology is a 'function' of economic relations, by which Lukács means that it is determined by them. But historical materialism is itself an ideology, the ideology of the proletariat, and is therefore itself merely a function of a certain type of society, capitalist society. The implication is that historical materialism, too, is an instance of 'false consciousness'.

Lukács could have followed the line taken by Marx in 1859 in the Preface to the *Critique of Political Economy*, and by Marx and Engels in an earlier work, *The German Ideology* (1845-6), arguing that historical materialism is not an ideology but a science.[51] This avoids imputing false consciousness to the Marxist by saying that although every ideology involves false consciousness, historical materialism is not an ideology. However, Lukács does not follow this line. He says that historical materialism is an ideology, and that it can and must be applied to itself. He avoids the imputation of false consciousness to Marxism by taking up the position that not every ideology involves false consciousness. Here, he is in line with more recent trends in Marxist thought, where there is a tendency for the word 'ideology' to be applied to any sort of theory whatever, true or false.[52]

Lukács' argument takes the form of a reply to the objection that historical materialism implies 'relativism'. He does not define the term, but seems to have in mind the view that it cannot be said that one theory is truer than another, it can only be said that each theory is relative to a specific stage of social development. Lukács offers two replies to the charge of relativism. In the first, written in 1919, he says that the truths of historical materialism are true within a particular socio-economic system, and as such have absolute validity. What is true of a given system, however, need not be true of all systems.[53] For example, historical materialism is primarily a theory of bourgeois or capitalist society. It can be applied to pre-capitalist society, though with some difficulty, and it has already seen that it cannot be applied to the future classless society, the 'realm of freedom'. Lukács' second reply, written in 1922, is something of a *tour de force*. To call something 'relative', he argues,[54] is to say that it is relative to something, and is to regard that to which it is relative as an absolute, i.e. as non-relative. Marxist dialectics, on the other hand, relativises everything, and it is therefore highly misleading to call it a 'relativism'. It is true that it resembles relativism in regarding man as the measure of all things; unlike relativism, however, it does not regard the nature of man as something fixed and unchanging.

But even if historical materialism is not self-refuting, the second of the two questions raised above still remains. This concerned human freedom, and it is important first of all to be clear about the question itself. Historical materialism is often called a form of historical determinism. It is a determinism, not in the sense that it declares that every human action is necessitated, but in that it states that the sorts of human activity that interest the historian — the great events, the major social changes — are necessitated. There is no doubt that Marx himself was a historical determinist in this sense. In the first volume of *Capital*, for example, he refers to the 'necessary' break-up of the existing capitalist state of affairs; he speaks of capitalist production begetting its own negation 'with the necessity of a natural process'; he says that the laws of capitalist production work with 'iron necessity'.[55] So there is clearly a problem whether a Marxist can allow that there is any scope for human freedom in any important historical event.

Lukács illustrates the problem by referring to the proletariat's achievement of self-consciousness. Is this, he asks,[56] no more than the law-governed consequence of the concentration of large numbers of workers in big factories, the mechanisation and standardisation of the labour process, and the levelling-down of the standard of living? He replies that it is not. The factors mentioned are indeed necessary conditions of the development of the proletariat towards class-consciousness, but they are not sufficient conditions. In other words, the proletariat could not attain class-consciousness without these economic conditions, but the economic conditions alone would not produce this class-consciousness. Proletarian consciousness, as has been seen, is connected with practice, with revolutionary activity; and this, says Lukács, is the *free activity* of the proletariat.[57] There is, according to Lukács, no material guarantee that capitalism will be destroyed. It is possible that the proletariat will not revolutionise society, but will adapt itself instead to the forms of bourgeois culture. In political terms, this means that it may allow itself to be seduced by social democracy, which involves a capitulation to the bourgeoisie.[58] If capitalism is to be superseded — if the forces at work within capitalism are not to advance blindly towards a total destruction of civilisation — the proletariat must become aware of its historical mission. The transition to the realm of freedom demands the conscious will of the proletariat.[59]

Clearly, Lukács is far from underrating the importance of free decision in history; on the other hand, he does not say that dialectics has no room for the notion of historical necessity. In the first place, he thinks that the bourgeoisie is totally subject to historical necessity. For example, he argues that unless the proletariat intervenes to change reality, contradictions in society will remain unresolved and will be reproduced in a more intensive form by 'the dialectical mechanics of development'. It is in this, he says, that the objective necessity of the process of development consists.[60] Second, he asserts that proletarian consciousness itself is an immanent consequence of the historical dialectic, and so is nothing but the expression of historical necessity. But he is quick to add that 'a dialectical necessity is by no means identical with a mechanical, causal necessity'.[61] However, he does not make clear just what is the nature of this dialectical necessity, and how it leaves room for the free acts of the proletariat. Perhaps what differentiates dialectical from mechanical necessity is that the former as an intrinsic connexion with rational action. Lukács is in effect saying that it is historically necessary that there should come into being a certain class, the proletariat, and that this class is such that the rational course of action for it to pursue is a revolutionary one, leading to the dissolution of class society. All this is historically necessary; what is not necessary is that the proletariat should act rationally. Whether or not it does so depends on its own free decision.

VI

In the course of this exposition of *History and Class Consciousness*, much has already been said about the self-knowledge of the proletariat, its class-consciousness. Nothing, however, has so far been said that has a bearing on the obvious question, how the content of this class-consciousness is to be discovered; that is, how one is to find out what the proletariat thinks about itself and its position in society as a whole. It does not seem that this can be discovered by means of empirical surveys among proletarians. According to Lukács, the proletariat is capable of *understanding* society as a whole, it is able to find the *correct* answers to complex problems of economics and sociology. But it is hard to believe that correct answers can be found simply by discovering what proletarians think about these problems.

Nor, indeed, does Lukács think that they can. When he speaks of class-consciousness in this context, he is not referring to what a class actually thinks. Class-consciousness, he says,[62] is neither the sum nor the average of what is actually thought or felt by the individuals constituting a class; rather, it involves the category of 'objective possibility'. In explaining this, Lukács begins by pointing out that men have certain positions in the productive process, and that these different positions determine various social types. This is a standard Marxist thesis, stated more clearly by Lukács elsewhere[63] in the form of the assertion that social class is dependent on position in the process of production. Now, for any such type or class it is possible to infer the thoughts and feelings that are appropriate to its position. That is, it is possible to infer the thoughts and feelings that men would have in a particular position if they were to grasp their situation properly. Class-consciousness just *is* 'the rational and appropriate reaction that is imputed (*zugerechnet*) in this way to a particular typical position in the process of production'.[64] Class-consciousness, then, has a hypothetical character; it is what certain people *would* think in certain situations, *if* they were to grasp these situations adequately. But Lukács insists that although class-consciousness has no psychological reality, it is not a mere fiction, for it has an explanatory function; by its means one can explain 'the painful path of the proletarian revolution'.[65]

In *History and Class Consciousness*, then, class-consciousness is an ideal, which also serves to explain social events. As such, it has some similarity to the notion of an 'ideal type' that is to be found in the works of Lukács' former teacher Max Weber.[66] Weber's exact meaning has been the subject of a great deal of discussion, but it may be roughly stated as follows. The natural scientist, in explaining physical nature, uses concepts such as that of an ideal gas, even though no actual gas behaves exactly like an ideal gas. In much the same way the sociologist, in explaining society, uses ideal types such as (for example) bureaucracy, capitalism, or even something so general as rational behaviour, whether or not any perfect instance of these has actually been found. What justifies the use of such ideal types is the fact that they can be used to explain observed events; if Lukács' concept of class-consciousness can be used in this way, then it too will be justified.

It cannot be said, however, that *History and Class Consciousness* shows in any detail how the concept of proletarian class-consciousness is to be used to explain 'the painful path of the proletarian revolution'. Moreover, there still remains the problem of discovering what, in any given social situation, this class-consciousness is — that is, what is the rational response to such a situation. It has been seen that one is not to look to what the proletariat actually thinks; where, then, is one to look? This is where

53

the Communist Party enters. By 'the Communist Party' Lukács meant a party of the type that Lenin had fashioned; a disciplined body of revolutionaries, submitting themselves to a collective will, committing their whole personality to the Party, and existing as a separate organisation — separate, that is, from the proletariat.[67] Lukács insists that the separateness of the Communist Party does not mean that it wishes to do battle for the proletariat and in place of the proletariat. It exists as a separate entity 'so that the proletariat can see immediately its own class-consciousness, given historical shape'.[68] Or, as Lukács said in his essay on Lenin (1924), the Communist Party is 'the class consciousness of the proletariat which has attained visible shape'.[69] It appears, then, that one will find the content of proletarian class-consciousness by looking towards the Communist Party.

Lukács' Party members may seem to resemble the Guardians in Plato's *Republic*. That is, they may be thought to be a chosen few, who alone have a true insight into the nature of reality, and whose business it is to rule over those who do not have this insight. This, however, is certainly not what Lukács meant. The Communist Party is indeed, according to him, in possession of the correct theory, and it is sometimes necessary for it to take up a position which opposes that of the masses. But Lukács insists that the Party is in constant interaction with the proletariat. Again, the obedience of the Party member is not a blind obedience; there must be interaction between the will of the members and that of the Party leaders.[70] This means that, when the Party approaches its task of leading the proletarian revolution, it is not a complete and finished organisation. As Lukács says in his essay on Lenin, 'The Party does not exist; it comes into being.'[71]

VII

One important theme of *History and Class Consciousness* has still to be discussed. The exposition given in section IV of Lukács' account of the history of modern rationalism covered as it were only one dimension of that account. It regarded Lukács as discussing rationalism simply in terms of the adequacy or inadequacy of its arguments, that is, simply in terms of the goodness or badness of the *reasons* that philosophers brought for their views. It was not wrong in this; Lukács does discuss philosophy in this way, as other Marxists do.[72] But Lukács, like other Marxists, also regards philosophy in the light of what *caused* philosophers to hold the views that they did.[73] The section in which he discusses modern rationalism is called 'The Antinomies of Bourgeois Thought', and the title is significant. By 'bourgeois thought' Lukács does not mean thought which simply happened to be developed during the bourgeois epoch; rather, he means thought which not only occurred during, but also bears the mark of that epoch. This thought, he argues, bears the mark of 'reification', which impresses its structure on the whole consciousness of man during this period.[74] Three questions arise here: what Lukács means by 'reification', how he regards reification as related to bourgeois thought, and what is the importance of the concept. The answers to these questions will occupy the remainder of this chapter.

Lukács discusses the nature of reification (*Verdinglichung*) in the first section of the essay on 'Reification and Proletarian Consciousness'. He takes as his starting point the section of *Capital* in which Marx discusses 'the fetishistic character of commodities'. Marx argues that when bourgeois economists discuss commodities — things whose character enables them to satisfy human wants — they make a fundamental mistake; they take the social relations of producers to the sum total of their labour to be a social relation of things existing outside them. In other words, a social relation between men has taken on the phantasmagoric form of a relation between things.[75] Marx finds an analogy in religion, where the products of the human mind appeared to the believer as independent objects. This is what Marx calls 'the fetishistic character of commodities', and his account of this is, according to Lukács, a discription of the basic phenomenom of reification.[76]

Marx is making the point that bourgeois economists go wrong in that they take as an eternal law of nature what is in fact peculiar to one form of production, the capitalist form.[77] Lukács agrees with this, but he goes further, developing the notion of reification in a way in which it is not developed in *Capital*.[78] He says that the fetishism of commodities, the 'basic phenomenon of reification', is important in that through it a man's activity, his own labour, becomes something that is objective and opposed to him. This opposition has both an objective and a subjective aspect. The objective aspect is that there comes into being a world of things and their relations (commodities and their movement in the market) whose laws can indeed be known by men and used to their advantage, but which men cannot modify.

The subjective aspect is that a man's own activity, his labour, becomes an object which is opposed to him, subject to objective natural laws which govern society, but which are alien to man.

As noted earlier, Lukács asserts that reification impresses itself on the entire consciousness of man during the bourgeois period; it follows that it impresses itself on bourgeois philosophy. Lukács' thesis is[79] that the contradictions to be found in modern rationalist systems — contradictions between subject and object, freedom and necessity — are formulations in philosophical terms of the society in which rationalist philosophers lived. In such a society, Lukács says, men constantly destroy and leave behind them 'natural' bonds, by which he means that the bourgeois epoch is one of an increasing mastery over nature. Yet at the same time men create a kind of 'second nature', whose laws are just as inexorable as the old irrational laws of nature. Here (though he does not state this explicitly) Lukács clearly has in mind the 'fetishism of commodities', the tendency to turn in social relations into objects governed by laws which have the necessity of natural laws. In sum, Lukács is saying that the failure on the part of bourgeois society really to master its world — its replacement of the nature that it has mastered by a 'second nature' which is just as inexorable as the old forces of nature were — is reflected in thought by bourgeois philosophy's failure to discover a subject which really produces its object, and to reconcile the contradiction between freedom and necessity.

When he wrote *History and Class Consciousness*, Lukács did not know of the now famous manuscripts which Marx wrote in Paris in 1844, but what he says about reification has a close similarity to some of the things which Marx said there about 'alienation' or 'estrangement'. Marx described a three-fold alienation of the worker in capitalist society: alienation from the products of his labour, from labour itself as an act of production, and from the very nature of man. What Lukács has said about reification, particularly in its subjective aspect, is close to the second of these, alienation from labour as an act of production. This, according to Marx, consists in the fact that labour is external to the worker, and that it is not his own property, but belongs to someone else.[80]

It may seem that Lukács has succeeded by his own efforts in recreating some of Marx's doctrines, at that time unknown to him or to the world at large. In fact, however, his views about reification owe a great deal to Georg Simmel's book *Die Philosophie des Geldes* (*The Philosophy of Money*, 1st edition, 1900).[81] In a section on the concept of culture,[82] Simmel had traced the effects on the worker of the division of labour. He argued that because the worker does not produce a whole, work ceases to be a living thing for him, and he ceases to see himself in his work. The same result is produced by the separation of the worker from the means of work, which are owned and shared out by the capitalist. Labour power becomes a commodity, and the worker is separated from it, as from something objective. Finally, the object produced becomes something which has a separate existence, and a character foreign to that of the producer. In sum, specialism produces an ever-increasing estrangement (*Fremdheit*) between the worker and his products, as the latter obtain an objective independence.[83]

In *History and Class Consciousness*, Lukács acknowledges his debt to Simmel somewhat obliquely, saying that *The Philosophy of Money* is 'very interesting and accurate in matters of detail',[84] but that Simmel is wrong in turning the manifestations of reification into something independent and permanent, a timeless type of human relations. However, the fact that Lukács borrowed from Simmel does not diminish the importance of what is said about reification in *History and Class Consciousness*. When Lukács looked back on the book in 1967 he said, quite rightly, that it owed its profound influence on intellectuals to the fact that it took estrangement to be the central problem of the critique of capitalism.[85]

Lukács' later attitude to *History and Class Consciousness* has been described in chapter 1, where it was pointed out that his public recantation of the views contained in the book was influenced by tactical considerations. But this should not obscure the fact that Lukács came sincerely to believe that the book was wrong in many respects. He felt it more important to emphasise the book's errors than to ask whether certain trends of thought contained in it were on the right lines; that, he said, was a question which he left to others.[86] This question will not be considered here, as our concern in this book is to expound rather than to criticise. However, we are concerned with the way in which Lukács' ideas developed, and when Lukács' later views are expounded in the remaining chapters it will be helpful from time to time to consider them in the light of *History and Class Consciousness*, and to ask which of these views represent a rejection, and which a development of certain aspects of the work.

4

Marxism and the History of Philosophy: *The Young Hegel* (1948) and *The Destruction of Reason* (1954)

I

The section on 'The Antinomies of Bourgeois Thought' in *History and Class Consciousness* was Lukács' first attempt to discuss the history of philosophy from a Marxist standpoint. In later years, he devoted two long books to the history of philosophy: *Der junge Hegel* (*The Young Hegel*: 1948), in which he examined Hegel's philosophy in detail from its beginnings until the publication of his first major work in 1807, and *Die Zerstörung der Vernunft* (*The Destruction of Reason*: 1954), a critical account of non-Marxist philosophy from the French Revolution until the middle of this century. Lukács regarded these two books as differing radically in approach from *History and Class Consciousness*,[1] and in discussing them it will be instructive to see in what respects they differ from the earlier work.

The Young Hegel might be thought to interest the student of Hegel rather than the student of Lukács. Certainly, it is the student of Hegel who will be interested in such questions as whether it is correct to speak of a 'theological period' in Hegel's development, and whether or not Hegel experienced an intellectual crisis during his stay in Frankfurt between 1797 and 1800. Nevertheless, the book is also an important one for the student of Lukács' thought. Lukács said later[2] that the first draft of the book, which he completed in 1937, was his first attempt to put into practice a plan which he conceived after he had grasped what was wrong with his approach in *History and Class Consciousness*. The plan was to investigate the philosophical connexions between economics and dialectics.

It is significant that Lukács speaks here of *philosophical* connexions. He does not have in mind the way in which the economic basis determines the ideological superstructure; the connexions between basis and superstructure could hardly be called 'philosophical', since philosophy itself belongs to the superstructure. Rather, by 'economics' he means the *science* of economics; the object of his study is, as he puts it in *The Young Hegel*, 'the methodological relation between philosophy and the conceptual mastery of social phenomena'.[3] He adds that this is not the only way in which the development of Hegel's philosophy can be approached; it can, for example, also be approached from the angle of developments in the natural sciences, such as chemistry. However, Lukács says that this way has already been followed, whereas his has not.[4]

In studying the relation between economics and philosophy in Hegel, Lukács does not regard himself as concerned with something that has no contemporary relevance. In *History and Class Consciousness*, his attitude to Hegel's dialectics was far from being one of total rejection, and this remained his attitude. Hegel's dialectics, he said in *The Young Hegel*, had an important as well as a weak side.[5] In establishing a connexion between economics and philosophy, Hegel was doing in an imperfect way what Marx was to do at a much higher level, both in terms of economics and of philosophy, in his *1844 Manuscripts*.[6] This is why *The Young Hegel* is of interest to the student of Lukács, as well as to the Hegelian scholar. Not only does the book give an example of Lukács' approach to the history of philosophy, but it also shows something of his ideas about the nature of that Marxist dialectic which is, in Hegelian terms, the 'sublation' of Hegel's — negating it, and yet preserving what is valid in it.[7]

II

In Lukács' discussion of the philosophical connexions between Hegel's economics and his philosophy, the central concept is that of labour. Here, Lukács is consciously following the views of the young Marx. In his *Economic and Philosophic Manuscripts* of 1844, Marx declared that Hegel's *Phenomenology of Mind* was 'the true birth-place and the secret of the Hegelian philosophy', and added that 'The great thing about Hegel's *Phenomenology* ... is that Hegel grasps the essence of *labour*'.[8] This, incidentally, is why Lukács' study of the young Hegel ends with a discussion of the *Phenomenology*, a book which is usually regarded, not as belonging to Hegel's youth, but as being the first work of his maturity.

In emphasising the part played by the concept of labour in Hegel's philosophy, Lukács is not so much contradicting as supplementing *History and Class Consciousness*. In *The Young Hegel*, he repeats his earlier views about the way in which classical German philosophy differed from the philosophy that preceded it. In the philosophy of the Renaissance and the Enlightenment, he says, mathematics and natural science were of primary importance, but classical German philosophy (anticipated by Vico) laid stress on activity. For Hegel, this activity consisted of the socio-historical activity of man, an activity which overcomes the sharp opposition of subject and object.[9] All this is familiar; but Lukács goes beyond what he had said in *History and Class Consciousness* when he examines more closely Hegel's views about the self-production of man in the historical process. Following the lead of Marx's *1844 Manuscripts*, he points out that it is Hegel's thesis that it is through labour that man becomes man.[10] This thesis is clearly displayed in the *Phenomenology*, but it is also present in some of Hegel's earlier lectures, in which he argues that labour means a break with the merely natural, instinctive life of man.[11]

For Lukács, Hegel's recognition of the part played by labour in the self-production of man is an aspect of his philosophy that has lasting value. But, as mentioned earlier, he regards Hegel's philosophy as having both a strong and a weak side. This two-sidedness, he says, can be seen in the *Phenomenology*, in the form of ambiguities that attach to what he regards as the key term in that work, the term *Entäusserung* ('alienation').[12] Of the three meanings that the word has, one is closely related to what has just been said about self-production of man; another, however, is connected with a feature of Hegel's philosophy that Lukács rejects. This is its idealism, its view that everything is, in some form or other, mind. Since Lukács came to believe that this ambiguity affected his own thought, it will be worth while to pursue the topic further.

Lukács states that in the first of its three senses, 'alienation' refers to the complicated subject-object relation that is connected with all labour, with all the economic and social activity of man. He has in mind here the relations between society and the individuals who make it up, his point being that although society may be said to have an objective existence and to have objective laws of development, it is not something other than the human beings who constitute it. In essence, this is the same as a point that he made when discussing the identical subject-object in *History and Class Consciousness*. There, he quoted with approval Vico's remark that we have made our own history; here, he uses almost the same words, saying that 'men make their own history'.[13] Lukács adds that Hegel took a great step towards the understanding of alienation of this kind, and although he does not specify the nature of the step, he doubtless has in mind Hegel's recognition of the importance of labour.

The second sense of 'alienation' refers to the specifically capitalist form of alienation, which Marx was later to call 'fetishism'. Alienation in this sense[14] is a consequence of the division of labour under capitalism, which leads to both the means of production and the products of labour opposing the worker as a power that is foreign to him. Hegel, says Lukács, had no clear views about alienation of this kind. He was well aware of the evil consequences of capitalism; he saw the way in which it created great wealth and great poverty, and led to hatred of the rich by the poor.[15] But he knew little about the economic basis of the division between rich and poor, and for this reason Lukács says that he had only certain 'intimations' of this type of alienation.

Hegel uses 'alienation' in a third sense, to mean the same as 'thinghood' or 'objectivity'. When he speaks of alienation (or, alternatively, of 'estrangement', *Entfremdung*) of this kind he does so in the context of his idealistic metaphysics, and more specifically in the context of his views about the identical subject-object. Substance, he says, is subject; that is, in a sense everything is mind (cf. chapter 3, section III). It is true that we find ourselves, or seem to find ourselves, confronted by objects which are quite independent of thought; really, however, such objects *are* mind in a self-estranged or alienated form. The *Phenomenology of Mind* traces the way in which the human mind comes to grasp this fact; it describes what Hegel calls the mind's 'return to itself'.[16] Lukács declares this view about the nature of objects to be a mere 'mystification'.

In his 1967 Preface to *History and Class Consciousness*, Lukács applied these distinctions to his earlier views about reification.[17] In *History and Class Consciousness*, he said, he had followed Hegel in equating estrangement or alienation with objectification (*Vergegenständlichung*). This gave unintended support to the view, held by Heidegger and others, that alienation is an eternal 'condition humaine', inseparable from the nature of man. This support, however, rested on a confusion. Objectification is indeed something that cannot be eliminated from the social life of humanity. Labour itself is an objectification; every human mode of expression, including speech, objectifies human thoughts and feelings. What Lukács really had in mind, however, was another sense of 'alienation', namely, that type of alienation which arises when a man's nature is deformed and crippled. Lukács did not think that such alienation was irremovable; on the contrary, he thought that socialism would abolish it.

III

It was said in section I that when Lukács speaks of the philosophical connexions between Hegel's economics and his philosophy, he does not have in mind the way in which the economic basis determines the ideological superstructure; that is, he does not have in mind here the doctrines of historical materialism. Nevertheless, as may be expected, he thinks that these doctrines can be applied to Hegel's thought, and although *The Young Hegel* does not contain a detailed discussion of the nature of historical materialism, of the kind to be found in *History and Class Consciousness*, it does contain some interesting examples of Lukács' use of the doctrine.

These are to be found when Lukács discusses what he calls the 'real connexions' of which philosophical connexions are only the surface.[18] When he reviews the course of his argument towards the end of *The Young Hegel*, he says[19] that his aim had been 'to show, in a concrete and historical way, what part the real contradictions of capitalist society had in the highest form of bourgeois philosophy, the idealistic dialectic of Hegel.' The relations between the two, he says, were extremely complex; however, it seems fair to say that he regards them as being of two main kinds. One kind of relation is that which holds between Hegel's thought and the economic and social backwardness of Germany — a Germany which was far behind England economically, and which was divided into many states in which feudalism was still strong. The other kind of relation is political rather than socio-economic; namely, the impact on Germany of the French Revolution and of the Napoleonic conquests which followed. As a Marxist, Lukács regards politics as belonging to the ideological superstructure, and so as being itself conditioned by the socio-economic basis. In the end, then, Hegel's philosophy is conditioned by this basis; but Lukács insists that it is important to grasp the way in which the influence of the basis is 'mediated'[20] by other factors such as, in this case, political events.

Before discussing Lukács' account in detail, one point must be stressed. He does not think that to discover the social origin of a theory is to refute it. As he himself remarks, the discovery of the social basis of the new astronomy of the sixteenth and seventeenth centuries has no bearing whatsoever on the truth of that astronomy.[21] As already pointed out, Lukács does not think that Hegel's philosophy is wholly devoid of truth, and in *The Young Hegel* he is concerned to discover the 'real connexions' that lie beneath, not only the weak side of Hegel's philosophy, but also its important side. His task, as he states it,[22] is two-fold. He has to show the origins of Hegel's idealism — that is, of what he regards as the weak side of Hegel's philosophy. But he also has to show how, despite the fact that it gives an abstract and partly distorted picture of reality, Hegel's philosophy also displays a masterly grasp of certain universal principles of activity and movement.

In giving his account of what lies beneath the strong side of Hegel's philosophy, Lukács draws attention to the impact of Napoleon on Germany. This, he says, produced contradictory results. On the one hand, French conquests destroyed the relics of feudalism, and as such were welcomed by many German thinkers.[23] Yet at the same time these conquests increased the dismemberment of Germany, and made it still weaker. It might be thought that Lukács would say that such a contradiction led to inconsistency and so to weakness in Hegel's thought. Quite the reverse is the case; Lukács sees this contradiction as a source of Hegel's strength, in that it led to that 'masterly grasp of certain universal principles' just mentioned. What happened, he says, is that between 1797 and 1800 contradiction occupied an increasingly central position in Hegel's thought, and was experienced by him as a moving power of life.[24] This idea was to receive its definitive formulation in Hegel's later works, which lie outside the scope of *The Young Hegel*; one may cite, however, the view put forward in *The Science of Logic* (1st edn, 1812-13) that everything is inherently contradictory; contradiction is the root of all movement and life.[25] Essentially the same view is to be found in classical Marxism. In *Anti-Dühring*, Engels says that it is only as long as we consider things as static and lifeless that we do not come across contradictions in them. The situation changes as soon as we consider things in their motion, their change, their life; motion and life are both contradictions.[26]

Lukács regards Hegel's idealism also as related to social contradictions, but in this case the relation is less direct; Hegel's idealism is traced, not to his awareness of these contradictions, but rather to his failure to discover their economic basis.[27] Lukács argues that Hegel, like other classical German philosophers and writers, took as his point of departure the contradiction between humanistic ideals and German bourgeois society, full of the relics of feudalism. He experienced these contradictions, and he pondered over them, but because the economic basis of these contradictions was not clear to him, he went astray in what Lukács calls 'idealistic constructions'. His failure to be clear about this basis was not a contingent matter; he *could not* be clear about it. The idealistic side of Hegelian dialectics, Lukács argues, could be overcome only by a socialist critique of capitalist alienation, and for this the time was not yet ripe, in that class struggles had not yet sufficiently developed in Germany.[28]

This, however, is only a part of Lukács' account of the factors determining Hegel's idealism. Lukács regards idealism as committed to a defence of religion; in this connexion, he quotes with approval Lenin's remark that philosophical idealism is the same as clerical obscurantism.[29] Consequently, his discussion of Hegel's idealism is closely linked with his account of Hegel's views about religion.[30] These views, he argues, are to be explained in the context of the German Enlightenment. He sees Hegel as following the general tradition of the Enlightenment, with its great stress on the human reason, and he is therefore opposed to philosophers such as Dilthey, who saw in Hegel a philosophical romantic, an irrationalist. There was, however, a significant difference between the French and the German Enlightenments. The leaders of the French Enlightenment, the *philosophes*, were strongly opposed to religion. Lukács argues that because of the backwardness of the country, such an attitude was not possible in Germany; the representatives of the German Enlightenment, therefore, did not attack religion, but tried to reconcile it with the principles of reason, and Hegel followed them in this.

It will be clear from all this why Lukács differed from the official view of Hegel put forward in Russia during the war, according to which Hegel's philosophy was the expression of feudal reaction against the French Revolution.[31] Nevertheless, Lukács is faced with a paradox, which he has to explain. He insists that Hegel never sympathised with reaction, but at the same time he has to admit that Hegel was no democrat — in contrast with his contemporary Fichte, whom Lukács regards as far inferior to Hegel as a philosopher. His explanation is that the conditions for a genuinely democratic movement in Germany — which means, the sharpening of class antagonisms and the rise of the proletariat — did not yet exist. Fichte's democratic views, then, could only be utopian; Lukács regards it as a point in Hegel's favour that he did not indulge in such utopianism, but stood 'with both feet on the ground of historical reality itself'.[32]

IV

In *The Young Hegel* Lukács had been concerned with bourgeois philosophy at what he regarded as its highest point; *The Destruction of Reason* deals with bourgeois thought in decline. The subject of the book is a trend of thought which Lukács calls 'irrationalism'. Irrationalism, he argues, is to be found in both sociology and philosophy, but he devotes most attention to its philosophical manifestations. It is also an international phenomenon, but because Germany was a particularly favourable ground for this trend of thought, and because German irrationalists had the greatest international effect, Lukács deals mainly with irrationalism in Germany. German irrationalism culminated in Hitler, and so Lukács can describe the subject-matter of his book as 'Germany's road to Hitler in the realm of philosophy'.[33] But irrationalism did not end with Hitler, and in an epilogue Lukács traces its course in the post-war world.

Lukács' aim is to write a Marxist history of philosophy; the first, he claims, of its kind.[34] As a Marxist historian, he sees himself faced by two tasks. First, and most obviously, he has to show how the 'real development of Germany'[35] was reflected in philosophy. It is not, Lukács says, sufficient to view the development of philosophy as something purely 'immanent', as Hegel did; that is, as if each problem posed or solved springs out of the inner logic of philosophical thought.[36] Rather, the various stages of philosophy have to be viewed as answers to the problems of the class struggle. In other words, the Marxist historian of philosophy has to relate philosophy, as part of the ideological superstructure, to the socio-economic basis. This, however, is not all that he has to do. Classical Marxism, as expounded in letters written by Engels towards the end of his life, insists that although the socio-economic basis undeniably determines the ideological superstructure, the superstructure can affect the basis — though the forces involved are very unequal, the economic one being much the strongest and most decisive.[37] This view has been widely accepted by Marxists, and Lukács is no exception. He says[38] that one of his tasks is to show how philosophical views — themselves the conceptual reflection of the real development of Germany towards Hitler — helped to accelerate this development.

In *History and Class Consciousness*, Lukács made it clear that he thought that historical materialism left room for human freedom (cf. chapter 3, section V), and this continued to be his view. His purpose in writing *The Destruction of Reason*, he said, was to enable the reader to 'learn, and be warned'.[39] This clearly implies that we can learn from the past, can learn to avoid the recurrence of something similar to Hitler's Germany; and this in turn implies that such a recurrence is something that we are free to avoid.

Lukács' determination to issue a warning gives his book a certain one-sidedness. He himself says[40] that irrationalism is only one important trend in reactionary bourgeois philosophy, which suggests that such philosophy may also have manifested some trends of which he approved. For example, it has been argued[41] that Nietzsche, whom Lukács regards as an arch-irrationalist, was as opposed as Lukács was to the reification of thought and reality. Lukács admits that Nietzsche's criticisms of contemporary art and culture were sometimes correct,[42] but he passes over this quickly in order to dwell on what he regards as Nietzsche's failings. In general, the picture of non-Marxist thought that *The Destruction of Reason* presents is uniformly black, and this monotony has doubtless contributed to the largely hostile reception that the book has received.

V

What has just been said about *The Destruction of Reason* raises two main questions. First, what exactly is that 'irrationalism' of which

Lukács speaks? Second, how does he relate the history of irrationalism to social and economic factors?

For Lukács, irrationalism has to be defined by reference to that which it opposes, reason; and to speak of reason in this context is to speak of dialectics. *The Destruction of Reason* does not contain a full and systematic account of the views about dialectics which Lukács held after *History and Class Consciousness*, but what is said in passing is enough to indicate their main outlines. The relation between irrationalism and dialectics, he says, can be explained as follows.[43] Objective reality is much richer and more complex than any concepts that we can form; it follows, therefore, that it is impossible to avoid what Lukács calls 'conflicts between thought and being', which is to say that at various times unsolved problems must arise. Irrationalism is in essence the supposition that problems which are not solved are in fact insoluble, and that we *cannot* obtain rational knowledge of reality. In place of rational knowledge, irrationalism postulates knowledge of some 'higher' sort, such as faith or intuition.

It will doubtless be asked what all this has to do with dialectics. The answer is that the problems in the face of which irrationalism retreats can be solved, and the solution is provided by dialectics. In the Hegelian language that Lukács uses,[44] irrationalism equates the 'understanding' (*Verstand*) with the 'reason' (*Vernunft*), and supposes that the limits of the understanding are also the limits of reason, so that anything not grasped by the understanding must be grasped, if at all, by some kind of super-rational knowledge. 'Understanding' and 'reason', in this technical sense, have not met us before, but they are closely related to Engels' distinction between the 'metaphysical' and the 'dialectical' modes of thought, discussed in chapter 3, section II. The former, it will be recalled, regards things and concepts as rigid and fixed; it accepts the law of contradiction as binding, and supposes that a thing either exists or does not exist, and that it cannot at the same time be itself and something else. This way of thinking is the work of what Hegel calls the 'understanding'. It is a one-sided and abstract way of thinking, whose limitations can be overcome only by dialectical thinking, which grasps the inherently contradictory nature of reality.[45] Thinking of this kind is the work of Hegel's 'reason'. Irrationalism, then, arises when it is thought that what cannot be grasped by understanding but can be grasped by reason — dialectical thinking — cannot be grasped by reason at all.

As described so far, the concept of dialectics contained in *The*

Destruction of Reason does not differ from the one to be found in *History and Class Consciousness*. There is, however, a fundamental difference between the two concepts. Whereas the notion of the identical subject-object is of the greatest importance in the dialectics of *History and Class Consciousness*, this is no longer the case in Lukács' later dialectics. Instead, stress is laid on the thesis that knowledge is a 'reflection' (*Widerspiegelung*) of reality. This point is made most clearly in *The Young Hegel*, in which Lukács says[46] 'The identical subject-object is the central methodological concept of objective idealism [idealism such as that of Hegel], just as the reflection in human consciousness of an objective reality which is independent of consciousness forms the central point of the theory of knowledge of philosophical materialism.' That human knowledge is a reflection of objective reality is repeated in *The Destruction of Reason*;[47] this view, however, is of less importance to Lukács' account of irrationalism than it is to his aesthetics, and a fuller account of it will be deferred until chapter 7.

The removal from Lukács' dialectics of the thesis of the identical subject-object has another aspect. It was pointed out earlier (chapter 3, section V) that this thesis led Lukács, in *History and Class Consciousness*, to deny that dialectics can be applied to the natural sciences. Now, however, Lukács follows Engels, and orthodox Soviet Marxism, in extending dialectics to the natural sciences. The philosophy of dialectical materialism, he says, sums up the principles and laws of the special sciences.[48]

The view that the limits of the understanding are to be transcended, not by the reason, but by means of some kind of alleged super-rational knowledge is fundamental to irrationalism, as Lukács understands it. Irrationalism, however, has other distinctive features. Lukács declares[49] that in almost every irrationalist there are to be found, besides the disparagement of reason and the glorification of intuition, the following motifs:

(1) An 'aristocratic' theory of knowledge. Super-rational knowledge, the irrationalist declares, is not to be obtained by anyone, but is the possession of a privileged few.
(2) The denial of historical progress. For Lukács, this is a mark of irrationalism in that history manifests certain laws, the laws of dialectics; so the irrationalist's assertion that there is no progress in history is another indication of his failure to think dialectically.

(3) The creation of myths. These myths are not just falsehoods (in the sense in which one might speak of the myth of Prussian invincibility), but are presentations in analogical or symbolic form of what are claimed to be super-rational truths. It is obviously Lukács' view that what can be thought, can be stated clearly and literally.

VI

Such, then, is the nature of irrationalism, as Lukács understands it. Before we can examine Lukács' views about its relations to social and economic conditions, we need to know something about its history simply as a trend of thought. We know that, for Lukács, irrationalism still existed when he was writing *The Destruction of Reason*; but when did it begin? His language here may cause confusion. He speaks sometimes of 'irrationalism' simply, and sometimes of 'modern irrationalism', which suggests that the latter is one form of irrationalism in general — just as, in *History and Class Consciousness*, what is called modern rationalism is one form of rationalism in general, which has existed at many times and in many forms.[50] However, this is not what Lukács means; for him, 'irrationalism' and 'modern irrationalism' are interchangeable terms. His argument is that irrationalism is essentially a reaction to dialectical thinking, and so its history can only begin with the origin of dialectics early in the nineteenth century; that is, in what Lukács regards as the modern era.[51] He admits that irrationalism had predecessors — for example, Pascal, who was a contemporary of Descartes, and Jacobi, who wrote at the time of the German Enlightenment.[52] But he regards these as forerunners of irrationalism rather than as irrationalists. For him, irrationalism begins with Schelling — a philosopher who was at first a friend of Hegel, but who later criticised Hegel's views — and his account of irrationalism begins with the formation of Schelling's thought in the years immediately following the French Revolution.

Since Lukács is primarily concerned with German irrationalism, he devotes his first chapter to 'Some distinctive features of the historical development of Germany'. He has said that the various stages of philosophy have to be viewed as answers to the problems of the class struggle; in this chapter, therefore, he sketches the history of class struggles in Germany, so providing an account of that 'real development of Germany' which was reflected in irrationalist philosophy. As far as the main part of his book is concerned — that is, before the Epilogue, which deals with irrationalism after the Second World War — this development ended with the coming to power of the Nazis. So the question with which Lukács is faced is, 'How did this happen? How was it that the forces of democracy were so weak in Germany?' As already mentioned, it was his view that irrationalism not only depended on the class struggle, but also affected its outcome. In this chapter, however, he is mainly concerned with that which influenced irrationalism, rather than with irrationalism itself as an historical influence.[53]

'Generally speaking', he says, 'the destiny and the tragedy of the German people lies in the fact that it came too late in modern bourgeois development.'[54] He had already referred to the backwardness of Germany in his book on the young Hegel, but whereas the historical background provided there begins with the French Revolution, in *The Destruction of Reason* Lukács begins his account with the transitional period lying between the end of the middle ages and the beginning of the modern era.[55] Industry and trade in Germany increased during this period, but the various independent German states had no common economic interests, and their economy was badly damaged by the change in trade-routes that followed the discovery of America and of the sea-route to India. The outcome of class struggles within Germany, culminating in the Peasant War of 1525, also contributed to the weakness of the country. According to Lukács, the peasants wanted to put an end to feudal absolutism, which was preventing the centralisation of power in Germany, and their defeat meant that the country continued to be divided and weak. So Germany became the battlefield of the European great powers, and suffered political, economic and cultural destruction.

Only in the eighteenth century, and especially in its second half, did the economic recovery of Germany begin,[56] and with it a strengthening of the bourgeoisie. In this condition, Germany went through the period of the French Revolution and the Napoleonic Wars. Napoleon's conquests only increased the dismemberment of Germany; however, there was a strong desire for national unity, and the struggle for such unity came to dominate the whole political and ideological development of Germany in the nineteenth century. But a special problem faced Germany. The other great European powers, and in particular England and France, had already achieved national unity under their absolute monarchies; in Germany, on the other hand, the bourgeois revolution had to lay the very foundations of national unity. So it had, at one stroke, to destroy well-established institutions and create new ones — tasks which, in other countries, had taken centuries. The special position of Prussia also raised a problem. Feudal, absolutist and bureaucratic, Prussia was also the greatest military power among the German states. Put simply, the question was whether German unity could best be achieved with the help of Prussia, or by its destruction. The second alternative, Lukács says, was the only one favourable to the development of democracy in Germany. However, the big bourgeoisie were inclined to compromise with Prussia, and Prussia in turn was compelled to support the development of capitalism.

After the revolution of 1848, Prussia moved towards what Engels called a 'bonapartist monarchy'.[57] This led to still further economic progress, though at the cost of a 'Prussianisation' of Germany, which meant a strengthening of its undemocratic social and political structure. By the time that Germany entered its imperialist period, that is in about 1890,[58] it had become a great capitalist power, yet democracy still did not gain ground. One reason for this was the political immaturity of the German people; further, the masses outside Germany had become disenchanted with bourgeois democracy, and this had an effect on Germany, and in particular on German intellectuals. The end of the German empire and the establishment of the Weimar republic after the First World War brought no move towards what Lukács regards as real democracy. It is true that the Weimar republic was ostensibly democratic; but, Lukács says, it was a bourgeois democracy, a union of all bourgeois forces against the growing threat of a proletarian revolution.

Lukács finally considers Hitler's rise to power.[59] Lenin had declared that 'in its economic essence, imperialism is monopoly capitalism',[60] and it is to monopoly capitalism that Lukács relates the spread of Fascism in Germany. As their power increased, monopoly capitalists were no longer content to restrict themselves to economic affairs, but demanded a leading role in all questions. Lukács now has to answer the problem, how they succeeded in their demands — a success which is the more puzzling in that, as he points out, widespread unemployment led to an anti-capitalist mood in the masses. Somehow, the monopoly capitalists had to turn this mood to their advantage, and Lukács says that only a radically irrationalist world-view, such as Fascism, was adequate to this task. To explain the spread of Fascism in Germany, Lukács refers to some new phenomena. The intelligentsia and the petty bourgeoisie — e.g. the small tradesmen and the shopkeepers — had seen the collapse of their former security of existence, and this led them to follow ideologists of despair such as Oswald Spengler, whose book *The Decline of the West* had a great success when it was published in 1919 and 1922. But despair was not confined to the middle classes; it was also the socio-psychological link between the masses and National Socialism, whose real effect on the German people began with the economic crisis of 1929. Not that despair was the only link. Out of despair there arose credulity, the expectation of miracles, and this led people to look to the 'God-sent genius'. Such a mood of credulity was nothing new; Lukács compares the belief in miracles that was common in the Graeco-Roman world during the Alexandrian epoch, and the belief in witches that was widespread during the seventeenth century. Common to all such periods of social insanity, he says, is the fact that they are periods of the destruction of an old social order and the birth-pangs of a new one. The rise of Fascism occurred during such a period of crisis in Germany.

VII

Against this background, Lukács places his account of irrationalist thought. It is impossible to discuss here all the philosophers and sociologists whom he criticises; it must be sufficient to state the main outlines of his account of irrationalist philosophy, concentrating on the four philosophers to whom he devotes most attention — Schelling, Schopenhauer, Kierkegaard and Nietzsche. In discussing Kierkegaard, Lukács may seem to have forgotten his intention to concentrate on irrationalism in Germany; but, as he points out, Kierkegaard can be placed within the context of German philosophy, both because it had a great influence on him and because he in turn influenced later German philosophers such as Heidegger. Lukács may also have had another motive. In his 1967 Introduction to *History and Class Consciousness*, he says that Kierkegaard played a considerable part in his early development, and that in the years immediately preceding the First World War he even planned an essay on Kierkegaard's critique of Hegel.[61] His discussion of

Kierkegaard in *The Destruction of Reason*, then, may in part be an attempt to settle accounts with this early influence on him.

Lukács divides irrationalism into two main periods;[62] the first of these ends roughly in 1871, and the second stretches up to the present. The irrationalist philosophies of the first main period have in common the fact that they are opposed to idealist dialectics, and in particular the dialectics of Hegel. Socially, the period is one in which the power of the bourgeoisie reaches its highest point, and then begins to decline. This leads Lukács to subdivide the period, the division occurring in about 1848. Before this date, the bourgeoisie was a rising and progressive class; irrationalist philosophy was an attack on the ideology of the bourgeoisie and a defence of the Restoration, the political reaction to the French Revolution. The chief exponent of irrationalism of this type was Schelling. But at about the time of the revolutions of 1848, the decline of bourgeois ideology begins. Though Lukács recognises some individual exceptions, he argues that bourgeois literature and art manifest a steady decline after 1848; in the field of the theoretical sciences the decline began even earlier. Since the end of the school of Ricardo in the 1820s, and of Hegelianism in the 1830s and 1840s, bourgeois economics and philosophy have, according to Lukács, produced nothing that is original and progressive. It is true that the natural sciences made enormous progress after 1848, but Lukács argues that the bourgeois methodology and philosophy of the sciences deteriorates. The irrationalist philosophy of the years immediately following 1848 is the philosophy of the bourgeoisie, now no longer progressive, but reactionary; Schopenhauer and Kierkegaard are its main representatives.

In saying that the second main period of irrationalism begins in about 1871, Lukács is again using the class situation as his principle of division. At about this time, many of the demands of the bourgeois revolution have been satisfied, and the new class, the proletariat, begins to display its increased power, a clear demonstration of which is provided by the Paris Commune of 1871. From about this time, it is the world-view of the proletariat — dialectical and historical materialism — against which irrationalism struggles. The most important philosopher of this period of irrationalism was Nietzsche.

It may seem strange that Lukács should begin his account of irrationalism with Schelling, since he regards Schelling's early philosophy as an important stage in the history of dialectics.[63]

Lukács argues, however, that idealisst dialectics, of which Schelling's was one type, had two sides.[64] One of these, the progressive side, was an approximation to dialectical materialism; the other, however, was close to mystical pantheism. In Schelling, the mystical tendency became steadily more important. This tendency in Schelling, Lukács argues, was linked with his doctrine of intellectual intuition. Even in the young Schelling, this had been associated with an aristocratic theory of knowledge, the connexion being the idea that intuition is for the few. At first, Schelling said that this intuition was manifested in the aesthetic attitude; later, however, the object of intuition became God.[65] Lukács was of course aware that Spinoza, whom he does not count as an irrationalist, had a theory of intellectual intuition, and that the object of this intuition was God; but he would have argued that in Spinoza this intuition is not (as it is in Schelling) a mystical vision.

In 1841, ten years after Hegel's death, the now elderly Schelling was appointed to the chair of philosophy at Berlin to counteract the influence of Hegelianism. It is important to be clear about the part which Lukács ascribes to Schelling in the class struggle of this period. Schelling was appointed by the reactionary Prussian authorities, led by Friedrich Wilhelm IV; that is, by the supporters of feudal absolutism. The ideas that he was to oppose were primarily those of the 'left Hegelians', those of Hegel's followers who formed the extreme left wing of bourgeois democracy.[66] In other words, Schelling was called upon to support feudalism against the pressure of the bourgeoisie. Not that Lukács thinks that the philosophy of the later Schelling was wholly wrong. He was right (as against Hegel) in giving being priority over consciousness, and in treating practice as a criterion of theory. But 'being' in Schelling is not viewed as dialectical materialism was to view it; it is turned into God, who is above reason.[67]

Schopenhauer's version of irrationalism is more highly developed.[68] It has already been mentioned that Lukács regards him as the first representative of purely bourgeois irrationalism, and connects him with economic and social conditions after 1848. This throws an interesting light on Lukács' conception of historical materialism. It is doubtless true, as he says, that Schopenhauer's philosophy first became influential after 1848;[69] but it is also a fact that his major work, *The World as Will and Representation*, was published long before this, in 1819. One naturally asks: how, then, can Schopenhauer's philosophy be regarded as determined by the social and economic conditions of its time? Lukács does not pose this question in so many words, but the answer that he would give is clear. He says that the seeds of later bourgeois development were already present when Schopenhauer wrote, and that it is an indication of his philosophical gifts that (like Kierkegaard and Nietzsche after him) he was able to anticipate later developments, thanks to 'the keenness of his conceptual ear'[70] for important symptoms.

Schopenhauer's importance, says Lukács, lies in the fact that he discovered a new way of defending capitalism: an *indirect* defence.[71] Broadly, the indirect apologist for capitalism does not try to smooth over the contradictions of capitalism, or argue them out of existence. Instead, he accepts these contradictions, but then says that these bad aspects of capitalism are features, not of capitalism as such, but of human existence in general, from which it follows that to struggle against them is senseless. In Schopenhauer, pessimism — the idea of the senselessness of human endeavour — is at the very centre of his philosophy. He drew a sharp distinction between appearance ('representation') and reality ('will'), and said that all historicity, and with it all progress, is mere appearance. (Hence, according to Lukács, Schopenhauer's bitter hatred of Hegel.)[72] Such is the philosophical basis of Schopenhauer's assertion of the senselessness of all political activity; his pessimism was also socially conditioned, in that it was an ideological reflex of the Restoration period. After the French Revolution had exhausted itself, everything seemed to be as it was before the revolution, and it was easy to be persuaded that all political effort was in vain.[73]

In his theory of knowledge, Schopenhauer develops Schelling's aristocratism, saying that the world as it really is can be grasped only by the genius.[74] His views about religion, however, contain something new and important. In Lukács' discussion of Schopenhauer there occurs for the first time the theme of 'religious atheism', which is to recur several times in *The Destruction of Reason*.[75] Schopenhauer proclaimed himself an atheist; but, Lukács says, his atheism was not hostile to religion. He rejected what he called 'low rationalism', and said that the 'deep mysteries of Christianity', and in particular the doctrine of original sin, were philosophically defensible. In this way, he provided a kind of substitute religion for those who had ceased to believe in the dogmatic religions. There will be more to say about religious atheism when we discuss Lukács' views about Kierkegaard.

Lukács regards Kierkegaard as the second of the two great pioneers of the indirect defence of capitalism. Like Schopenhauer, Kierkegaard was slow in achieving world-significance; only between the two world wars, when existentialists such as Heidegger took up his ideas, did he become a decisive influence upon philosophical irrationalism. In Kierkegaard, then, as in Schopenhauer, Lukács finds the conceptual anticipation of later development.[76] The difference between their philosophies is to be traced to the fact that Schopenhauer wrote during the Restoration period, whereas Kierkegaard wrote when Hegelianism was coming to an end and materialist dialectics was beginning. This meant that Schopenhauer could dismiss Hegelianism as sheer nonsense, whereas Kierkegaard had to oppose Hegel in the name of a new type of dialectics, which Lukács regards as pseudo-dialectics.[77]

The attitudes of Schopenhauer and Kierkegaard to Hegel's dialectics may be summed up as follows. Both attack it for enshrining the view that human history displays real progress, and that the laws that govern this progress can be discovered. But whereas Schopenhauer declares the notion of real progress, and indeed of real change of any kind, to be senseless, Kierkegaard is merely agnostic; human beings, acquainted as they are with only a small part of history, cannot discover the laws that govern the whole. In place of the idea of an objective world-history, whose laws can be grasped, Kierkegaard offers what Lukács calls a 'mythicised pseudo-history', whose focal point is the life of Jesus Christ. What matters to the Kierkegaardian individual is his relation to Christ; the rest of world-history is quite irrelevant, as having no bearing on the salvation of the individual soul.[78]

The fact that Kierkegaard proclaimed himself a Christian, whereas Schopenhauer was a professed atheist who derived inspiration from Buddhist rather than Christian sources, may seem to be an important point of difference between them. Lukács would say, however, that this difference is insignificant. Kierkegaard, like Schopenhauer, believed in nothing, and his philosophy, like Schopenhauer's, is a religious atheism — though Kierkegaard himself was unaware of this.[79] Lukács realises that this may sound paradoxical; but, he asks, *in what* does Kierkegaard's religious man believe? Kierkegaard's Christianity is one of extreme subjectivity;

for him Christianity is a matter not of doctrine, but of practice, of the following of Christ, the 'how' as opposed to the 'what'. Again, there is no religious congregation to give guidance; religion is a matter of inwardness, and the religious man lives, as Kierkegaard puts it, 'incognito'. So Kierkegaard's religious man has as a guide only what he finds in himself; and this, says Lukács, is nihilism and despair.[80]

Religious atheism was not something purely personal to Kierkegaard, nor even a local Danish matter; it was, says Lukács, the spontaneous expression of the feelings of a group of deracinated bourgeois intellectuals, and is to be found in writers who were quite independent of Kierkegaard, such as Dostoevsky. But although it was a spontaneous expression of feeling, it also acquired a social function. The reactionary bourgeoisie were able to turn it into a defensive weapon, whereby bourgeois intellectuals were diverted away from the abandonment of religion and the adoption of the outlook of dialectical materialism, and towards the religious defence of the existing social order.[81] Here one may object that, even if one grants that Lukács has correctly described the social function of religious atheism, this is not the same as showing it to be false. Lukács would agree. He himself says early in *The Destruction of Reason* that it is one thing to show the genesis and function of a doctrine, and quite another to refute it.[82] However, he believes that Marxism does provide a refutation of religious atheism. Such atheism, he argues, arises out of the senselessness of modern life.[83] Now, we saw earlier that it is a feature of the indirect defence of capitalism that it regards characteristics that are peculiar to capitalism as typical of human life in general; and this, Lukács would say, is the error that is committed by religious atheism.[84] The feelings of senselessness and of despair from which it arises do not attach to the human condition as such, but only to one phase of human history, the capitalist phase.

We have noted a number of differences between the philosophies of Schopenhauer and Kierkegaard, but we have still to mention what Lukács regards as Kierkegaard's chief original contribution to irrationalism. This is the concept of what Lukács calls 'sham activity'.[85] Whereas Schopenhauer's pessimism had led to a withdrawal from action, Kierkegaard stressed the importance of action, and criticised German idealist philosophy — not, Lukács says, without justification — for its contemplative attitude. But the action which Kierkegaard recommends is not *social* action, and so

Lukács regards it as sham action, a mere caricature. Lukács adds that this concept of sham activity contributed to the influence of Kierkegaard's philosophy between the two world wars. The existentialists not only took over Kierkegaard's religious atheism, but they also made use of his concept of activity. They removed from activity everything social and historical, and claimed in this way to reach true reality, in which a man can find his freedom.[86]

The next step in the history of irrationalism was taken by Nietzsche. This was a step towards irrationalism of a more militant kind. Just as Schopenhauer anticipated the development of the class struggle after 1848, so Nietzsche, whose career as a writer ended in 1889, anticipated the needs of the bourgeois intelligentsia of Germany's imperialist epoch.[87] Nietzsche recognised that the bourgeois epoch was becoming more decadent, and undertook to show the way to overcome this tendency. The best of the intellectuals of the imperialist epoch also wished to overcome decadence, but they shrank from aligning themselves with the proletariat. Nietzsche's social task was to 'save' or 'redeem' such intellectuals in a way which enabled them to retain the pleasant feeling of being rebels without having to break with the bourgeoisie. For Nietzsche, the chief enemy was socialism, and Lukács claims that we must grasp this fact if we are to understand the general structure of his world-view.[88]

Before expounding Nietzsche's thought, Lukács makes some interesting observations about his philosophical style. Among the typical features of irrationalism that Nietzsche manifests is one that has not so far been illustrated: namely, his tendency to express his thought in myths. Lukács connects Nietzsche's use of myths with his historical position.[89] Nietzsche, the leading philosopher of imperialist reaction, had no experience of imperialism, and so his expression of what was to come could only come in utopian, mythical form. Nietzsche's historical position also explains his aphoristic method of writing. Lukács returns to a topic first discussed in *The Soul and the Forms* — the nature of the essay — when he says that it is a general phenomenon that thinkers who can observe a social development only in its origins prefer the essayistic, aphoristic form. In this respect, Nietzsche is in the tradition of writers such as Montaigne and La Rochefoucauld — writers for whom, incidentally, he expressed admiration.[90]

With Nietzsche, the indirect defence of capitalism takes a new form. Schopenhauer had argued that all action (and therefore action against capitalism) was valueless; Nietzsche, on the other hand, called for action — and not for sham action of the kind that Kierkegaard advocated.[91] This call for action is to be found in Nietzsche's moral philosophy. Nietzsche's famous demand for a 'transvaluation of all values' meant, above all, that the instincts should be freed. This, says Lukács, was an idealisation of the egoism of the decadent bourgeoisie. As he puts it, 'The declining bourgeoisie must unchain everything that is evil and bestial in man, to win militant activists for the preservation of its dominance.'[92] This is an indirect defence of capitalism in that Nietzsche does not try to minimise the evils of capitalism; rather, he accepts them, and indeed he glorifies them. He lays stress on the barbaric features of capitalist man, as 'properties of that type which must be the object of moral endeavour, if humanity — that is, capitalism — is to be saved'.[93] This is clearly an ethics for the ruling class, and it is accompanied in Nietzsche by a passionate opposition to the morality of the oppressed. The struggle between the two systems of morality is, according to Nietzsche, the basic feature of all history. So it may be said that Nietzsche (unlike direct apologists for capitalism) does in some measure acknowledge the existence of the class struggle. He does not, however, have any clear ideas about class; for him, the conflict is between higher and lower *races*. Lukács sees in this an anticipation of Fascist race theory.[94] It is true, he says, that Nietzsche did not stress the supremacy of an 'Aryan' race; it is also true that he speaks of race in a very general and mythical way. Yet from his race theory he drew the same barbaric consequences as the Nazi theorist Alfred Rosenberg drew from the views of Houston Stewart Chamberlain, so there is no essential difference between Nietzsche and Fascism on this issue.

Like Schopenhauer, Nietzsche proclaimed himself an atheist; like Schopenhauer, he is an atheist of a special kind, a religious atheist. But there is a difference. Nietzsche's atheism is not based on the view that the world-picture presented by the sciences is inconsistent with the concept of God; instead, his atheism has a moral basis. When Nietzsche says, in a well-known passage, that 'God is dead',[95] he means that the concept of God is incompatible with the new morality, in which 'Everything is allowed'.[96] This distinguishes Nietzsche's attack on Christianity from that of the philosophers of the Enlightenment. They had attacked it as the support of feudal absolutism; Nietzsche attacks it as a form of slave-morality, the ideological forerunner of democracy and socialism. In sum,[97] 'When Nietzsche appears in the character of the Antichrist, he really wants to destroy socialism.'

When Lukács comes to the end of his account of Nietzsche, he is not yet half-way through *The Destruction of Reason*, but the main lines of his argument have already been laid down. As he himself says, Schopenhauer, Kierkegaard and Nietzsche are the great exponents of the indirect defence of capitalism; their successors did not add anything that is essentially new.[98] The remaining philosophical stage on the way to Fascism can, therefore, be dealt with quickly. This is the trend of thought called 'life-philosophy', whose influence on the thought of the young Lukács has already been noted (chapter 2, section I). Lukács distinguishes two chief phases in the history of life-philosophy. The first extends from the origins of life-philosophy, in the thought of Wilhelm Dilthey (1833-1911), as far as the beginning of the First World War. Up to this time, there was no acute crisis in imperialism; the seeds of crisis were indeed there, but they were still latent. The second phase of life-philosophy comes after 1918, when the crisis in imperialism becomes acute.[99] The main representatives of the first phase are Dilthey and Simmel; of the second, Heidegger and Jaspers.

To see how Lukács relates life-philosophy to social conditions, it is necessary first to consider his account of its immediate predecessor, the neo-Kantian school of philosophy (cf. chapter 1, section I). He sees this as the expression of bourgeois confidence in continued capitalist development, which leads to a rejection of all questions about 'world-views' and a restriction of philosophy to logic, theory of knowledge and psychology. Neo-Kantian theory of knowledge was agnostic, and on the basis of this it rejected as unscientific and metaphysical the world-view of the German workers, dialectical materialism.[100] However, the latent crisis of the imperialist period led to the need of a world-view, and it was the task of life-philosophy to satisfy this need. It retained the agnosticism of neo-Kantianism, and denied the existence of a reality that is independent of thought, but it opposed the neo-Kantians' concentration on the categories of the 'understanding' — roughly, those of the natural sciences. These, it argued, were too thin and poverty-stricken; in their place, life-philosophy appealed to the fulness of life, of 'lived experience' (*Erlebnis*). Socially, life-philosophy was of use to the bourgeoisie, in that the anti-capitalist mood of the intelligentsia was increasing; life-philosophy, with its contrast between the living on the one hand, and the dead and mechanical on the other, 'deepened' all the real problems of the age, and turned the attention of the intelligentsia away from their social consequences. In this respect, its social function was similar to that which Lukács ascribes to religious atheism; and indeed, Lukács argues that the philosophy of Simmel enters into the mainstream of religious atheism.[101] Again, the agnosticism of life-philosophy undermined belief in historical progress, and in the possibility of a radical democratisation of Germany.[102]

The First World War produced a radical change of mood in Germany, and with this, life-philosophy also underwent a change. The world had collapsed in ruins, and 'in the wilderness there stands, in dread and anxiety, the solitary ego'.[103] It was natural that in such circumstances the philosophy of Kierkegaard, based as it was on the despair of extreme subjectivism, should become topical. A renaissance of Kierkegaard's philosophy was proclaimed by Heidegger and Jaspers, leading figures in the existentialist movement. Their philosophy differed from previous life-philosophy by its mood of despair; it differed from that of Kierkegaard by the fact that it attacked dialectical materialism instead of Hegelian dialectics. There was another important difference between Kierkegaard and existentialism. Although one finds in the existentialists the same turning away from social activity that is to be found in Kierkegaard, as in Schopenhauer before him, the feeling of despair that is expressed by Heidegger could easily turn into desperate revolutionary activity. 'It is no accident', says Lukács, 'that Hitler's agitation constantly appeals to despair.'[104]

Although life-philosophy is the stage of irrationalist philosophy that immediately preceded, and indeed was contemporary with, the rise of Nazism, Lukács does not assert that Nazism drew exclusively on this source. In his view,[105] the most important prop of the philosophy of Fascism was race theory, and he devotes a whole chapter of *The Destruction of Reason* to this topic. However, his account of life-philosophy completes his account of Germany's road to Hitler in the realm of philosophy proper, and it is now time to make a few general comments on this account. It has been seen how, for Lukács, German irrationalism is the reflection in philosophical terms of the class struggle. However, it was said in section IV that

Lukács regarded irrationalism as not only dependent on the 'real development' of Germany, but also as accelerating that development. His argument for this conclusion is quite simple. His view is that life-philosophy, the final stage of German irrationalist philosophy, helped to create an atmosphere in which Fascism could flourish — an atmosphere of distrust in reason, of disbelief in historical progress, and of the credulous expectation of marvels. This atmosphere was not the creation of a few years; it was the outcome of the development of German irrationalism from Schopenhauer onwards.[106]

One concluding point. Hegel spoke of 'the cunning of reason', by which he meant that a person's conscious purposes may differ greatly from the outcome of his actions; the individual may follow his own particular passions, but the outcome of his actions forms part of a rational pattern, which the individual himself does not see.[107] Lukács might have spoken (though in fact he did not) of a 'cunning of unreason'. He says that it would be ludicrous to suppose that thinkers such as Dilthey and Simmel were conscious precursors of Fascism; but whatever their intentions, they contributed to that atmosphere of distrust in reason which helped Fascism to grow.[108] Much the same, he argues, can be said of the relations between the existentialist movement and the Nazis. Heidegger compromised with the Nazis, Jaspers did not; but their personal attitudes are irrelevant. It remains true that, by the very content of their philosophies, they prepared the way for Fascism.[109]

5

Marxism and Literary Criticism:
1 The Literature of the West

I

It is perhaps for his Marxist literary criticism that Lukács is best known. It is true that this fills only a little over four of the seventeen volumes of his collected writings;[1] still, this is a substantial amount of work, which covers a period of nearly forty years — from articles in *Die Linkskurve* (1931-2: cf. chapter 1, section IV) to a short book on Solzhenitsyn published in 1970. It also forms a remarkably unified whole, and the task of the pages which follow will be to present in a systematic form its main outlines. The task is a complex one, and will require more than one chapter. As the social and economic background of Russian literature differed considerably from that of the rest of European literature, it will be convenient to discuss Lukács' account of Russian literature separately in chapter 6 and to devote the rest of the present chapter to what will for convenience be called the literature of the West.

First, however, there is some preliminary work to be done. One of the aims of this book is to place Lukács within his intellectual context, and in the case of his Marxist literary criticism this involves the performance of two tasks. First, it has to be shown how much there is in this criticism of what may be called 'classical' Marxism — that is, the views expounded in the writings of Marx and Engels. Second, it is also necessary to place Lukács' criticism within the context of what was regarded as Marxism in the Russia in which Lukács took refuge after 1933; that is, in the context of what may briefly be called Stalinism. It was mentioned in the first chapter (section IV) that Lukács claimed that his concessions to Stalinism — in particular, his recantation of views put forward in *History and*

Class Consciousness — were made to enable him to wage a kind of guerilla warfare on behalf of his views about literary criticism. Clearly, it is important to see what Stalinist literary criticism was.

The assertion that there exists something that may be called the literary criticism of classical Marxism may be met with surprise or scepticism. It is of course true that Marx and Engels wrote no treatise on aesthetics or criticism. However, Lukács' friend Lifschitz was able to compile from their writings whole books of excerpts that deal with art and literature.[2] Much of this material is of no great weight; nevertheless, the fact remains that from the writings of Marx and Engels it is possible to construct at any rate the outlines of a theory of literature.[3]

One may take as a starting point the famous passage from the Preface to the *Critique of Political Economy* already quoted in chapter 3, section V, in which Marx distinguishes within society between a basis and a superstructure. The basis, the 'mode of production of material life', conditions the superstructure, which includes politics, religion, philosophy and also art. In the Preface, written in January 1859, Marx does not explain how art is conditioned by the basis, but something is said about this in the Introduction to the *Critique of Political Economy*, written in 1857 but not published until 1903.[4] Here, Marx considers Greek art, and in particular the Greek epic. His thesis is[5] that certain social conditions gave rise, and alone could give rise, to Greek art. He argues that Greek mythology was not only the storehouse from which Greek art derived its materials but was also its basis; now, underlying Greek mythology, and therefore Greek art, there was a certain view of nature and of social relations. When material conditions changed — e.g. with the invention of printing machines — the conditions necessary for epic poetry disappeared, and so the epic had to cease. It is in this way that art is part of the superstructure; but Marx makes it clear that he does not think that to say this is to explain art away. He remarks that although Greek art and the Greek epic are associated with certain forms of social development which now belong to the past, they still give us pleasure and in some respects are still regarded as an ideal. Marx explains this by saying that Greek art has the charm of the child, of the historical childhood of humanity, and this charm is not affected by the fact that this period will not recur. Whether this explanation is correct is not important here. What is important is that Marx recognises that the value of a work of art is not tied to its epoch, so that the work becomes valueless once the epoch has passed; on the contrary, the art of a past epoch can still appeal to us, and still has value.

Classical Marxism does not hold that the artist is merely a passive reflector of social conditions, as can be seen from the fact that it lays down rules about what the artist should do, rules which would be pointless if the artist's work is totally necessitated. The main source of information about these rules is provided by two letters of Engels. In a letter to the novelist Margaret Harkness, written in April 1888, Engels implies that the artist should strive for realism, and explains what he means by this term. Realism, he says, implies not only truth of detail, but also the faithful reproduction of 'typical characters under typical circumstances'. The notion of a type also appears in the other of the two letters mentioned, written to the authoress Minna Kautsky on 26 November 1885. Complimenting Frau Kautsky on her characterisation, Engels remarks, 'Each of them is a type, but at the same time a determinate individual, a "Dieser" [a 'this'] as old Hegel would say.'[6]

The concept of realism, and the concept of a type which is an integral part of it, are of fundamental importance in subsequent Marxist criticism, and in Lukács' works in particular. So, too, is what Engels says in these letters about *Tendenzdichtung* — literally 'tendentious literature', but perhaps better translated as 'didactic literature'. Writing to Miss Harkness, Engels says that he approves of her not having written a didactic novel (*Tendenzroman*), glorifying the social and political views of the author. In his opinion, the more the opinions of the author are hidden, the better for the work of art. Not that (as he wrote to Frau Kautsky) he disapproved of the didactic novel as such; his point was simply that the novel's thesis (*Tendenz*) must spring directly from the situation and the action themselves, without explicit reference being made to them. In this connexion, Engels makes a very important point when writing to Miss Harkness. He has said that the opinions of the author should not be stated explicitly, and he goes on to say that the realism of which he has spoken may crop up in spite of the opinions of the author. Balzac, for example, gives in *La Comédie humaine* a realistic picture of French 'society', describing the ever-increasing inroads of the rising bourgeoisie upon the society of nobles that had been reconstituted after 1815. Now, Balzac was politically a legitimist, and his sympathies were with the nobles; yet, as an artist, he went against his own class-sympathies and political prejudices, in that he saw the necessity of the downfall of his beloved nobles and saw the real men of the future. This, says Engels, is one of the greatest triumphs of realism. The distinction that is drawn here between the conscious political attitudes of an author and the world-view that is implicit in his work is of great importance in Lukács' literary criticism; so, too, is the view that a statement of acceptable political attitudes is not sufficient to ensure excellence in a literary work.

II

From 1934 onwards, official literary theory in the USSR had as its cornerstone the doctrine of 'socialist realism', which was propounded by the veteran novelist Maxim Gorky and by the important Party functionary A.A. Zhdanov at a congress of Soviet Writers held in August 1934.[7] Socialist realism contains several of the elements of classical Marxist literary criticism, but with some additions and with a significant change of emphasis. Engels had said that he had no objection to a 'tendentious', i.e. a didactic, novel, provided that the opinions of the novelist are not paraded. In Socialist realism, there is a greater emphasis on didacticism. Stalin had said that the writer must be an 'engineer of the soul', and Zhdanov said that this meant that the writer has a part to play in the transformation of society. He must give a faithful portrayal of life in its revolutionary development, and this involves transforming and educating the working man in the spirit of socialism.[8] The main addition to classical Marxist literary theory that was provided by socialist realism was the concept of 'revolutionary romanticism'.[9] Gorky criticised what he called bourgeois romanticism as being divorced from reality and leading to a despairing nihilism; however, he said that there is also a kind of romanticism which promotes a revolutionary attitude towards reality. Zhdanov associated such 'revolutionary romanticism' with 'the loftiest heroism and grandiose perspectives', and declared it to be an integral part of socialist realism.

   In the early days of the Russian Revolution there was much debate about the relations between proletarian culture and the culture that preceded it. Adherents of the so-called 'Proletkult' movement said that proletarian culture was totally new, constituting a clean break with the past.[10] This view was rejected by Lenin, and at the 1934

Congress Zhdanov said that to be an engineer of the soul meant mastering literary technique, taking over in a critical way the literary heritage of all epochs. The proletariat, he said, was the sole heir to the best that is contained in the treasure-house of world literature. The inheritance of the proletariat may also be described[11] by saying that socialist realism is the heir to what Gorky called 'critical realism', which, he said, was of value to Communist writers. By 'critical realism' Gorky meant the works of writers who were apostates from the bourgeoisie, depicting in a critical way its life and traditions. He evidently regarded critical realism as covering a very long period, since the examples he gave of Russian critical realists ranged from the dramatist Griboyedov (1795-1829) to his own contemporary Bunin (1870-1953). Soviet critics have continued to use the term 'critical realism' in this very wide sense.[12]

III

It is now time to turn from the intellectual context of Lukács' literary criticism to that criticism itself. We will begin by asking how Lukács views the relations between historical materialism and literature. The answer is not a simple one. As may be expected, Lukács insists that the writer must be seen in his historical and social context; the problem is, just what this involves. It was pointed out in Section I that classical Marxism did not view the writer merely as a passive reflector of social conditions, but thought it worth while to lay down canons for literature. Lukács, who never tired of proclaiming to writers the correct course to follow, was clearly of the same opinion. He must therefore have believed that there is a middle way between supposing a writer to be wholly determined by social forces, and supposing that such forces have no influence whatever on what he writes. The question is, what is this middle way?

One of Lukács' favourite quotations[13] is a couplet from Goethe:

Und wenn der Mensch in seiner Qual verstummt,
Gab mir ein Gott zu sagen, was ich leide.

(And if man is dumb in his torment,
A god gave me a voice to say what I suffer.)

In more prosaic terms: the writer expresses clearly what the mass of inarticulate mankind cannot. In Lukács' interpretation, this does not mean that the artist expresses his own feelings and no more. The artist's saying what he suffers is indeed an expression of self-consciousness; but this self-consciousness is also a consciousness of that whole social process in which the artist's work is just one factor.[14] Further (as we know from what has already been seen of Lukács' views about dialectic), this social process is not a random affair; it is a law-governed process, with a direction — in fact, it is a *progress*. One may perhaps see, in this connexion between the self-consciousness of the writer and his awareness of the nature of social process, a trace of the view about the self-consciousness of the proletariat put forward in *History and Class Consciousness* (cf. chapter 3, section IV).

The writer, then, has to be aware of the nature of society, and indeed has to grasp society as a totality.[15] But he must not present society and its laws in an abstract way; the characters and situations that he portrays must not be mere illustrations of some abstractly conceived general law.[16] A character which serves as an illustration can perfectly well be replaced by another, and it would be a poor writer indeed whose characters are replaceable in such a way. Instead, the writer must create characters and situations which Lukács (following Engels) calls 'types'. Lukács stresses that when he speaks of a 'type' he does not have in mind a mere average, a statistical mean.[17] A type is not something that is devoid of individual traits; neither, on the other hand, is it something purely individual, with no relation to what is universal. The type binds together general and particular, in the sense that through the character and the events in which the character is involved the author presents the universal laws that govern society.[18] The author does not simply state these laws; he brings them home to the reader through the medium of the concrete individuals whose lives he portrays.

A writer who creates types in the sense just explained is called by Lukács a 'realist'. This must not be misunderstood. For Lukács, to speak of realism is not to speak of one style among others; realism is a mark of any work of literature that is worthy of the name.[19] In particular, realism is not to be confused with a flat, photographic reproduction of everyday life; for example, Lukács regards the fantastic tales of Balzac and E.T.A. Hoffmann as great works of realistic literature.[20] Realism, then, covers a variety of styles, and so Lukács can say that in calling a writer a realist he is not necessarily holding up his style as a model to be imitated.[21]

The Marxist critic, Lukács says, will state which literary works satisfy the criteria of realism, and will show how they do so. Since Lukács thinks that realism is a desirable characteristic of works of art — indeed, his view is that only realist works are *genuine* works of art — it may be said that in stating which literary works are properly called 'realist' the critic is *evaluating* works of art. Lukács adds that the critic does not only evaluate; he also explains.[22] It is obvious that literature has a history, and Lukács regards it as part of the critic's task to explain why literature changes; why new genres come into existence and why, during a given period, realism flourishes or declines. All this has to be done on the basis of the doctrines of historical materialism. The writer not only portrays a socio-historical whole, he is also part of such a whole, and is affected by it;[23] in particular, he is affected by the class struggles of his epoch. It is the business of the literary critic to explain the writer by reference to his socio-historical context. Let us now see, in outline, how Lukács carries out these two tasks of explanation and evaluation.

IV

Lukács asserts that realistic literature has been produced by both bourgeois and socialist writers. That he should assert this of socialist writers is not surprising, but it may seem strange that he should grant the existence of bourgeois realists. We have seen that realism implies a grasp of totality; but in *History and Class Consciousness* (cf. chapter 3, section IV) Lukács argues that the bourgeoisie, by virtue of its very nature as a class, is incapable of grasping a totality, which is something that only the proletariat can achieve. Lukács' explanation of the existence of bourgeois realism is that some bourgeois writers were capable of grasping a totality after a fashion, though their knowledge of this totality was class-limited and their dialectics were only instinctive.[24]

Most of this chapter will be concerned with Lukács' views about the literature of the bourgeoisie. When discussing Lukács' account of the history of philosophy, we saw (chapter 4, section VII) that he regards 1848 as a watershed in the history of the bourgeoisie. Before that date it is still a rising and progressive class; afterwards, it becomes increasingly reactionary.[25] As might be expected, this is also reflected in the history of bourgeois literature. The great period of bourgeois realism is in the years before 1848; after that, realism becomes increasingly difficult for bourgeois writers to achieve, and anti-realist types of literature flourish.

The pre-1848 era is subdivided by Lukács into the periods before and after the French Revolution. He regards the French Revolution as the 'heroic period' of the bourgeoisie,[26] by which he seems to mean that the revolution, with its ideals of liberty and equality, is the ideological summit of the history of the bourgeoisie, constituting the culmination of the Enlightenment.[27] But the hopes of the French Revolution were soon extinguished, and it became clear that, as Lukács puts it, the 'kingdom of reason' was really the kingdom of the bourgeoisie.[28]

Lukács has little to say about the literature of the bourgeois epoch before the French Revolution, and most of what he does say about it covers roughly its last twenty-five years in Germany.[29] Of the major literary figures to whom he devoted an extensive study, the first in time is Goethe, whom he discussed in a number of essays which make up part of the volume entitled *Goethe and his Age* (1947). Lukács regards Goethe as a transitional figure between the periods immediately before and after the French Revolution. More specifically, he comes between, and contains elements of, two intellectual movements: the Enlightenment, and the beginnings of modern dialectical thought. This is what Lukács has in mind when he says that Goethe was the heir to the Enlightenment, but that he also overcame it.[30] Lukács is aware of the fact that, in regarding Goethe as an heir to the Enlightenment, he is being controversial. The argument against him can be put simply as follows. The young Goethe is acknowledged to have been a member of the German literary movement known as the 'Storm and Stress' movement. The writers belonging to this movement (Lukács' critic will continue) rebelled against the understanding and exalted the feelings; as such, they opposed the Enlightenment and were precursors of the Romantic movement. Before Lukács' reply to this objection is stated, it must be stressed that for him, the issue is not a trivial one. It will be seen later that he regards romanticism as a reactionary school of thought; the thought of the Enlightenment, on the other hand, was progressive, for in asserting the primacy of reason and opposing religion it was opposing feudalism. So in linking Goethe with the Enlightenment Lukács is linking him with what he regards as a progressive trend of thought.

Lukács does not deny that the young Goethe belonged to the 'Storm and Stress' movement, but he argues that it is a mere legend that this movement and the Enlightenment were opposed to each other. The mere fact that the members of the Enlightenment acknowledged only that which withstands the test of human reason does not, says Lukács, mean that they disregarded man's emotional life. For example Lessing, one of the leaders of the German Enlightenment, attacked the tragedies of Corneille precisely because they disregarded human feelings.[31]

Another respect in which Lukács sees Goethe as an heir to the Enlightenment is in his proclamation of the ideal of the full development of the human personality. Lukács argues that the problem of the free and full development of the human being is at the heart of Goethe's *Werther* (1774), one of the most important works of the 'Storm and Stress' movement. Here, Goethe shows the way in which the capitalist division of labour hinders such development by fragmenting the human personality, turning a human being into a lifeless specialist. The same problem, Lukács argues, is taken up in the novel *Wilhelm Meister's Apprenticeship* (pub. 1795-6), in which Goethe criticises not only the capitalist division of labour but also the constraints that are imposed by social rank.[32] It is worth adding that this ideal of full human development is not, for Lukács, something that belongs to the dead past; on the contrary, he regards it as part of the living heritage of Marxism,[33] and it plays a part in his own ethics (cf. chapter 8, section V).

But Goethe, in Lukács' view, was not simply an Enlightenment thinker; rather, he moved from Enlightenment thought to dialectical thought. When Lukács' views about the young Hegel were discussed, it was seen (chaper 4, section III) how he ascribes the beginnings of dialectics in Germany to the country's economic and political backwardness. Because of the lag in its capitalist development Germany was not yet ready for a bourgeois revolution, and could react to the French Revolution only in an ideological way — above all, in philosophy.[34] This Germany was Goethe's Germany; Lukács regards it as significant that the first part of Goethe's *Faust* was completed at about the same time (1806) as Hegel's *The Phenomenology of Mind*. It is in *Faust* that Lukács finds Goethe's dialectical thinking most clearly expressed.[35] Here, Goethe expresses his awareness of the contradictory nature of reality, and in particular of capitalism. Lukács would think it too crude to regard

Goethe's Mephistopheles as the representative of capitalism; nevertheless, he argues that the diabolical side of capitalism comes to the fore in Mephistopheles' character. To regard capitalism as diabolical is not of itself a mark of dialectical thinking; what is dialectical in Goethe is, according to Lukács, his recognition in *Faust* that capitalism is both diabolical and progressive.[36] Not that Lukács regards Goethe as in any way a revolutionary. Though Goethe sympathised with the aims of the French Revolution he objected to its methods, and in general his thought was evolutionary rather than revolutionary.[37]

This account of Goethe's relation to the Enlightenment and to the history of dialectics may seem to have concerned Goethe's thought rather than his art. Lukács would argue that the two cannot be separated; however, his discussion undeniably turns to Goethe's art when he considers the relation of Goethe's work to the realism of the eighteenth and early nineteenth centuries. He again sees Goethe as a transitional figure.[38] In articles first published in Russian in 1934-5 Lukács called the earlier phase of realism the period of 'the conquest of everyday reality'.[39] It is the period of such writers as Defoe, Fielding, Richardson, Smollett, Lesage, Restif, Marivaux and Laclos. In this period the bourgeoisie, now the economically dominant class, sees its own class destiny portrayed in literature, and above all in the novel, which Lukács (following Hegel) calls the 'bourgeois epic'.[40] The fantasy which typifies the preceding phase of the novel — for example, the works of Rabelais and Cervantes — disappears, and the action and characters become realist in a narrow sense of the term. This is also a period of bourgeois confidence, and in the literature of the period the factor of progress is emphasised more than at any other stage of bourgeois development.

Goethe comes between the realism of this period and the realism of Balzac. Lukács sees Goethe's novel *Wilhelm Meister's Apprenticeship* as particularly significant. He argues that although it retains many features of the eighteenth-century novel, it also manifests tendencies that were to become important in the nineteenth century — in particular, the concentration of the action in dramatic scenes, a trait which was typical of Balzac.[41] This raises a point about Lukács' literary criticism which is not restricted to his account of Goethe, but is of general importance. Lukács does not say that Balzac had read Goethe, nor is he interested in the question whether Balzac had read anyone who had read Goethe. He is scornful of those critics who hunt down the effects of one individual writer on another; their efforts, he says, contribute nothing to our understanding of a writer.[42] To understand literature, we have to see it in its economic and political context; in the case of Goethe's writings, we have to see them in the context of the bourgeois ideals that were incorporated in the French Revolution, and the loss of those ideals.

But although Lukács sees Goethe as a transitional figure, he also sees him as in one respect the end of an era. He agrees with Heine that with the death of Goethe, the 'artistic period' (*Kunstperiode*) comes to an end.[43] By 'the end of the artistic period' Lukács means what he calls the destruction of the unity and beauty of the world of forms, the end of formal perfection in bourgeois literature.[44] The word 'beauty' is one of the vaguest terms of aesthetic appraisal, but Lukács uses it in a relatively precise sense. Beauty, for him, is a classical ideal, associated with the ideas of proportion and harmony; he cites as paradigms of beauty, besides the works of Goethe, those of Mozart, Raphael and Pushkin.[45] Goethe's adherence to the classical ideal of beauty is what differentiates his type of realism from Balzac's. Lukács' views on Balzac will be our concern shortly; first, however, there is something to be said about his account of another predecessor of Balzac, Sir Walter Scott.

V

Just as Lukács relates Goethe to social and political conditions at about the time of the French Revolution, so he argues that the same conditions are intimately connected with the historical novels of Scott. Lukács discusses Scott[46] in the first chapter of what is perhaps his richest and best-organised book of Marxist literary criticism, *The Historical Novel* (1955). It is with Scott, says Lukács, that the historical novel in the strict sense begins; any so-called historical novels before Scott are historical only in respect of their purely external choice of theme and costume.[47] This makes it clear that Lukács is using the term 'historical novel' in a restricted sense. A novel is not historical simply by virtue of being about the past; something more is required of it. What this 'more' is, can be seen by going further into Lukács' views about Scott.

Waverley, the first of Scott's historical novels, was published in 1814. Lukács argues that it is no mere coincidence that the historical

93

novel should have originated at about the time of the fall of Napoleon.[48] The French Revolution and the rise and fall of Napoleon had made history a mass experience on a European scale, as the nations of Europe underwent more upheavals than they had previously experienced in centuries. Again, the wars of the period were fought by mass armies instead of by small professional armies; consequently, the nature and purpose of the wars had to be explained to the masses, which involved an explanation of the historical circumstances of the struggle. Besides this, the new wars destroyed the separation of army from people, and brought about a great widening of horizons. Lukács sums up by saying that during this period there were 'concrete possibilities' for men to grasp their own existence as historically conditioned, and to see in history something that deeply affected their everyday life. The phrase 'concrete possibilities' is significant. Lukács does not mean that the rise of what he calls 'historical consciousness'[49] occurred in a mechanical way; what he means is that the circumstances were right for it.

It is in the context of this newly arisen historical consciousness (which, it need hardly be added, is also related to the origins of modern dialectical thinking) that Lukács places the historical novels of Scott. This also shows what Lukács means by a 'historical novel'. Scott's novels do not simply describe past events; they express what Lukács calls a 'historicised attitude to life', the idea that the problems of contemporary society can be understood only if that society's. prehistory is understood.[50] Of itself, this does nothing to explain Scott's greatness as an artist. This greatness is displayed in Scott's realism. Engels had spoken of the 'triumph of realism' in Balzac, by which he meant (cf. section I) that Balzac as an artist went beyond his own consciously held political opinions. In the same way, Lukács argues, Scott was a realist despite his own political and social views.[51] What Lukács means is this. As a patriotic and conservative petty aristocrat, Scott approved of the progress that capitalist Britain had made. This was genuine progress, but it necessarily involved much social ruin, and Scott as an artist saw and portrayed this, displaying his sympathy with the past social formations — in particular, the Scottish clans — that had been destroyed. It was by virtue of the interpenetration of these two sides of his character that Scott was a realist;[52] that he was able, just as Goethe was, to grasp the contradictory nature of capitalist reality.

But, as was pointed out in section III, an artist must do more than

94

simply grasp the nature of reality; he must also bring it home to the reader. The historical novel, as Lukács puts it, must 'make the past live', must 'bring the past close to us and enable us to experience it in its true reality'.[53] Scott does this by creating characters which are 'types' in the sense discussed in section III, i.e. such that great historical trends are manifested in them in perceptible form.[54] What is particularly interesting here is Lukács' account of how Scott is able (as a realist must be able) to portray a totality. Lukács draws attention to the fact that Scott's heroes are always more or less mediocre, average British gentlemen. Partly, this reflects Scott's own political views, his preference for a 'middle way' between extremes. But the mediocre hero has a more important artistic function. Standing between warring extremes, but also in contact with them, he enables Scott to portray the totality of the social forces of a given epoch.[55]

A portrayal of a social totality of the kind with which Scott was concerned must involve a portrayal of both its upper and lower strata, and the complex interactions between them. Scott portrays important historical figures, such as Mary Stuart in *The Abbot* and Louis XI in *Quentin Durward*, and these too are types, presented in such a way that their individual traits of character are brought into a live relation with their epoch.[56] But Lukács agrees with Heine's view that Scott's real strength lay in his presentation of the life of the people.[57] Scott's aim, Lukács argues, was to show the human greatness that is always latent in the people, and is set free by great social crises. This can be seen clearly in the character of Jeanie Deans in *The Heart of Midlothian*. In this novel, Scott does not simply tell a story of a sudden blaze of heroism; he brings out the historical character of this heroism. The historical events portrayed are not a mere framework for the story of Jeanie Deans (as they are, Lukács argues, in the case of Klärchen in Goethe's *Egmont*, or of Dorothea in his *Hermann and Dorothea*). Rather, they provide an opportunity for her to exercise her latent powers — powers that are not just hers, but are latent in the people as a whole. Lukács adds that revolutions are great periods of mankind because in and through them such realisations of human capacities become widespread.[58]

VI

The way in which Lukács relates Scott's historical novels to the rise of historical consciousness in Europe raises two related questions.

First, why had there been great historical dramas long before this rise of historical consciousness? Second, why was this rise not accompanied by a resurgence of historical drama? Lukács tries to give an answer to these questions in the second chapter of *The Historical Novel*, and in doing so he is led to reflect on the nature of certain literary genres.[59] He does not argue that there is a direct causal relation between the social conditions of the early nineteenth century and its literature, such that these conditions necessarily gave rise to the historical novel, and only to it. His argument is in essence that the novel is the only genre in which the new historical consciousness could receive adequate literary expression.

It was mentioned earlier (section IV) that Lukács regards the novel as a form of the epic — namely, the bourgeois epic. In *The Theory of the Novel*, Lukács had declared epic poetry and the novel to be subforms of what he called 'the great epic' (cf. chapter 2, section IV). He retains this terminology in *The Historical Novel*. Both drama and great epic, he says, present the objective, outer world; this is what differentiates them from the lyric. Further,[60] great epic and drama both give a *total* picture of this objective reality; this is what differentiates them from other genres of the epic, of which Lukács mentions the *novella*, a genre about which there will be more to say later (chapter 6, section VII). How, then, is drama distinguished from the great epic, and more specifically from the novel? Lukács concentrates on the difference between the novel and tragedy.[61]

In *The Theory of the Novel*, Lukács had distinguished between an 'extensive' and an 'intensive' totality, relating the great epic to the former and drama to the latter (chapter 2, section IV). He does not draw the distinction in precisely these terms in *The Historical Novel*, but the way in which he does draw it seems at any rate loosely related to his earlier distinction. Drama and the novel, he says, both aim at the presentation of a totality, the totality of a stage of the development of humanity; they differ in that in the novel this totality is presented in the context of the surrounding world of things which form the objects of its activities, whereas in drama the totality is concentrated around the dramatic collision.[62] Lukács cites *King Lear* as an example. Shakespeare, he says, portrays in the relations of the characters the movements and trends which spring from the break-up of the feudal family. These form a completely closed system, an exhaustive totality. What are not included are the entire life-surroundings of parents and children, the material basis of the family and its growth and decline — features which a novelist would portray. In short, drama simplifies and generalises, by grouping all manifestations of life around a great collision.[63] Of course the novel, too, portrays great collisions; but in the novel they occupy the position which is theirs in the total process of life; they are not the centre round which everything else is grouped.[64]

This difference between drama and the novel is reflected in their different approaches to characterisation. It was mentioned earlier that Lukács stresses the mediocrity of Scott's heroes. This, he says, is no merely personal quirk on the part of the novelist; the hero of a historical novel *must* be a 'middle of the road' individual if the author is to portray all the factors of development in the whole society of the time. Drama, on the other hand, tries to characterise the most general traits of an epoch, and this is possible only if all the typical features of the epoch have been assimilated into the characters. That is, the dramatist has to create characters who 'in their own self-contained personalities can bear and reveal in sensible form the fullness of their world'.[65] Such a character, Lukács concludes, cannot be a mediocre individual, but must be someone of historical importance.

It is now possible to answer the questions with which this section began. These were: why did the upsurge of historical consciousness early in the nineteenth century produce historical novels and not historical dramas, and why were there historical dramas before there was such an upsurge? Lukács answers the second question by reference to the historical plays of Shakespeare.[66] These arose out of the break-up of the feudal system, and Shakespeare had deep insights into the important collisions of this age. But he was not primarily interested in the causes of the decline of feudalism; what interested him were the human collisions that sprang from this decline, and the forceful historical types among the representatives of a declining feudalism and among the new humanists. Drama, Lukács implies, is the apt artistic means for the portrayal of such collisions and such types. Lukács' answer to the first question can easily be seen. The upsurge of historical consciousness led to the historical novel precisely because the novel is the artistically apt way of portraying a *process* of change, the *origin* and *causes* of a trend.

In the second chapter of *The Historical Novel* Lukács is chiefly concerned to distinguish the genres of the novel and the drama as such; when he cites the historical novel he does so as an example of the novel and not as constituting a separate genre. Indeed, at the end of the chapter he declares that there is no independent genre which can properly be called 'the historical novel', or for that matter one which can be called 'the historical drama'.[67] What he means is this. The historical novelist, he has argued (section V), is trying to understand the present, and his interest in the past is directed to the provision of a genuine prehistory of the present. In so doing, he portrays the totality of a process of social development.[68] But this is what is done by any novelist worthy of the name; that is, by any novelist who may be called a 'realist'. Each genre, in Lukács' view, is a distinctive reflection of reality, and a historical novel by Scott, say, reflects reality in essentially the same way as any realistic novel; there is no difference in the 'facts of life' portrayed.[69]

All this applies to what Lukács calls the 'classical' historical novel, which arises out of the upsurge of historical consciousness after the French Revolution.[70] However, Lukács is prepared to recognise the existence of the historical novel as a separate genre in other epochs; epochs in which the conditions for a correct understanding of the present do not exist.[71] In Europe, this happens after 1848, when bourgeois writers cease to be able to recognise the real social roots of development, and sharply separate the present from the past.

VII

However, our survey of Lukács' account of the literature of the West has not yet reached the period after 1848. Between Scott and the period of bourgeois decline there comes the extremely important figure of Balzac. It was mentioned in section IV that Lukács sees Balzac as beginning a new phase of realism after Goethe. What this new phase is can perhaps best be seen by considering Lukács' account of the relations between Balzac and Scott. Lukács says[72] that Balzac continues the historical novel, in the sense of a consciously historical conception of the present, and transmutes it into a higher type of realistic novel. In his early historical novel *The Chouans* (1829) Balzac had portrayed past history in the spirit of Scott, but he went beyond Scott when, in the bulk of the *Comédie humaine*, he portrayed the present as history. This change, Lukács argues, had its social and historical causes.[73] Scott lived during a period of British history when the continued progress of the bourgeoisie seemed certain, and so he could look back calmly on the crisis of its prehistory. Balzac, on the other hand, lived through an age of revolutionary upheaval in France, where social antagonisms came to a head in the July Revolution of 1830, and it was inevitable that he should focus his attention on the contradictory character of the whole contemporary social structure. With the July revolution, belief in the inevitability of progress came to an end, and the problem then became the understanding of contemporary bourgeois society itself. Balzac approached this problem with a historical consciousness; but once this consciousness weakened among writers, as it did after 1848, the decline of the bourgeois novel began.

Lukács follows Engels in seeing in Balzac the 'triumph of realism'; that is, he sees Balzac the artist as overcoming his own political prejudices. Politically, Balzac was a legitimist, a supporter of the aristocracy. As an artist, however, he had a firm grasp of what Lukács calls the 'contradictory progressiveness' of capitalism;[74] he saw that capitalism, despite the way in which it crippled the individual, constituted a higher stage than the feudal order for which the aristocracy stood. Such a triumph of realism, Lukács says, is to be explained by reference to the talent and the honesty of the writer; that is, his capacity to grasp reality in all its complexity, and his having the courage to portray the world as he sees it.[75]

As may be expected, Lukács sees Balzac as a creator of 'types', in the sense of the term discussed in section III. In this context, he has some important things to say about romanticism. The romantic movement was in full swing in France whilst Balzac was writing, and the 'types' that Lukács finds in Balzac's novels may seem to have connexions with romanticism. As was mentioned earlier, a type is not an average character, but binds together the general and the particular. In order to do this, that is, in order to manifest in an individual the contradictions of bourgeois society, Balzac intensifies these manifestations to an extreme degree. So we find among his characters representatives of ultimate extremes, such as Vautrin. Vautrin — the arch-criminal who becomes chief of police — is a larger-than-life figure who might seem to be an example of the 'demonic hero' of romanticism. But the issue, says Lukács, is not so simple. True, the romantics employed exaggeration, but for them exaggeration was an end in itself. Balzac on the other hand, as a realist, employed exaggeration to evoke the fundamental contradictions of a society.[76]

However, Lukács seems unwilling to say, firmly and without

qualification, that Balzac was not a romantic. At this stage, it will be opportune to look more closely at his views about romanticism. Romanticism, says Lukács, was the expression of an attitude towards the development of bourgeois society after the French Revolution. It was a revolt against capitalism, and more specifically against the capitalist division of labour and its consequences.[77] But it was a one-sided response to capitalism; the romantic did not see capitalism's progressive side, and because of this he looked back to the Middle Ages, which he saw as an epoch in which the economy was orderly and the artisan was a whole man and not a fragmented being. Politically, romantic enthusiasm for the Middle Ages was manifested as support for the restoration of feudal absolutism. This also meant an opposition to the ideals of the French Revolution, and the Enlightenment of which it was the culmination.[78] Now, Lukács declares that Balzac was not a romantic in the strict sense of the term, since he was aware of capitalism's progressive side; on the other hand, he was aware of the force of the criticism that the romantics directed against capitalism. Put in terms of Hegelian language, what Balzac tried to do was to 'sublate' romanticism, preserving what was sound in it and casting aside what was false.[79]

Lukács views about romanticism play a part in an interesting contrast that he drew between Balzac and Stendhal, which appears in one of the chapters of a book that he published in 1952 under the title of *Balzac and French Realism*.[80] Unlike Balzac, Stendhal completely rejected romanticism; he was, Lukács says, a true disciple of the philosophers of the Enlightenment. If, then, we regard the two writers on the level of their consciously held views, Stendhal must be declared to be the more progressive. Yet despite his confused and reactionary world-view, Balzac in his writings portrayed the period between 1789 and 1848 much more completely and perfectly than Stendhal did. More than this: there is in Stendhal an element of romanticism of a kind which is not to be found in Balzac. Balzac shows the price that has to be paid for finding a niche in the society of his day; he shows how the rise of capitalism leads to the utter debasement of the human being. But none of Stendhal's characters is at heart sullied or corrupted. This, says Lukács, is the deeply romantic element in Stendhal, and is due to his refusal to accept the fact that the heroic period of the bourgeoisie was over. Balzac, then, was not only the greater realist of the two, but was also in the last analysis the less romantic.

VIII

Two years before Balzac's death there occurred the widespread revolutions of 1848, the year that Lukács regards as initiating the decline of bourgeois literature. Lukács does not mean that these revolutions were the direct cause of the decline; rather, they manifest the increasing power of the proletariat and a decrease in the power of the bourgeoisie. In effect, Lukács argues that the decline of bourgeois literature resembles the decline of bourgeois philosophy; the writer is no longer capable of grasping the nature of reality, and so is no longer capable of what Lukács calls 'realism'.[81] In explaining this incapacity, Lukács makes use of a thesis that he had first put forward in *History and Class Consciousness*. There (cf. chapter 3, section IV) he had asserted the unity of theory and practice, by which he meant roughly that knowledge is practical; to understand is to act. Similarly, when speaking of literature, he says that great realists of the first half of the nineteenth century, such as Goethe, Balzac and Stendhal, were able to grasp the nature of reality because they were active in public life. After 1848, however, writers withdrew increasingly from public life in order to preserve the integrity of their aesthetic ideals in the face of a society which, they felt, was hostile to art. As a result of this they became mere observers instead of participants, and so became less and less capable of understanding the nature of social reality.[82]

After 1848, Lukács argues, realism is gradually supplanted by 'naturalism'. This transition from realism to naturalism is complete by the time of Zola (Flaubert is regarded by Lukács as a borderline case),[83] and it is in the person of Zola that naturalism can most conveniently be studied. It should be stressed, however, that naturalism is by no means a purely French phenomenon, nor is it restricted to the nineteenth century; it will be seen later that Lukács regards it as a fundamental trait of European 'modernist' art of the twentieth century.

The naturalist writer, it need hardly be said, does not think dialectically, and it is perhaps most helpful to approach naturalism by contrasting it with dialectical thinking. It has been seen already (chapter 3, section III) that a central idea of Lukács' dialectics is the idea of a concrete totality; that is, the view that particular things and events have to be seen as parts of a whole, a whole which is concrete and not an abstraction. With naturalism, however, the idea of a concrete totality is destroyed and falls apart into two segments. On the one hand, the naturalist represents particulars in a purely photographic way, and fails to display their relationship to a whole.[84] On the other hand, it would not be correct to say that Zola sees the world simply as a chaos of particulars; he believes that he has found the most important laws that govern reality, and this is why he believes that his is the scientifically correct way of writing. But the laws in question remain abstract, as Zola fails to find the 'mediations' (cf. chapter 4, section III) that connect them with particulars.[85] Another feature of dialectics is the emphasis that it lays on change, and on contradiction as the principle of change. Zola, on the other hand, regards society as a harmonious entity and portrays social evils as diseases attacking its organic unity, instead of seeing capitalist society as something that is essentially contradictory, as Balzac did. Further, when Zola poses social problems he simply describes them as social facts, as results, and does not depict the forces that produced them.[86]

The naturalist's failure to connect particulars with general laws is manifested in his failure to create types. In place of the type, the naturalist usually substitutes the merely 'average' character.[87] If — as Zola did — he has an urge to go beyond the mere average, he then turns into a romantic. Lukács adds that this coexistence of the flat reproduction of everyday life with romanticism is not a chance one. Such romanticism is the guilty conscience of naturalism — its uneasy recognition that life does have its poetry and is not uniformly grey.[88]

Despite all this, Lukács is far from denying Zola's greatness as a writer,[89] but he says that Zola is great only in so far as the writer triumphs over the theorist. As a writer, Zola was conscious of the greatness — the inhuman greatness — of the life of his epoch, and in almost every one of his works he was able to produce genuinely realistic episodes. But these are only episodes. Zola the writer could not master Zola the theorist sufficiently for realism to permeate an entire novel.

IX

Writing in the late 1950s, Lukács said that all the avant-garde literature of the preceding fifty years was basically naturalistic in character.[90] This may seem a wildly paradoxical assertion. What is there in common, one may ask, between a novel by Zola and (say) the last chapter of Joyce's *Ulysses*? Lukács would reply that of course there are differences in style between the naturalistic novel of the nineteenth century and avant-garde literature of the twentieth, but these differences are superficial. What is important is what Lukács calls the 'immediacy' of naturalism. It has already been seen that naturalism, according to Lukács, fails to relate to a concrete whole the particular persons and events which it describes. The naturalist concentrates his attention on facts — which means *experienced* facts — and does not try to connect these with anything else. This leads him to represent the world as it appears to his characters. He does not try to relate their experiences to objective reality; rather, the limits of their experiences are the limits of the work itself.[91]

Such immediacy is, according to Lukács, a basic feature of the avant-garde literature of this century. It is, for example, typical of expressionism, a trend which was influential in Germany between about 1910 and 1925.[92] The expressionist movement had as members not only writers, but poets and musicians as well, and it is perhaps in the works of such artists as Kokoschka, Nolde, Grosz and Dix, and also in some of the early music of Schoenberg, that the most important contributions of expressionism to art are to be found.[93] Lukács, however, concentrated on the literary movement, attacking it in some celebrated articles written in the 1930s (cf. chapter 1, section IV, n.35). Expressionism was not a movement which had clearly defined principles, and it cannot be said that Lukács helped to define it more accurately; his main aim in these articles was polemical, his intention being to show that expressionism was not (as it was claimed to be) a progressive movement, but was reactionary.

Expressionism, Lukács said, took as basic the experiences of the individual. It did not attempt to connect these experiences with an orderly, objective reality; indeed, it regarded objective reality as mere chaos.[94] This distinguished expressionism from Marxism. The expressionist was bitterly opposed to the bourgeoisie, but this opposition was not, according to Lukács, based on the knowledge of objective social trends, but was of a romantic kind. Its class basis was not the proletariat, but the petty bourgeoisie, whose feelings of despair, of being lost in the machinery of capitalism, it raised to a new level.[95] Lukács adds that a romantic opposition of this kind could easily turn, and indeed did turn, into a critique of capitalism from the right, a demagogic critique of the kind to which Fascism owed much of its mass appeal. So he regards expressionism as an ideological ancestor of Fascism.[96]

Naturalism, according to Lukács, is also a basic feature of other avant-garde literary movements, such as symbolism, the 'new objectivity' and surrealism.[97] What he has in mind here can be illustrated by what he says about Joyce. Lukács speaks of Joyce as a surrealist, his reason for this being that in his view, surrealism in literature means primarily the 'stream of consciousness' novel, of which Joyce's *Ulysses* is one of the most famous examples.[98] It is easy to see why Lukács should regard such novels as naturalistic; they display the same 'immediacy' as expressionist works do. But it is important to draw a distinction here. Lukács points out that the mere fact that a writer uses, as Joyce did, the technique of interior monologue does not of itself make him a surrealist. Thomas Mann, for example, was not a surrealist, yet in chapter 7 of *Lotte in Weimar* he uses the technique of interior monologue to describe Goethe's thoughts. The difference between Mann and Joyce is that in Mann the interior monologue is simply a technical device, which Mann uses to go beyond the immediacy of Goethe's sensations and to relate them to his social and intellectual environment. In Joyce, on the other hand, the technique of free association is an aesthetic principle which governs the construction of the work.[99] For Mann, there is an objective reality to which the flux of Goethe's thoughts and feelings is related; for Joyce, the flux *is* the reality.

But it would be wrong to suppose that, in Lukács' view, every modern writer is either a realist or a naturalist. It has been seen already that he finds traces of realism in Zola; similarly he argues that among the avant-garde, Franz Kafka stands between the two extremes of realism and naturalism. Lukács' views on Kafka are to be found in a book first published in 1957, *Die Gegenwartsbedeutung des kritischen Realismus* (*The Contemporary Significance of Critical Realism*).[100] It has already been pointed out that Lukács says that naturalism fails to connect the particular with the universal, fails to see the general law in the particular case. One aspect of this, says Lukács, is that the naturalist fails to distinguish between significant and insignificant detail. For the naturalist, all details are equally significant, or equally insignificant. Kafka, on the other hand, has a selective attitude to detail, and in this respect he resembles the realists. Indeed, if one takes realism to mean an original and powerful conception and reproduction of a world, then Kafka is one of the greatest realists.[101]

But when one considers the nature of the world that Kafka has conceived, and the principles that govern his selection of detail, then it becomes clear that he is not a realist. The nature of Kafka's world, Lukács says, is shown by a powerful image towards the end of *The Trial*; it is a world viewed from the standpoint of a trapped and struggling fly. It is a world that is coloured by a feeling of *Angst*, of dread in the face of a strange and hostile reality.[102] Lukács does not deny that there is such a feeling, or that it is widespread in modern society; what he denies is the correctness of Kafka's interpretation of this feeling. According to Lukács, the real subject-matter of Kafka's writings is the hellish character of modern capitalism and man's impotence in the face of it. The true realist recognises that this is only one epoch of social history, which will — or at any rate, which can — be replaced by another, the epoch of socialism, in which the alienation that Kafka expresses so vividly will cease. Kafka, on the other hand, believes that he is describing something permanent, and is saying something about the human condition as such.[103] This attitude of despair in the face of reality is very like that of existentialism, and indeed Lukács argues that, like Heidegger and other existentialists, Kafka is a religious atheist, worshipping the void created by the absence of God.[104]

This non-realistic side of Kafka is reflected in his artistic methods. For Lukács, another way of saying that Kafka is religious is to say that he denies that human life has any immanent meaning; his dominant concept is the religious one of transcendence — in his case, of a transcendent nothingness. Now, the aesthetic category which is most suitable for the presentation of transcendence is that of allegory, and Kafka's artistic method is basically that of allegory.[105] Kafka is unable to raise the individual to the level of the typical; he cannot find the perceptible link between the individual and the universal. In short, Kafka's artistic methods are not those of the realist.

X

In the last two sections we have been considering what Lukács regards as the decline of bourgeois literature; speaking of the avant-garde literature of the twentieth century, indeed, Lukács uses the harsher term 'decadence'.[106] But Lukács does not regard the story of Western literature after 1848 as one of unrelieved decline. In the first place, this epoch also sees the birth of Marxism, and therefore of the possibility of what Lukács calls 'socialist realism'. Second, there are in western literature after 1848 many writers who are examples of what Lukács (following orthodox Soviet doctrine: cf. section II) calls 'critical realism'. To speak of 'critical realism' is to speak of the work of bourgeois writers who, despite their lack of a Marxist standpoint, may still be called realists. For Lukács, the terms can be applied to some writers of the period before 1848,[107] but it is by no means restricted to these. Flaubert, for example, is said to be a critical realist, and parts of Zola's works are said to satisfy the standards of critical realism. Other examples from French literature are Anatole France and Romain Rolland; from English and American literature Shaw and Dreiser may be mentioned.[108] Lukács gave particular attention to critical realism in German literature, and three chapters of his *German Realists of the 19th Century* (1951) are devoted to writers active after 1848 — Wilhelm Raabe, Theodor Fontane and the Swiss writer Gottfried Keller. But the German critical realist for whom Lukács had the deepest regard was Thomas Mann. Introducing his book on Mann (*Thomas Mann*, 1st edn 1949; English trans., *Essays on Thomas Mann*, 1964) Lukács said that it summed up a discussion in which he had been engaged over a lifetime.[109] The book is a collection of articles, and is not claimed to give a complete or systematic account of Mann's writings; nevertheless, it shows clearly enough why Lukács valued them.

In the last section, it was seen that Lukács criticised avant-garde literature because of its 'immediacy'. The modernist writer, he argues, takes a subjectivist attitude, in that he treats the experiences of his characters as if they constituted the world. It might be thought that Thomas Mann, too, displays this attitude; that his novel *The Magic Mountain*, for example, conveys the message that time is subjective. Lukács denies this. Mann, he says, takes subjectivism as a theme, not as a principle. In *The Magic Mountain*, he brings out the fact that the experience and measurement of time differ for the patients in the tuberculosis sanatorium (the 'magic mountain') and for people in the world below; nevertheless, he insists that the magic mountain belongs in real time. Mann, says Lukács, 'treats the subjective aspect *as* subjective, and so can insert it organically into his own objective representation of the world'.[110] In the same way (cf. section IX), Mann's use of interior monologue does not imply subjectivism on his part. He does not regard a stream of sensations *as* reality; rather, he relates them *to* an objective reality.

Mann's works, then, do not display the 'immediacy' that is typical of modernist literature; neither, again, do they display the transcendence that Kafka portrays. Mann, says Lukács, is always 'of this world' (*diesseitig*). The place and time of his novels, with all their details, present in a concentrated form the essence of a concrete socio-historical situation. The consequence of this is that Mann never treats the present in isolation; it always appears as a part of the life-process of humanity, with a clearly recognisable 'Whence?' and 'Whither?'[111] In other words, Mann (like such critical realists as Scott and Balzac) has a firm grasp of the historical nature of reality, and indeed in *The Historical Novel* Lukács says of two of Mann's novels about modern society, *Buddenbrooks* and *The Magic Mountain*, that they are much more *historical* than many historical novels written in this century.[112]

This is related to another respect in which Mann differs from modernism. The avant-garde writer, says Lukács, has no 'perspective' on the fate of mankind. When Lukács speaks of a 'perspective' he means a view of the future which is more than a mere utopia, in that it is objectively based, but which is not fatalistic, in that it sees the future as depending on the thoughts and actions of human beings.[113] Mann has a perspective: namely, that socialism is unavoidable if humanity is not to be swallowed up by barbarism. By virtue of having a perspective, then, Mann belongs to realism and not to the avant-garde. But his perspective is only abstract; it says little or nothing about the nature of socialism, and is silent about the problems of the transition from present-day society to a future society. This, Lukács argues, is because Mann was not a Marxist. The hero of Mann's *Doctor Faustus*, he says, has found the road that leads to Marx, but neither he nor his creator travelled that road.[114] So although Mann was a realist, he was only a critical, not a socialist realist.

XI

It is easy to infer Lukács' views about socialist realism from what has just been said. The socialist realist has a perspective, one that is provided by scientific socialism, i.e. by Marxism.[115] This perspective is a concrete one, and implies a consciousness of the totality of society in its movement, and of the direction and the important stages of this movement. Of course, such a consciousness was also possessed by critical realists, but Lukács stresses that in the case of socialist realism there is no contradiction between a writer's artistic vision of society and his consciously held world-view, as there is for example in the case of Balzac. This correct view of social life provides the possibility of a qualitative leap;[116] that is, the possibility of a realistic literature which is different from and higher than critical realism. But it only provides a possibility; Lukács emphasises that a study of Marxism, and even membership of the Communist Party, is not sufficient to produce a socialist realist.[117]

All this is very general, and one naturally looks to see what Lukács had to say about the actual writings of socialist realists. It so happens, however, that he had little to say about the works of socialist realism that belong to what we have called Western literature. He mentions such writers as Becher, Brecht, Eluard and Aragon,[118] but did not devote a detailed study to any one of them. For a number of years, indeed, his attitude to Brecht was one of hostility (cf. chapter 1, section IV, n. 37); however, it is important to be clear about this. Lukács' opposition to Brecht relates only to the didactic works that he wrote in the late 1920s and early 1930s — he mentions specifically *Die Massnahme (The Measures Taken)* and Brecht's adaptation of Gorky's *The Mother*.[119] Lukács objected to these works precisely because of their didacticism, their attempt to impose intellectual schemata on the spectator, which turned Brecht's characters into mere spokesmen. But Lukács argued that the plays which followed Hitler's rise to power are in a different category; works such as *Mother Courage, The Caucasian Chalk Circle* and *The Good Person of Szechwan* are, he said, literary achievements of the highest order. In place of something that had only allegorical significance they present us with genuine, dramatic types.[120]

Lukács hoped to devote a detailed study to Brecht, but circumstances prevented this.[121] To see his views about socialist realism in a more concrete form, it is necessary to turn to his account of Russian literature.

6

Marxism and Literary Criticism: 2 Russian Literature

I

In Lukács' view, the social background of Russian writers differed significantly from that of their contemporaries in the rest of Europe. The development of capitalism, and with it the formation of the proletariat as a class, began much later in Russia than in Western Europe, and 1848 was not the watershed for Russian history that it was for other European states. For Lukács, the event in Russia that corresponds to the European democratic revolutions of 1848 is the revolution of 1905.[1] This followed an epoch of peasant revolution, which was due to the irruption of capitalism into Russian serfdom, and which was initiated by the liberation of the serfs in 1861.[2] The revolution of 1905, like those of 1848, ended in defeat, but its defeat did not allow the bourgeoisie time to establish the rule of their own ideology, and the proletarian revolution triumphed in 1917.[3]

It is against this background that Lukács sets his account of Russian literature. His main work in this field is contained in the volume *Russian Realism in World Literature* (4th edn, 1964). As he himself points out in the preface to an earlier edition (1951), there are many gaps in his account.[4] Of nineteenth-century imaginative writers, he discusses only Pushkin, Gogol, Chernishevsky, Dostoevsky and Tolstoy; he also devotes an essay to some nineteenth-century Russian literary critics. Not only, then, is there no detailed treatment of such writers as Griboyedov, Lermontov, Nekrasov and Goncharov, but even Turgenev and Chekhov go almost without mention. When dealing with twentieth-century Russian writers, Lukács devotes articles only to Gorky, Fadeyev, N.J. Virta, Sholokhov, Makarenko, Platonov, A.A. Beck and

Solzhenitsyn.[5] Many famous novelists, highly praised by the Soviet regime, are discussed only briefly or not at all — one may mention Ehrenburg,[6] Alexei Tolstoy, Fedin, Furmanov, Katayev, N. Ostrovsky and Paustovsky. There is no discussion whatsoever of any Soviet poets. Lukács' silence may sometimes be the silence of disapproval, but this can hardly apply in all cases. In the preface to *The Historical Novel*,[7] Lukács ascribed his failure to discuss the Russian historical novel to a lack of translations, and perhaps this accounts for other gaps in his treatment of Russian literature. But whatever the reasons may have been, Lukács was unable (as he admits)[8] to give a total picture of Russian literature. As there is no total picture to be presented, it is justifiable to concentrate on topics of the most general interest. The rest of this chapter, then, will be confined to a discussion of Lukács' account of those whom he calls 'the most famous Russian realists',[9] Dostoevsky and Tolstoy; of his views about socialist realism, as exemplified by Gorky and Sholokhov; and finally of his account of Solzhenitsyn.

II

In discussing Dostoevsky and Tolstoy, Lukács makes use of a distinction which was often met in the last chapter; namely, between the views that writers present in their works and their consciously expressed opinions. If, Lukács says, we approach Dostoevsky and Tolstoy by way of the views that they expressed in articles, letters and diaries, we shall have to regard them as reactionaries.[10] Lukács' method, on the other hand, is to start from the social basis that determined their character as writers and to look for what their works objectively represent, their real intellectual content. When viewed in this way, he argues, Dostoevsky and Tolstoy appear as anything but reactionaries.

Lukács' article on Dostoevsky is a short one, written during the war (1943) for an American journal.[11] In *The Theory of the Novel* Dostoevsky had been presented (cf. chapter 2, section VI) as a writer who transcended the form of the novel. For Lukács the Marxist, on the other hand, Dostoevsky is a novelist, and a realistic one; indeed, Lukács declares *Crime and Punishment* to be a 'masterpiece of realism'.[12] The question is, what is the specific nature of this realism? Lukács says that Dostoevsky's importance lies in the fact that he posed problems — not as an abstract thinker poses problems, but through the medium of his characters and what happens to them.[13] These problems were not just his problems, but were the problems of an epoch; moreover, he posed them before everyday life did. It has been seen already (chapter 4, section VII) that Lukács regards Schopenhauer, Kierkegaard and Nietzsche as anticipating problems and movements which came after them; in the same way, he says that what has given Dostoevsky's works their lasting effect is their artistic anticipation of the spiritual and moral development of the civilised world.[14]

What Lukács means is this. Dostoevsky, in his view, is the first and greatest artistic portrayer of the modern capitalist big city.[15] It is true that Defoe, Dickens and Balzac had portrayed the big city before him; but Dostoevsky was the first, and so far the unsurpassed portrayer of the spiritual deformation that is necessarily brought about by life in the modern big city. This is where the element of anticipation enters. In Dostoevsky's time, St Petersburg was not a big city in the sense in which London and New York already were, and his genius lay in the fact that he could recognise in the germ and portray artistically the development that was to come. It was said just now that Lukács sees Dostoevsky's writings as posing problems; the main problem that they pose, in his view, is that of going beyond the limits that deform the soul and distort life. This can be seen most clearly in a distinctive feature of Dostoevsky's heroes. They experiment on themselves; they act, not so much for the sake of the effects produced, as for the sake of knowing themselves. In *Crime and Punishment*, for example, Raskolnikov commits robbery and murder, not for the sake of the money that he steals, but to find out if he has the spiritual capacity to become a Napoleon. Such experiments on the self, Lukács argues, are desperate attempts to go beyond the limits imposed by capitalism.[16]

Dostoevsky's explicit answer to the problem was an appeal to the Orthodox Church. Here, however, we meet the distinction that Lukács draws between the propagandist and the artist. Dostoevsky the propagandist might speak as a conservative, but the content of his work is rebellious in character, a revolt against the moral and spiritual deformation of man that has been produced by capitalism.[17] Again, although Dostoevsky preached faith, as an artist he did not believe that such faith was possible for his contemporaries. It is his atheists who display genuine depth of thought, genuine fervour in their search; really, then, Dostoevsky is not an orthodox Christian, but (as Lukács says in his philosophical works) is a 'religious atheist'.[18]

We have spoken of the problem that Dostoevsky posed in his writings. Lukács insists that he did not pose this problem in any merely contemplative way. In section VIII of the last chapter it was seen how Lukács draws a distinction between the writer who merely observes society and the writer who participates in a progressive social movement, and how he argues that it is only the latter who can achieve genuine realism. In the 1946 preface to *Russian Realism in World Literature*, Lukács argued that Dostoevsky was connected with a progressive popular movement. Although he has associated Dostoevsky with the big cities, he does not say that his roots were in the urban proletariat, doubtless because this class was only in the process of formation when he wrote. Lukács says instead that Dostoevsky's roots were in the suffering 'plebeian' strata of the cities — that is, in the people rather than in the proletariat.[19] The notion of a 'plebeian' point of view will meet us again when we consider Lukács' account of Solzhenitsyn in the last section of this chapter.

III

Lukács' chief work on Tolstoy is a long essay entitled 'Tolstoy and the Development of Realism'.[20] In this essay, as in his essay on Dostoevsky, he emphasises the point that realism is not possible for a mere onlooker; the realist must participate in a progressive social movement.[21] But whereas Dostoevsky was connected with the plebeian strata of the big cities, Tolstoy's realism had its roots in the Russian peasantry. Following Lenin, Lukács sees Tolstoy's art as the mirror of the revolutionary peasant movement that occurred between the liberation of the serfs in 1861 and the revolution of 1905.[22] He adds that the peasant movement was also responsible for a weakness in Tolstoy, namely the presence in his world-view of reactionary prejudices, such as his view that the only right attitude is the religious one.[23] Despite this, Lukács insists that the peasant movement was on the whole healthy and progressive.

Like Lenin, Lukács regards the peasant movement not as something independent, but as an aspect, a 'moment' of a bourgeois revolution.[24] Russian capitalism, as it developed during the second half of the nineteenth century, had a specific feature which Lenin termed its 'Asiatic' character. It was a type of capitalism in which antiquated methods of production survived, together with obsolete social and political conditions.[25] More specifically, Russian capitalism tended not to eliminate the worst features of Tsarist autocracy, but merely to adapt them to capitalist interests, turning aristocrats into bureaucrats. This increased the deadness and rigidity of social structures, and accounts for the fact that Tolstoy presented social structures as much more lifeless and inhuman than the Western realists of the first half of the nineteenth century did. Even Tolstoy's aristocratic characters, who might be thought to have some influence, regard social institutions as finished, dead. In *War and Peace*, for example, the old Prince Bolkonsky has retired in anger and disappointment, and the careers of his son Andrei and of Pierre Bezukhov are presented as chains of disillusionment.[26]

But despite this, Tolstoy's novels must be differentiated from such novels of disillusionment as Flaubert's *L'Education sentimentale*. Flaubert, Lukács argues, is not engaged in a real struggle with the capitalist world. He sees the meaninglessness of life in capitalist society and the falseness of bourgeois ideology, but is unable to escape from 'the dilemma of the co-existence of impotent subjectivity and meaningless objectivity'.[27] In Tolstoy, on the other hand, the disappointment that is presented is not always purely negative, in that he often uses it to present the fact that reality is richer than his characters suppose. This is because Tolstoy, thanks to his connexion with the peasant movement, never identified capitalist reality with reality itself.[28] Though he might portray the finished and lifeless character of social institutions in Russia, he did not regard this state of affairs as fixed for ever; like all realists, he saw reality not as static, but as in motion.[29]

The fact that Tolstoy portrays his heroes as living in a 'finished' world affects their nature as types. A type, as was seen in the last chapter, is not an average character in average situations. Such characters are to be found in naturalistic works; but the realist, who aims at displaying in an individual the essence of a great social trend, has to create a character who is an extreme, or place a character in extreme situations.[30] Now, the development of Russian society in the second half of the nineteenth century drove Tolstoy towards making his characters more like the average; nevertheless he was able, as Lukács puts it, to swim against the stream and create genuine types.[31] Sometimes, as in *The Death of Ivan Ilyich*, he placed an average character in an extreme situation that tears away the masks of everyday bourgeois life. Sometimes, when his material permitted, he created a character who is by no means average — for example, Anna Karenina, whose character and fate typify the contradictions of modern bourgeois love and marriage.[32] Often, however, the 'finished' character of Russian society prevented this, and then Tolstoy has to present the extreme, not as the actual pursuit of some course to its end, but as a *possibility*. His heroes do not, for example, break with their own class. The possibility of a breach may be considered, but the decisive step is never taken. Nevertheless, each 'extreme possibility' reveals a contradiction between social existence and consciousness — between, say, the opinions of such characters as Bezukhov, Levin and Nekhlyudov, and their actual way of life as parasitic landowners. In this way, extreme possibilities are closely linked with the great problems of Russian social development, and this is how Bezukhov and the others are types.[33]

It has just been said that the fact that Tolstoy's characters move within a strictly limited sphere of social life posed a problem about types, a problem that he solved by his method of 'extreme possibilities'. Lukács argues that the same fact influenced him in another, and perhaps equally important way.[34] In *The Theory of the Novel*, Lukács had said that Tolstoy's novels verged on the epic (cf. chapter 2, section VI). Similarly, in 'Tolstoy and the Development of Realism' he says that after Balzac had tended to give the novel the concentration of drama, Tolstoy pointed the novel again in the direction of the epic. It was, Lukács argues, the fact that Tolstoy's characters move within a limited sphere that made it possible for him to achieve greater epic calm and stability than was possible for Balzac.

IV

Tolstoy, in Lukács' view, is the last great classic of Russian bourgeois realism; we come now to the writer whom Lukács regards[35] as the first great classic of socialist realism, Maxim Gorky. Lukács' major work on Gorky is an essay entitled 'The Human Comedy of Pre-Revolutionary Russia'.[36] The comparison with Balzac that is implicit in the title is only rough. As Lukács remarks, Gorky rarely connected his writings with each other in the way that Balzac did; his work is a 'human comedy' only in that there is a deep historical and social connexion between the various characters and destinies that he portrays.[37] As the title suggests, the connexion is provided by pre-revolutionary Russia, the Russia during which there matured the crisis that led to the October Revolution of 1917.

Lukács has said that a realist must be an active participant in a progressive social movement, and he sees Gorky as having his roots in the proletariat and poor peasantry.[38] But there is a distinction to be made here. Gorky's art was always realistic, but his realism was not always *socialist* realism. The socialist realist, by definition, does not participate blindly in a struggle; rather, his is a *conscious* struggle, based on knowledge of the direction of social development. Consciousness of this sort is not displayed by Gorky's earliest writings, which portray the spontaneous rebellion of hopeless despair. It was only later, as a result of Gorky's increasing participation in the revolutionary working-class movement and his experience of the 1905 revolution, that despair was replaced by consciousness. The turning-point is provided by his novel *The Mother* (1907), which portrays the activities of proletarian revolutionaries.[39]

As a literary critic, Lukács has to ask what difference this achievement of consciousness made to Gorky the writer. To answer this, he has first to consider the problems that faced Gorky as a young man. Gorky began his literary career during the period of the birth of modern Russian capitalism and the dissolution of the old feudal order.[40] His early works portray the disintegration of a society; they show how 'the old Asiatic form of capitalism in Russia turned human beings into sullen ɛnd ill-natured hermits and individualists — beings which vegetated in their own confined shells'.[41] How, in such conditions, was realism possible? Gorky did not close his eyes to the brutality and fragmentation of Russian life, to what he called its 'zoological individualism', its boredom and apparent immobility. Instead,[42] he divided this immobility into an uninterrupted series of movements, of desperate explosions, fits of elation and depression. By a chain of such short, dramatic scenes he portrayed the protest of human beings against their environment, together with their relapse into apathy or despair. This does not mean that Gorky did what Lukács accused the 'modernist' writer of doing — namely, that he regarded reality as a chaos, and the individual as a mere bundle of fragmentary sense-impressions. His method of working with short scenes did not prevent him from portraying the whole man in the process of development,[43] but it did mean that he had to present a character through a number of facets, had to illuminate his characters gradually from all sides in the sequence of short scenes.

Such was the artistic method of the young Gorky; with *The Mother* there came a radical change of style.[44] In this novel, Gorky portrays the proletarian revolution, not simply as a perspective on the future, but as a present reality that transforms human beings. As a result, Lukács argues, the events of the novel are pictured with an epic breadth. This new style can still be discerned in Gorky's later novels, in which he returned to bourgeois themes. Such themes did not permit epic treatment of the kind to be found in *The Mother*; the facet-like characterisation that was typical of the early works had to remain. Yet the general movement (*Gesamtgang*) of the later novels became grandiose, calm, epic. This is not to say that the epic calm of the later works in any way lessens their accusatory character. But the accusations are no longer the diatribes of a man who is in the thick of the fight; they are 'the lofty generalisations of the humanistic counsel for humanity, who is bringing a charge against the whole of capitalism'.[45]

V

Gorky's literary career spanned the last years of Tsarist Russia and the first years of the Soviets. Of the Russian socialist realists whose work falls wholly within the Soviet epoch, the most important to be considered by Lukács is Sholokhov. (The reason for not giving this title to Solzhenitsyn will be seen shortly.) Lukács devoted two major articles to Sholokhov: the first, originally published in Hungarian in 1949, dealt with his first novel, *The Quiet Don*, and the second, first published in 1952, considered the first part of *Virgin Soil Upturned*, a work that did not appear in its entirety until 1960.

Because of the comprehensive picture that it gives of a stage of the development of society — the changes in the Russian village during the civil war — *The Quiet Don* has been compared with *War and Peace*. Lukács says that the comparison is only superficial.[46] *War and Peace*, he argues, reflects the relative stability of its epoch, and this is manifested in Tolstoy's preference for broad and detailed scenes. Sholokhov, on the other hand, portrays the first stages of the dissolution of old forms of life, and his literary method is a linking together of short, truncated scenes. This is a continuation, not of Tolstoy's method, but of the 'facet' technique of Gorky that has already been described.[47] It was mentioned in the last section that this method might seem to resemble certain modernist techniques; Lukács holds, however, that just as in Gorky's case, so also in Sholokhov's there is a fundamental difference between modernism and realism.[48] The modernist, following Zola's doctrine that literature should reflect the 'how' and not the 'why', has given up the attempt to discover the causes of social change and of human actions in general. Sholokhov, on the other hand, uses his method of short, striking scenes to portray the complex relations of cause and effect in everyday life.

Lukács said of Tolstoy (cf. section III) that he turned the novel in the direction of epic. He also regards *The Quiet Don* as an epic, an epic of a transitional kind. Its specific nature can best be brought out by following Lukács' account of the changes made to the figure of the hero in the novel of socialist realism. As was seen in section V of the last chapter, the hero of the bourgeois realistic novel is a mediocre character; his function, Lukács says, is to act as a kind of litmus paper, making visible the chemistry of social change.[49] But Gregor Melyekhov, the hero of *The Quiet Don*, is no such litmus-paper hero. The waves of events, says Lukács, roll over the mediocre hero; he is the passive victim of a social process.[50] In a very real sense, Gregor is passive too; but this is shown most clearly in those of his actions which spring from his own initiative. Is Gregor, then, a tragic hero? Certainly, Lukács regards the heroes of tragedy as exceptional individuals (cf. chapter 5, section. VI), but he says that Gregor, though an exceptional man, is not a tragic hero. Tragedy is a conflict that is insoluble, and not just one that this or that individual cannot solve.[51] Behind the personal conflict there is always a collision of social forces, and the nature of this collision determines whether a personal conflict is a tragedy or not. In *The Quiet Don*, there is no insoluble conflict of social forces. A social conflict there is, but it has a solution — socialism — and the village eventually follows the path to socialism. The fate of Gregor, who follows the wrong road and ends by destroying himself, does not parallel the fate of his class. Gregor, then, is not a tragic hero. But there is one other literary genre whose hero is an exceptional individual, and this is the epic. Gregor, according to Lukács, is an epic hero.[52] As such, however, he is a transitional phenomenon. *The Quiet Don* has left behind the mediocre hero of the bourgeois novel, but its hero is not yet the consciously acting hero of the new socialist epic. Here one might perhaps expect Lukács to contrast Gregor with Davydov, the Communist hero of *Virgin Soil Upturned*, the first part of which had already been published when Lukács wrote his essay on *The Quiet Don*. Instead, he cites Levinson, the hero of another novel that deals with the civil war, Fadeyev's *The Nineteen*.[53] Levinson, a Communist Party member, is the commander of a guerilla unit. Both subjectively and objectively, Lukács says, he is the real initiator and director, a typical representative of the coming victory.

Virgin Soil Upturned is a novel about the impact of collectivisation on a Cossack village. Lukács' essay on the first part of this novel appeared first in the 1952 edition of his book *Russian Realism in World Literature*. In the preface to this edition, Lukács expressed his agreement with the view of the Hungarian Communist Party, put forward in the years 1949-50, that no people could solve the problems of its literary development if it failed to learn from Soviet literature.[54] Lukács said later[55] that this expression of agreement was a tactical retreat in the face of Stalinism, and that he was able to use his analyses of Soviet writers to mount an indirect attack on official literature. Certainly, some of the most interesting parts of the essay on *Virgin Soil Upturned* consist of attacks on a number of unnamed novelists from the Soviet Union or from satellite countries. Lukács brings two main charges against these novelists: the first concerns their misuse of the 'happy ending' and the second is a more general charge of abstractness.

Some modern critics, Lukács says,[56] object to the 'happy ending' that is to be found in nearly all Soviet literary works. Lukács replies that there is a distinction to be drawn here. The 'happy ending' with which inferior modern bourgeois writers provide their works is a falsification of reality, a way of presenting insoluble problems as solved. The optimistic charcter of socialist works, on the other hand, springs from a correct reflection of a great world-historical process. However (Lukács goes on) some justification for the reproach can be found in the works of some Soviet writers, in which social processes are represented in a schematised way. In such works there is no conscious falsification of social processes, but there is an unjustifiable simplification, which degrades the optimism manifested by genuine social realists to a trite 'official optimism'.[57]

Later in the essay, Lukács remarks on what he calls the 'puritanism' of the style of *Virgin Soil Upturned* — the fact that it is very sparing with figures and events — and on the density of the diction.[58] These stylistic features, he says, spring from Sholokhov's deep recognition of the complexity of the relations between the individual and his class — relations in which class is always the dominant factor, and what is merely personal is subordinate. In this way, Sholokhov is able to express all the individual traits of his characters, whilst retaining the dominance of the general tendency of social development that works in them like a driving force. But, Lukács adds, there are great dangers in this method of representation, dangers that only a master can surmount. These are the dangers of monotony, of failing to translate the idea-content into a living form, and of turning characters into abstract schemata. Such dangers are especially great, says Lukács, in countries where socialist realism is taking its first hesitant steps.[59] He expressly excludes the Soviet Union, but one may suspect that this is one of the tactical moves of which he spoke later.

VI

This is an opportune moment at which to discuss in greater detail Lukács' views about the Stalinist attitude to literature, and about Stalinism in general. The chief single source of information about his views on Stalin is a letter written to the Italian Communist Alberto Carocci in 1962,[60] but other works written after 1956 — in particular, the last chapter of *The Meaning of Contemporary Realism* contain some valuable material.

First, let us ask what is to be understood by the term 'Stalinism'. For some Communists, Stalinism is the opposite of Trotskyism; it is the belief, upheld by Stalin in the 1920s and afterwards, that socialism is possible in one country within a world which otherwise is non-socialist. In this sense of the term, Lukács did not reject Stalinism. He argues that in defending the doctrine of socialism in one country Stalin was defending a Leninist doctrine which was perfectly correct.[61] But there is a Stalinism of a different kind, and this was rejected by Lukács. This is the Stalinism which was summed up in a phrase made popular by Russian Communists during and after the Party Congress of 1956: 'the cult of personality'. This cult, said Lukács, led to the destruction of discussion within the Party, and to the use of organisational measures, going as far as judicial action, against any opposition.[62] Systematically and contemptuously, Stalin's regime destroyed every trace of humanity, and the political development that was supposed to justify Stalin's decrees degenerated into hypocrisy and terror.[63]

Lukács had asked himself, and had tried to answer the question, 'How was Fascism possible in Germany?' One might perhaps have expected him to try to answer the question, 'How was Stalinism possible in Russia?', but he does not. He does not deny that the origin and continuance of the cult of personality had a social basis that must be investigated, but he says that this is a task for Soviet experts. He restricts himself to pointing out the theoretical and cultural effects of the personality cult, and also the method that was implicit in it.[64]

In his letter to Carocci, Lukács begins by considering what may seem a very abstract question about method.[65] The Stalinist method, he says, tends to exclude mediations as far as possible, and to bring matters of fact into an immediate relation with theoretical propositions of the most general kind. What he means here can perhaps be seen most easily by way of a contrast that he draws between Lenin and Stalin. He takes as an example Lenin's concept of the tactical retreat. The necessity and usefulness of such a retreat can be grasped only (as Lenin grasped it) in the context of the concrete power-relations of a given time; it cannot be derived directly from universal principles. But this was just what was attempted by Stalin, who tried to justify all his measures by presenting them as immediate and necessary consequences of Marxist-Leninist doctrines. This must not be taken to mean that Lukács thought of Stalin as a head-in-the-clouds theorist, with no regard for practicalities. In fact, he thought that Stalin had too little, rather than too much regard for general principles. His theoretical pronouncements were often pseudo-theoretical 'justifications' of tactical measures, many of which were valid only for a short time.[66] This meant a reversal of the correct relations between science and political decisions.[67] The classics of Marxism thought it evident that science should provide the material for propaganda and agitation; for Stalin, on the other hand, the needs of agitation — i.e. of getting decisions accepted — determined what science should say and how it should say it. So Lukács accuses Stalin of 'subjectivism'.[68] He says that it is true that in his last work on economics Stalin criticised what he called 'economic subjectivism' — that is, the attempt to realise economic aims directly, without troubling about the relevant objective laws. But his own cult of personality had fostered the growth of such subjectivism in the Soviet Union.

We turn now to the effects that Stalinism had on literature. It was seen in the last section that Lukács was critical of much Soviet literature, but it was not made clear there whether he thought that its weaknesses were due to failings in the authors themselves, or were consequences of Stalinism. There is no doubt that he took the latter view. The point made just now about the failures of Stalinism to provide mediations between universal and particular is relevant here. When Lukács' views about Western literature were discussed in the last chapter, it was seen (section VIII) that he argues that such a failure is to be found in what he calls 'naturalism'. Similarly, he says expressly that the Stalinist exclusion of mediations led to naturalism in much Soviet literature.[69] There are, as may be expected, differences between bourgeois and Soviet naturalism. The former sort expresses the inability, or the unwillingness, to raise oneself above the merely factual character of the individual experience; in Soviet naturalism, the particular case is a mere illustration of an abstract truth. Yet both are species of the same genus. Stalinist theorists might talk about the virtues of 'socialist realism', but the rules that they prescribed led to a form of naturalism.

Mention has already been made, in connexion with Lukács' views about Zola, of his thesis that romanticism is the bad conscience of naturalism (chapter 5, section VIII). In a similar way, Lukács connects Soviet naturalism with 'revolutionary romanticism', one of the features of the Party's official theory of literature.[70] Stalinism, he says, not only degraded the genuine portrayal of reality to mere naturalism, but where real poetry had withered into prose it produced the poetry-substitute of revolutionary romanticism. He adds that it is true that Lenin, in his pamphlet 'What is to be done?', had spoken of the revolutionary's need to dream. But the dream of which Lenin speaks is the passionate and clear sight of what can come from sober and realistic revolutionary measures — indeed, of what *must* come from them, if they are properly conceived and carried out. The dreams of revolutionary romanticism, on the other hand, are merely subjective.

Soviet literature, Lukács argues, was also damaged by another feature of Stalinism: namely, the primacy that it gave to immediate political measures, to agitation and propaganda. It has been seen (chapter 5, section II) that Stalinist literary theory stressed the importance of 'types', and this might seem to agree with Lukács' own views. But, Lukács says, when one considers what the 'type' really meant in much Soviet literature, it is clear that it has turned into a political category. The writer's task became the illustration of Party directives,[71] and what he produced cannot properly be called realistic literature, nor can his characters properly be called 'types'.

VII

Of the Russian writers who have opposed Stalinism, the one to whom Lukács devoted most attention is Solzhenitsyn. He wrote an essay on *One Day in the Life of Ivan Denisovich* in 1964; in 1969 he added an essay on Solzhenitsyn's novels *The First Circle* and *Cancer Ward*, and published the two as a book in 1970.[72]

We have mentioned already Lukács' views about some of the literary genres — more specifically, drama and the novel (chapter 5, section VI). His essay on *Ivan Denisovich* (for so we will abbreviate *One Day in the Life of Ivan Denisovich*) brings into prominence his views about another genre. This work belongs to a genre for which Lukács' term is the German word *Novelle*. Some translators render this as 'short story', but the translation that will be used here is 'novella'.[73] In its favour, it may be pointed out that *Ivan Denisovich* can hardly be called a *short* story; further, as Lukács himself would remark, length is not the important factor. A long novella may sometimes be longer than a short novel; the difference between the two genres is one of aim.[74] As has been seen, the novel aims at the portrayal of a totality; in so doing, it presents a totality of types, which contrast with and enrich each other, and occupy their correct place in a time-sequence. The novella, on the other hand, starts from a particular case — usually an extreme one — and does not attempt to portray the totality of social reality. It can therefore dispense with the social origins of the characters, of their relations to each other, and of the situations in which they act. It needs, in Lukács' language, no 'mediations'.[75]

One may object that Lukács has criticised much Soviet literature precisely for its lack of mediations. The answer is twofold. First, Lukács was criticising Soviet novels, and it does not follow that what is a weakness in a novel is a weakness in a novella. The second point is more important. In saying that the novella needs no mediations, Lukács might give the impression that the individual case that it portrays is pictured in complete isolation. But this is not what he means. In his essay on *Ivan Denisovich* he stresses that a novella, to be a success, must portray a particular case that is *characteristic*, in that it is possible only in a particular society at a particular stage of development.[76] In an essay on Gottfried Keller, first published in 1939, Lukács brought out the specific nature of the novella in another way, by saying that it concentrates in a perceptible form the social and moral features of a whole complex of problems. 'It is', he says, 'in the extraordinary case that the law appears in a sensible perceptible form',[77] and what the novella presents is one particular point of the transformation of individual into law. It seems to be this that Lukács has in mind when he says that in Solzhenitsyn's novella, the day in a Stalinist concentration camp is a 'symbol' of Stalinist everyday life, indeed of the Stalinist era in general.[78] Lukács is careful to add that *Ivan Denisovich* is not a symbolist work in the sense in which, say, Flaubert's *The Temptation of St Anthony* is a symbolist work. Such works, in Lukács' view, belong to a decadent literature; in them, unimportant details are given an exaggerated significance and are turned into bearers of abstractions.[79] Symbolism of this kind is just another form of naturalism, and Solzhenitsyn's novella is not a naturalistic work.

In his essay on *Ivan Denisovich*, Lukács argued that the work represented a beginning, a first exploration of a new reality — which was post-Stalinist Soviet society.[80] He left open the question whether Sozhenitsyn himself would bring about the re-birth of socialist realism; his second essay, in which he discusses Solzhenitsyn's first two novels, is devoted to answering this question. His answer is that, in these novels at any rate, Solzhenitsyn has not done so. Solzhenitsyn's critique of Stalinism, Lukács says, confines itself to the damage done to the integrity of the individual. This is a 'plebeian', not a socialist point of view; it is close to Tolstoy, to the world-view presented (for example) by Platon Karatayev in *War and Peace*.[81] A socialist world-view, on the other hand, would stress that in periods which do not give honest reformers and critics an opportunity to act, such people *must* become alienated. Socialist realism also has a perspective, and Solzhenitsyn sometimes gives the impression of a lack of perspective. His heroes achieve a kind of self-deliverance, but they remain imprisoned in pure subjectivity, in that the leap into activity does not even seem possible for them.[82]

Writing in 1969, Lukács said that a failure on Solzhenitsyn's part to rise above the level of a plebeian world-view would limit his literary stature.[83] All the same, this would not detract from his tremendous historical achievement — namely, of having shown himself a worthy successor to the important plebeian tradition which was one of the foundations of the greatness of Russian literature.

7

A Marxist Philosophy of Art: *The Specific Nature of the Aesthetic* (1963)

I

In the years which followed his return from exile after the Hungarian revolution of 1956, Lukács worked on two major projects — a Marxist aesthetics and a Marxist ontology of social existence. The aesthetics was to have had three parts. The first of these was published in 1963 under the title of *Die Eigenart des Ästhetischen* (*The Specific Nature of the Aesthetic*).[1] Its task was to establish the distinctive categories of aesthetics by making clear the nature of what Lukács calls 'aesthetic behaviour' (*Verhalten*);[2] in particular, its relations to science and religion. This part of the aesthetics dealt with its problems in an abstract way; the task of the second part, which Lukács provisionally entitled *Kunstwerk und ästhetisches Verhalten* (*The Work of Art and Aesthetic Behaviour*) was to make more concrete the specific structure of the work of art by discussing in greater detail problems such as those of the relation of form to content and technique, as well as problems about the creation and appreciation of works of art. The third part of the work was provisionally entitled *Die Kunst als gesellschaftlich-geschichtliche Erscheinung* (*Art as a Socio-historical Phenomenon*). In contrast to the first two parts, the standpoint that would have predominated in the third part would have been that of historical, not of dialectical materialism, as Lukács concentrated his attention on the historical factors that determine the origins and development of the various arts. The second and third parts of the work were never written, but it is important to realise that they were planned, so that one can put in a proper perspective the relative abstractness of the first part.

Although only one part of a projected whole, *The Specific Nature of*

125

the Aesthetic is an enormous work, comprising more than 1,700 pages. A full account of it cannot be given here,[3] but an attempt will be made to bring out its main points. The first task must be to consider the way in which Lukács sees the aims and methods of aesthetics. In inquiring into the specific nature of 'the aesthetic', Lukács is in effect starting from the position that there are certain types of human behaviour that may be called 'aesthetic', such as the creation of works of art, and the appreciation of such works *as* works of art and not (say) as a useful investment. What, he asks, is it that differentiates such activities from others? All this may seem clear, but it conceals two difficulties. It was in effect suggested that Lukács regards aesthetics as being about the question, 'What is art?' But it may be pointed out that some aesthetic theories treat as primary the question 'What is beauty?' and are led to discuss the relations between the beauty of a work of art and natural beauty; consequently, it may be asked what are Lukács' views on this matter. The answer is that Lukács argues that to treat the concept of beauty as central (as, for example, Hegel did) leads to distortions. Lukács does not deny that man's emotional attitudes to nature have influenced art, but he says that there is no place in aesthetics for a category of natural beauty.[4] Aesthetics, for Lukács, deals exclusively with the works of man.

The second difficulty is more important. It was said just now that Lukács' aesthetics is concerned with works of art; the problem is, however, that words like 'art' or 'work of art' are used with varying degrees of stringency. The point may be brought out most clearly by an example. What the ordinary reader counts as a novel, a critic may not; he may say that such and such a work, though advertised as a novel and appearing in those sections of libraries that are devoted to novels, is not a *real* novel. Now, there is no doubt that Lukács uses the term 'novel' in a narrow sense; for example, it has already been seen (chapter 5, section V) that not every work that would generally be called a 'historical novel' would be recognised by Lukács as such. The question, then, is this: when Lukács tries to discern the specific nature of the aesthetic, when he inquires into the creation and appreciation of works of art, does he understand the term 'art' in a wide or a narrow sense? It cannot be said that he raises this question explicitly, but it gradually becomes clear that *The Specific Nature of the Aesthetic* is not concerned with everything that would be termed a work of art in popular usage. For example, Lukács remarks in passing[5] that all art is in essence realistic. This view, which has already been met in the context of his literary criticism (chapter 5, section III) is such as to rule out many works which would normally be called 'works of art'. But the point is perhaps made most clearly in chapter 12, in which Lukács argues[6] that the central category of aesthetics is what he calls *Besonderheit*. This will be discussed in detail in section V: for the moment, it is enough to say that the concept in question is closely connected with the notion of a 'type', which is central to Lukács' literary criticism. It is clear, however, that many so-called novels and dramas do not contain types, and so are not instances of what Lukács calls the central category of aesthetics.

It comes to this, then; in investigating the specific nature of the aesthetic, Lukács is leaving out of account many works that would commonly be called works of art, and is discussing only those that satisfy his critical standards. Some examples have just been mentioned from Lukács' literary criticism, but it should be said at once that the examples given in *The Specific Nature of the Aesthetic* cover the whole range of art — not only literature, but also music and the fine arts. In all these cases, Lukács is prepared to say that what commonly are called 'works of art' may not deserve the name. This raises the problem of the relation between Lukács' criticism — in particular, his literary criticism, which constitutes by far the greatest part of his critical work — and his aesthetics. Is the aesthetics meant to provide a basis for his criticism, giving proofs of the correctness of what is said in his critical works? There is no suggestion from Lukács that this is so; rather, his aesthetics shows what his criticism involves, in the sense that it places his criticism within a wider conceptual context. It is worth noting that what Lukács does here has a rough parallel in the aesthetics of modern linguistic philosophy. Some linguistic philosophers think that aesthetics is properly the study of what critics say; it is the attempt to find the rules that govern critical language.[7] It could be argued that this is what Lukács, too, is doing. But there are important differences between his aesthetics and those of modern linguistic philosophers. One obvious difference is that Lukács, unlike the linguistic philosopher, writes from the standpoint of dialectical materialism. Again, the linguistic philosopher distances himself, as it were, from the critic; he talks about the language of various critics, but need not be committed to any of their critical views. Lukács, on the other hand, is committed, in that the criticism that he discusses is his own.

This has advantages and disadvantages. The advantage is that Lukács has had first-hand experience of what he is talking about. The disadvantage is that in talking about his own critical standpoint, he may give a one-sided answer to the question 'What is art?' But as our concern is with the nature rather than with the truth of Lukács' views, the question of a possible one-sidedness cannot be pursued here.

We have spoken of the aims of aesthetics, as Lukács understands them; its methods will of course be those of what he regards as Marxist dialectics. Lukács stresses, however, that it is not immediately clear how these methods are to be applied in the field of aesthetics. The classics of Marxism, he says, do not provide even the skeleton of an aesthetics; there can be no question of constructing a Marxist aesthetics by a mere exposition of texts.[8] The Marxist aesthetician, then, must to some extent work on his own. Yet he is not original in what he does, in that the methods that he employs are derived from a study of the whole body of the Marxist classics. Indeed, he owes a debt to more than these. In being true to Marxism, the Marxist aesthetician is adhering to the great intellectual traditions that preceded Marxism — Lukács mentions in particular Aristotle and Hegel.[9] There will be occasion to speak later (section IV) about what Lukács' aesthetics owes to Aristotle, but it will be useful to say something now about its relations to Hegel's aesthetics, as this will make more concrete the nature of Lukács' method. Lukács says of Hegel's aesthetics that, despite its weaknesses, 'the philosophical universalism of its conception, the historico-systematic character of its synthesis is an enduring model for the design of any aesthetics'.[10] There are two elements here — universalism (which is clearly linked with totality) and history — that have met us repeatedly in our study of Lukács' dialectics. Totality is a constant theme throughout *The Specific Nature of the Aesthetic*. As to history, it might be thought that this should belong to the third part of Lukács' aesthetics, which would have been devoted to historical rather than dialectical materialism, but this is not so. Lukács argues that the two branches of materialism cannot be rigidly separated, and in the early pages of the first part he argues that reality is essentially historical, and that the philosophical analysis of a phenomenon cannot be separated from a historical inquiry into its origins. The nature of art, then, must be discussed in close connexion with its origins.[11]

II

After these preliminaries about the aims and methods of Lukács' aesthetics, it is time to discuss their content. It will be helpful to begin by considering further the relations between Lukács' aesthetic theories and those of Hegel. Lukács valued Hegel's aesthetics not only for the reasons just mentioned, but also for the stress that it laid on the content of a work of art.[12] Hegel viewed art as one of the three forms of 'Absolute Mind', the other two being religion and philosophy.[13] These are the three highest forms of mental activity; what matters here is that, despite their differences, all are ways of apprehending reality. Roughly, art presents reality in sensible form; religion works through the medium of *Vorstellung,* often translated as 'representation', but perhaps more clearly rendered as 'pictorial thought'; philosophy works through the medium of pure conceptual thought. This is, to repeat, a rough way of conveying Hegel's meaning, but it is sufficient to bring out the point that matters for Lukács — namely, that the very same reality that is grasped by philosophy in purely conceptual terms is presented by art in the form of perceptible objects. As a materialist, Lukács of course rejects Hegel's views about the fundamentally spiritual nature of this reality; he also rejects Hegel's view that the three stages of Absolute Mind form a hierarchy, with art as the lowest and philosophy as the highest stage.[14] But that the artist may be regarded as in a sense putting forward a view about the nature of reality is fundamental to Lukács' aesthetics.

Lukács expresses this by saying that a work of art is a kind of reflection (*Widerspiegelung*), copy (*Abbild*) or imitation (*Nachahmung, Mimesis*) of reality.[15] Not all these terms are strictly equivalent; imitation is a species of reflection or copy, in that it is that type of reflection that involves behaviour.[16] However, in so far as art is an imitation, it is also a reflection, and for this reason Lukács uses these terms interchangeably when speaking of art. It must be stressed that for Lukács, art is just one kind of reflection among several. It was mentioned in chapter 4, section V that in *The Young Hegel* and *The Destruction of Reason* Lukács put forward the view that human knowledge is a reflection of reality. In *The Specific Nature of the Aesthetic* he adds that this is true both of everyday and of scientific thought; further, even magic and religion may be said to imitate or reflect reality after their fashion.[17] Clearly, our first task must be to see what Lukács means in general by a 'copy' or 'reflection'; it will then be possible to consider the distinctive nature of that kind of copy that a work of art is.

The view that thoughts and sensations are copies of reality is part of the theory of knowledge of classical Marxism, as expounded by Engels; it was emphasised by Lenin, particularly in his attack on philosophical idealism, *Materialism and Empirio-criticism* (1908).[18] Neither made clear in what precise sense a thought or sensation is a copy, though Lenin showed that he did not have in mind a photographically exact likeness, when he said that a sensation of green is a reflection of ether vibrations of a certain frequency. In what he has to say on this issue, Lukács does not go beyond Lenin.[19] But despite the sketchy nature of the theory offered, the point that is being made is fairly clear. Lukács (like Engels and Lenin) is saying that our ideas are true or false, not simply by virtue of their coherence or non-coherence with other ideas, but by virtue of their relations to the external world. To call an idea a copy is not necessarily to say that it is true; as we have seen, magic may be said to reflect reality in a way. A true idea, we may infer, is a good copy, a false idea is a bad one; but the point is that such ideas are about the external world, and their truth or falsity is measured by their relation to it. In other words, Lukács is rejecting the theory of truth put forward by Hegel and other philosophical idealists. But, as we have seen, he would not deny that Hegel's aesthetics contains, within its idealist shell, the kernel of an important truth: namely, that the artist is (in a broad sense of the word 'say') saying something about the nature of reality.

The next question must be, 'What is the nature of this "saying" ?' Or, to use Lukács' terminology, 'what distinguishes a work of art from other types of reflection?' In answering this, we shall also be providing the answer to a question that is posed by Lukács' literary criticism. It has been seen that he argues (cf. chapter 5, section III) that the imaginative writer must grasp the nature of a social totality. This leads one to ask what distinguishes the imaginative writer from the social scientist or historian, who may also be assumed to have such a grasp. The answer that is contained in *The Specific Nature of the Aesthetic* is long and laborious. True to his belief that the nature of art can be discussed only in connexion with its origins, Lukács devotes a great deal of space (in fact, his first five chapters) to an account of the origins of art — and not only of art, but also of religion and science, all of which he regards as developing out of magic.[20] One may have doubts about the success, and even about the necessity, of this genetic account of the nature of art. As Lukács himself admits, we can only make hypotheses about the origins of art; 'We must stress', he says at the beginning of his fourth chapter, 'that we know practically nothing about the real historical origins of art.'[21] It follows that if Lukács' account of the nature of art rested on his account of its origins, it would rest on very insecure foundations. Fortunately for Lukács, however, the essence of what he says about the nature of art does not imply any specific view about its origins. In what follows, therefore, we will leave aside the historical parts of *The Specific Nature of the Aesthetic* and concentrate on outlining the very considerable amount that remains. This does not mean that Lukács' first five chapters can be ignored; on the contrary, they contain as it were the ground-plan of his theory of the nature of art, and most of the passages to be discussed in the next section come from these chapters.

It was mentioned earlier that the types of reflection from which Lukács has to distinguish art are magic, religion and science. It is perhaps the distinction between art and science — a term which Lukács uses in a broad sense, to include history[22] — that throws most light on Lukács' views about the nature of art, and this will provide the main theme of the next three sections. We shall return in section VI to the question of the relations between art, magic and religion.

III

According to Lukács, one major difference between science and art is that science tries to 'de-anthropomorphise'; its aim is 'to represent objects and their relations as they are in themselves, independently of consciousness'. Aesthetic reflection, on the other hand, 'proceeds from the world of man and is directed towards it'.[23] Clearly, this needs expansion. When Lukács speaks about the de-anthropomorphising character of science, he has in mind partly its rejection of attempts at explaining natural phenomena as, however remotely, the effects of a personal force or forces. He also has in mind the use of instruments, such as the telescope and microscope, to free human beings from dependence on their own unaided senses.[24] In saying that art is anthropomorphic,[25] Lukács does not mean that the artist necessarily believes in personal forces that govern nature; it will be seen later (section VI) that he thinks that art is as hostile to religion as science is. He means that what the artist creates 'appears in a way which corresponds to the contemporary state of the inner and outer development of mankind', which has the consequence that every work of art has in it 'the historical here and now of its origin'.[26] This must not be misunderstood. Lukács does not just mean that a work of art is historically determined. Certainly, he thinks that it is so determined, but so is a scientific discovery.[27] What he means is that the 'here and now' which is manifested in a work of art is essential to that work, whereas it does not matter to a scientist when and where a discovery was made.

More light is thrown on the anthropomorphic character of the work of art by another way in which Lukács distinguishes art from science. Science, he says, is the consciousness of reality, whereas art is the self-consciousness of humanity.[28] One might object that this does not differentiate art from the science of history, which Lukács regards as man's consciousness of himself as the producer of himself.[29] Lukács would reply that the difference is that a work of art transforms the past into an 'experienced present', making the historical here and now come alive. We are conscious of our temporal distance from the work of art, yet there is also present an element of 'It is our case that is in question' (*Nostra causa agitur*).[30] In this way, the work of art awakens in a man the self-consciousness of humanity, which is also *his* self-consciousness. The person who appreciates a work of art and experiences its reflection of objective reality as his own concern thereby finds himself, achieves self-consciousness in what Lukács calls the highest sense of the word.[31]

How, then, does a work of art enable a man to achieve self-consciousness? Here we reach another feature of the work of art: its evocative character. What Lukács says on this topic needs careful analysis. He often says that art evokes feelings, emotions or passions;[32] but it is important to realise that in Lukács' view such evocation, though it may be necessary for a work of art, is not sufficient to constitute such a work. In the first place, the reading of a scientific work may arouse feelings in the reader — feelings of admiration, say — but the scientific work is not for that reason a work of art.[33] The emotional effects of a work of art must not be unintended, but must be the result of a conscious direction (*Leiten*) on the part of the artist.[34] Second, what the work of art evokes are not emotions of just any kind. In a discussion of the problems of natural beauty in chapter 15, Lukács points out that a wife's portrait may arouse feelings in a husband, without being a work of art in the strict sense.[35] It may be added that even if the portrait had been painted with the intention of arousing certain feelings, it still need not have been a work of art.

What, then, does a work of art evoke that is sufficient to make it a work of art? We have seen the importance of the concept of totality in Lukács' literary criticism, and it comes as no surprise when he says in *The Specific Nature of the Aesthetic* that the work of art must evoke the experience of a totality, the experience of a *world*.[36] Lukács' reason for saying this is that he regards the way to self-knowledge as going through knowledge of what is external to one, knowledge of the society in which one lives.[37] Such knowledge (by virtue of Lukács' views about dialectics) must be knowledge of a totality. But there is a complexity here. The world that a work of art evokes is not a world that is given, but a world that man creates; it is his own world, a world of man.[38] It is (so we may perhaps paraphrase Lukács) the objective world as reflected by man. This appears to be the point that Lukács makes in a section entitled 'Alienation and its Return to the Subject', which forms part of his seventh chapter. Here, Lukács adapts to his own purposes one of Hegel's views. Hegel had held (cf. chapter 4, section II) that objects are really the mind in a self-estranged or alienated form; the return from alienation is the mind's realisation of this fact. Lukács rejects this as a theory about the nature of the external world, but says that something similar holds in the case of aesthetics. By 'alienation' here he means the path that leads from the subject to the object-world; he means, that is, that a man can know himself only in knowing the world that surrounds him. By 'return' he means the penetration of the aesthetic object with 'the special character of the subject'.[39] The point is that if we were to make only the first move — that is, from subject to object — our state of mind would be that of the scientist; it is only with the return to the subject, only with the achievement of *self*-consciousness, that we have the experience of a work of art. But it must be stressed that the achievement of self-consciousness involves a 'return'; it cannot be obtained by direct introspection alone, but must involve a knowledge of the external world.

So far, attention has been concentrated on what a work of art evokes, that is, on its effects upon its audience; little has been said of it from the standpoint of the artist. It is clear from what has already been said that the artist does not simply reproduce reality as it is given

immediately to him. Neither, however, is it a distinctive feature of
the artist that he selects from given phenomena what is essential; for
this is something that the scientist does too. What is peculiar to the
artist is his positive or negative attitude (*Stellungnahme*) towards the
object that is reflected in the work of art, an attitude that is also
evoked in the audience.[40] This attitude is not something that is added
to the artistic reflection of reality; it is inseparable from it. There is in
the work of art, Lukács says,[41] 'an inseparable simultaneity of
reproduction and attitude, objectivity and taking sides
[*Parteinahme*]'. This simultaneity, he goes on, constitutes the
historicity of a work of art. A work of art 'does not simply fix an
independent fact, as science does, but eternalises a moment of the
historical development of the human race'. With this, we can return to
the starting point of this section: the point that art is
'anthropomorphic' in that, unlike the sciences, it has in it the
'historical here and now' of its origin.

IV

It has now been seen how a work of art, by evoking a world in the
recipient, leads him to self-consciousness. In his eighth and tenth
chapters Lukács argues that it does much more than this: it turns the
recipient into what he calls 'der Mensch ganz', and it produces in
him a 'catharsis'.

Lukács distinguishes between 'der ganze Mensch' ('the whole
man') and 'der Mensch ganz'. It does not seem possible to find a short
English phrase that will render the second term adequately; for lack
of a better, the phrase 'man's totality' will be used. The distinction
that Lukács has in mind is this. Let us suppose a man, in the course of
his everyday life, responding to the external world through his
senses, but doing so in a relatively undifferentiated way — i.e. not
concentrating his attention on anything. A man in this state, in
which no one sense, as it were, dominates the scene, is termed by
Lukács 'the whole man'. This phrase, as will be seen, has no ethical
connotations; it merely refers to a state of human awareness. Now
suppose the man to concentrate on something, in a way that he
might express by saying 'I am all eyes' or 'I am all ears'. (In German:
'Ich bin ganz Auge','Ich bin ganz Ohr').[42] This is a case of what
Lukács calls 'der Mensch ganz', a phrase that he seems to use with
the implication of the use of 'ganz' in the sentences just quoted. This

experience is common in everyday life, and it is also produced in the recipient by art, working through what Lukács calls a 'homogeneous medium' — for example, visibility in the case of the fine arts, audibility in the case of music, and gesture in the dance.[43] The difference is that in the case of everyday life, this concentration of attention is short-lived, and is determined by an immediate practical end. In the case of art, on the other hand, the concentration of attention that is produced is long-lasting, and there is also a suspension of immediate practical ends. This suspension, Lukács argues, is what lies behind Kant's celebrated views about the 'disinterestedness' (*Interesselosigkeit*) of the experience of a work of art. The phrase, however, can be misleading, in that it suggests that the experience of a work of art is a purely disinterested contemplation, having no bearing on what a man does. Lukács argues that this is not so. The ends that are suspended by art are only *immediate* ends, and their suspension eventually leads back to everyday, practical life. Nevertheless, Lukács adds, it leads only rarely to the furthering or impeding of specific practical ends.[44]

There will be more to say about the practical effects of a work of art later in this section, after we have seen how Lukács develops what he says about man's totality into theory about the 'cathartic' nature of art. Here, we are moving into territory which verges on that of ethics. Lukács thinks that there is a basic difference between ethical and aesthetic behaviour, in that the former is practical and directed towards reality itself; its medium is life itself, human activity. Art, on the other hand, aims at a reflection of reality.[45] However, Lukács also holds that the two are intimately related, and these relations are made clear in what he says about catharsis.

Many years before, in *The Soul and the Forms,* Lukács had quoted with approval Matthew Arnold's dictum that poetry is a criticism of life (cf. chapter 2, section II). He makes a similar remark when discussing catharsis in *The Specific Nature of the Aesthetic,* though he extends it to cover art in general.[46] When he speaks of catharsis, he is not using the term in the relatively restricted way in which it is used in Aristotle's *Poetics* — a 'purification' that is confined to tragedy among the arts, and to pity and fear among the emotions. He has in mind a more generalised kind of catharsis, of the type described in the eighteenth century by Lessing: a 'transformation of the passions into virtuous powers [*tugendhafte Fertigkeiten*]'.[47] What Lukács means here can perhaps best be approached by way of his literary criticism.

We have seen how Lukács repeatedly praises those writers who portray a *whole* man; not a whole man in the sense of 'der ganze Mensch', but whole in the sense of complete, all-sided, as opposed to merely fragmented. Such writers are Tolstoy and Balzac, whose struggle for the integrity of man, incidentally, is mentioned in *The Specific Nature of the Aesthetic*.[48] This ideal of wholeness may seem hard to reconcile with Lukács' view that each work of art is directed towards 'man's totality'; for, as Lukács himself points out, man's totality can make actual only *one* aspect of the 'all-sided man'. The answer is that although the unity and wholeness of the all-sided man cannot be produced by one work of art alone, the experience of a variety of such works takes us step by step towards such a wholeness, even if the ideal is never completely realised.[49] The catharsis of which Lukács speaks just *is* this transformation, by means of the experience of works of art, of the individual into the integral, all-sided man. Lukács sums up its nature by saying that it is[50]

> A shaking of the recipient's subjectivity, such that the passions that manifest themselves in his life receive new contents, a new direction, and are purified in such a way that they become the spiritual basis of 'virtuous powers'.

Rilke, Lukács says, had made essentially the same point about the work of art in his poem 'An Archaic Torso of Apollo', which presents the statue as telling the onlooker, 'You must change your life'.[51]

In a section entitled 'The Aftermath [*das Nachher*] of the Receptive Experience', which follows his account of catharsis, Lukács returns to the question of the practical effects of the work of art. On the one hand, he does not want to say that a work of art has no social consequences; on the other, he rejects Stalin's view of the writer as 'the engineer of the soul'.[52] He finds a way out of the dilemma by saying that the work of art does not alter the recipient's immediate practical aims, which are suspended during the aesthetic experience. The change that it produces affects the whole man, and only when this change is strong enough do there follow changes in his concrete aims. In other words, the social role of art is — as the Greeks saw — a 'spiritual preparation' (*seelische Vorbereitung*) for new forms of life.[53]

V

So far, nothing has been said about the relation of Lukács' aesthetics to a fundamental concept of his literary criticism, that of the 'type'. The function of the type, it will be recalled, is to bind together general and particular (chapter 5, section III). It is by means of the creation of types that the author portrays, not a mere collection of disjointed particulars, but a law-governed totality; at the same time, the laws in question are not portrayed in an abstract way, but are manifested through the medium of concrete characters and events. In his aesthetic theory, Lukács connects the type with a category which he calls *Besonderheit,* which will be translated here as 'speciality', using this word in the sense of a special feature or characteristic.[54] The category of speciality is the subject of the twelfth chapter of *The Specific Nature of the Aesthetic;* Lukács also devoted to it a whole book, *Über die Besonderheit als Kategorie der Ästhetik (On Speciality as a Category of Aesthetics),* which was originally intended to be the second part of his aesthetics, but which did not fit into his scheme and was therefore published separately.[55]

In view of the importance of the concept of the type in Lukács' criticism, it is not surprising that he should declare the related category of speciality to be the central category of aesthetics.[56] It is important to realise, however, that he does not think that this category is restricted to aesthetics, and it will be helpful to begin by considering its general nature before discussing its place in the context of aesthetics. To understand speciality, Lukács argues, it is necessary to see it in relation to two other categories, *Allgemeinheit* ('universality') and *Einzelheit* ('individuality'). Hegel was the first to explore this problem in all its aspects, and Marx developed his ideas, removing from them their idealist distortions.[57] A passage from the Introduction to Marx's *Critique of Political Economy*[58] illustrates clearly what Lukács has in mind. Marx is here describing economic method, and says that the economist must start from the real and concrete (in Lukács' terms, 'individuality'). But this, in its 'immediacy' — i.e. regarded as merely given, and not seen in relation to anything else — is a mere abstraction; it is therefore necessary to generalise its components and bring them to a universal concept (i.e. to 'universality'). From this point, thought must retrace its steps until it reaches the real and concrete again, 'but now, not as a chaotic representation of a whole, but as a rich totality of many determinations and relations'. Commenting on this, Lukács points out that the movement from individual to universal, and from universal back to individual, has many intermediate stages, many 'mediations'. Such a 'linking field of mediations'[59] constitutes what Lukács calls 'speciality'.

It is now possible to follow Lukács' discussion of speciality as an aesthetic category. He begins by saying that he has already pointed out the main differences between art and science — namely, that although both aim at an adequate reflection of reality, science tries to 'de-anthropomorphise' whereas art is anthropomorphic. He then says that in order to grasp the importance of the category of speciality for aesthetics, it is necessary to go more thoroughly into the anthropomorphic nature of art. In outline, his view is that what is peculiar to the aesthetic sphere is that here, speciality is not simply a mediation between universality and individuality, but is an 'organising mean'. This has the consequence that artistic reflection does not (as is the case with scientific reflection) move from individuality to universality and back; rather, as a 'mean', speciality is both the starting-point and the end of the movement. 'So we have to do, not with a cross-movement between the two extreme categories, but with a movement between centre and periphery.'[60]

Obviously there is much here that needs clarification. It emerges from his discussion that what Lukács has in mind involves the familiar Hegelian notion of *Aufhebung*, 'sublation' (cf. chapter 2, section VII). To speak of 'speciality' in the case of a work of art is, according to Lukács,[61] to say that the work 'sublates' the two extremes of universality and individuality; that is, that the rational features of these extremes are preserved, but what is contradictory and defective in them is cancelled. Described in greater detail, Lukács' position is as follows. Universality is 'sublated' into speciality in that there appear in the work of art, as an important 'power of life', the universal laws of which man makes use in mastering his environment. These are sublated in that art relates such powers directly to man; not to an abstract 'man in general', but to the concrete destinies of concrete men.[62] The way in which art sublates individuality into speciality needs a more elaborate account. Lukács begins with a general thesis about the nature of knowledge. Consider some individual thing, as it is presented immediately to us. This thing has very complex relations to others, but in so far as it is presented to us immediately — that is, in so far as we perceive it as something that is just given to us — we are not aware of these relations. The relations are *there* — we discover them, we do not invent them — but they are present in a merely implicit form.[63] Both science and art try to sublate the limitations that result, making explicit the relations that are only implicit in the individual as presented immediately, but they do so in different ways. Sublation, it should be recalled, involves both cancellation and preservation. Now, art differs from science in that art places greater stress on the preservation of the elements of individuality, making 'the humanly relevant nature of the individual appear, in these new connexions, in a more visible, experienceable and understandable way than could be grasped in its original form'.[64]

It is easy to see how all this is related to Lukács' concept of the type. To say that the work of art manifests the category of speciality just is to say[65] that it contains types, which link the universal and the individual. One point should be emphasised. Just as Lukács says that the category of speciality is not peculiar to the aesthetic, so he also says that the category of the type is not peculiar to it. Science, as well as art, seeks the typical; the difference between the two is that science tries to generalise as far as possible, raising the typical to the level of the universal, and this means that it tries to operate with as few types as possible. The reason for this, according to Lukács, is that science is concerned with the knowledge of objective reality, just as it is. Art, on the other hand, is concerned with the self-knowledge of man, and this leads to a plurality of types, such as we find in writers such as Balzac, Tolstoy and Chekhov.[66] It is in this way that Lukács' account of speciality provides, as he promised, a deepening of the concept of the anthropomorphic character of the work of art.

VI

So far, attention has been concentrated on Lukács' views about the ways in which art differs from science. As mentioned in section II, he also distinguishes art from magic and religion, which, like it, are reflections of reality. Lukács' views on magic need not detain us long. Briefly, Lukács holds that magic differs from religion in that magic displays a lower degree of generalisation, and the boundaries of the inner and outer world are less clear; further, the magician's way of handling unknown powers is in a way technological, and lacks the ethical relation to reality that religion has.[67] Magic differs from art in that, although both are anthropomorphic and have evocative aims, in magic the evocation serves immediate practical ends, such as success in battle or the hunt, whereas for art the aim of evocation is human self-awareness.[68]

What is said in *The Specific Nature of the Aesthetic* about the relations between art and religion is of greater importance. Lukács touches on this topic in the earlier chapters of the book, and devotes to it the book's long final chapter, 'Art's War of Liberation'. His account does not add to his aesthetics anything of fundamental importance, but it makes his views about religion clearer, and it also contains some challenging views about religious art.

Art resembles religion in that both are anthropomorphic,[69] but there are several differences between them. One is that religion ascribes absolute reality to the products of its reflection, whereas art does not ascribe any objective reality to its creations.[70] Now, if this were the only difference — if art involved no attitude towards that to which religion ascribes objective reality — then art and religion, though different from one another, would not be opposed, just as art and science are not opposed to each other. However, Lukács regards art as not only different from, but also opposed to religion, just as science is opposed to religion. This is because religion claims to deal with the transcendent, whereas art, like science, is 'this-worldly' (*diesseitig*).[71] By 'transcendence' Lukács means a type of existence that is higher and more real than the earthly existence of men. Lukács appears to regard this concept as a way of reifying human ignorance. In his view, the religious man supposes that the not-yet-known is something unknowable by rational means, and accessible only to faith.[72] This accounts for the struggle between religion and science, a struggle in which religion has constantly to retreat as scientific knowledge advances,[73] and there is a corresponding struggle between art and religion, which Lukács describes as 'art's war of liberation'. There is a difference, however, between the ways in which art and science reject transcendence. Whereas for science the supposedly transcendent is relative and no more, a 'merely provisional not-yet of knowledge', in art it appears as 'the signature of a momentary historical situation'.[74] As such — as a component of a world-picture — it is *historically* relativised, seen in relation to human development. In other words, art's 'this-worldliness' is linked with its anthropomorphic character.

Religion and art also differ by virtue of their relation to what

Lukács calls 'particularity'. Religion, he says, preserves particularity, whereas art (like science) sublates it.[75] What he means is that a man's religious endeavours are directed towards his own salvation, as a particular individual. Even a saint who devotes his whole life to the redemption of others, Lukács argues, is aiming at his own spiritual salvation. Art, on the other hand, sublates particularity by its movement from the individual to speciality.[76] Lukács adds that it is only by the sublation of particularity, and the rejection of an other-worldly redemption, that human self-fulfilment is possible. Needless to say, such self-fulfilment cannot be brought about by art alone, in isolation from social conditions; only under socialism will the religious need come to an end.[77]

The upshot of this is, as Lukács puts it, that 'in its objective intention, art is as hostile to religion as science is'.[78] This remark needs some comment. In the first place, the word 'objective' is important here. An artist may think that he is serving religion by his work, and his public may think the same. But, says Lukács, if we pay attention to the work itself and not to the artist's views about it, we shall find that if it is a real work of art, then it is hostile to religion.[79] The second point can be introduced by a phrase just used: 'if it is a real work of art'. When Lukács says that art is hostile to religion, he is using the term 'art' in a restricted sense, in which not everything that would normally be called a work of art would be recognised by him as such.

Considerable dissatisfaction may be felt with this view. Let it be granted, it may be said, that much so-called religious art is of little or no aesthetic value; yet surely works such as the religious pictures of Rembrandt, or Bach's Passions, are works of art? Lukács would reply that these are certainly works of art, but that in an important sense they are not *religious* works. Their themes are taken from the Christian religion, but they are far from 'other-worldly'. For example, the conflicts portrayed by Bach's Passions — Jesus or Barabbas, Peter's crisis of conscience, etc. — are very much of this world.[80] But it is important not to over-simplify here. Although Lukács maintains firmly that art in the proper sense of the term is this-worldly, and therefore opposed to religion, he is also prepared to say that there are works of genuine aesthetic value that are properly called religious. Such works are what Lukács calls 'allegories'.[81] He regards an allegory as a work of art (in a broad sense of 'art') in which there is no essential connexion between the perceptible nature of the objects depicted and their meaning. In other words, every allegorical interpretation is more or less arbitrary.[82] The connexion between allegory and religious art is made by way of that mode of representation that Lukács calls 'decorative' or 'ornamental'. Ornament is evocative, and it reflects reality, but it does so in an abstract way, its structural elements being such abstract forms of reflection as rhythm, symmetry and proportion.[83] The concept of the ornamental or decorative is wider than that of the allegorical, but Lukács argues that when the decorative mode of representation is made to express a content, then there arises something allegorical. In certain elements of decorative form, Lukács says,[84]

> there appears an empty space between the power of sensuous evocation, which is necessarily lessened, and the immediate lack of content. This empty space seems to be filled by the transcendent content that is prescribed by religion; for through it the weakening of objectivity seems no longer to be a defect, but to be the necessary reflection of the distance that separates everything earthly from the transcendent. This is the basis of the continued aesthetic effect of significant allegorical works of art, such as the best mosaics of Byzantine art, much Oriental art, some of the works of Calderon, etc.

But it must be stressed that Lukács does not regard this as art in the full sense. For him, art in the true sense of the term is that sort of reflection whose aim is to enable men to reach self-awareness; this, as has been seen (section III), can be achieved only by the evocation of a world, and Lukács holds that ornament is 'world-less'.[85] The same is true of allegory, and it is precisely this fact, that makes allegory so suitable for religious art, that prevents it from being art in the full sense of the term.

VII

Although this book on Lukács is expository rather than critical, if it is to give a rounded account of his aesthetics it must say something about the reply that he would have made to a possible objection. This objection springs from the emphasis that his aesthetics lays on the content of a work of art. Lukács' views about the nature of art, it may be said, are plausible with respect to works of art which have a content, such as is often the case with the novel, drama, painting and sculpture. In such cases, Lukács' aesthetic theory may not be the whole truth, and indeed it may not be the truth at all, but at least it has some semblance of truth. But how can it even plausibly be applied to music? What does music reflect? What types, in Lukács' sense of the term, can be found in a musical work? In the fourteenth chapter of *The Specific Nature of the Aesthetic,* which is entitled 'Marginal Problems of Aesthetic Mimesis', a long section is devoted to music and the problems that it raises.

In brief, Lukács' answer is that music reflects a man's feelings, his inner life.[86] Since Lukács holds that it is wrong to draw an absolute distinction between copying and expression, he also says that music *expresses* feelings.[87] This needs amplification and comment. It must be stressed at the outset that Lukács does not imply that a composer's music necessarily copies or expresses *his own* feelings: he does not imply, for example, that a composer must feel sad whilst he writes a lament. It is significant that, in the course of his discussion of music, he refers to *Klageweiber,* professional mourners.[88] Their weeping and wailing need not express their own grief — the dead person may be unknown to them — but they do express or imitate *grief.* We may put Lukács' point about music, then, by saying that in his view music expresses *feelings,* rather than what happen to be a composer's feelings whilst writing a piece of music.

Lukács' view that music imitates feelings raises a problem of its own, in that it appears to be inconsistent with the rest of his aesthetics. A main feature of this aesthetics is the connexion between a work of art and a man's awareness of society and of its development; feelings, on the other hand, seem to be personal and private. Lukács would reply that feelings are linked with the external world; a man's inwardness, he says, is a product of the socio-historical development of humanity.[89] So music, as Lukács says repeatedly, is a double mimesis — a copy of feelings, which in turn copy the objective world.[90] In saying this, Lukács is not stating what he regards as a distinguishing feature of music;[91] as suggested earlier (section III), he appears to hold that any work of art, in evoking a world of man, is in a sense evoking the objective world as reflected by man. The purpose of the reference to double mimesis is not to distinguish music from other arts, but rather to show that it shares with other arts the feature of reflecting objective reality. Where music differs from the other arts is in respect of emphasis. In music, the subjective aspect is very strong, in that feeling predominates: the world of real objects and their relations is barely perceptible.[92] But Lukács would add, although barely perceptible it is still there, to be discerned in the work.

The fact that music is a double mimesis in the sense explained makes it possible for Lukács to find in music the category of speciality. Music, he argues,[93] cancels out the merely individual, in that it eradicates the purely personal circumstances of its origin; on the other hand, since it can have no verbal character, it is incapable of grasping universality in conceptual terms. All the same, one can speak of a language of music, and this language is more than an inarticulate stammering of mere bursts of feeling. To say this is to say that music is governed by the category of speciality, which raises itself above the merely individual and extracts 'typical traits from every particular phenomenon'.[94] In the case of music, the phenomena in question are feelings, and Lukács' point seems to be that music does not merely express feelings, but presents them as the feelings of certain people at a certain stage of human development. Music, as Lukács puts it, reproduces and evokes 'the problems of the moment of its personal and historical origin, from the perspective of its enduring significance in the development of humanity'.[95] In this way, Lukács is able to give an account of music that is in line with his aesthetic theory as a whole.

8

The Ontology of Social Existence

Our survey of Lukács' thought ends with the major work of his last years, *Zur Ontologie des gesellschaftlichen Seins* (*The Ontology of Social Existence*).[1] 'Social existence' is one of the two main types of existence recognised by Lukács, the other being natural existence. Since Lukács regards the term 'natural existence' as equivalent to 'nature',[2] it may be inferred that by 'social existence' he means 'society'. His reason for using the term 'social existence' here is doubtless that society, like nature, has objective existence, and is not a mere mental construct. The same reason may lie behind his use of the term 'ontology' in this context. The word literally means 'the theory of existence'. Traditionally, it has connexions with metaphysics, and in this sense it means the study of existence *as* existence, i.e. existence in its most general or abstract nature. However, it has been seen that Lukács is hostile to any merely abstract approach, and so it is hardly likely that this is what he means by the term. In the light of what he says about knowledge as a 'reflection' of reality,[3] it is much more probable that when he speaks of the 'ontology' of social existence, he is implying that in studying society one is not imposing thought-categories on reality, but is discovering what is objectively *there*, existing independently of the mind that studies it.

But having made clear the meaning of the term 'ontology', one is still left with questions about the nature of ontology as a discipline. Does Lukács regard it as a branch of science, or of philosophy, or of neither? In non-Marxist thought, it has for some time been customary to draw a sharp distinction between the social sciences on the one hand, and the philosophy of the social sciences on the other.

The former are empirical; that is, they are in the last resort based on experience. In the case of the social sciences, to speak of experience is in the main to speak of mere observation; experiment is largely ruled out by the very nature of the subject. The philosophy of the social sciences, on the other hand, is in a broad sense linguistic, dealing with what may be called the grammar (or perhaps better, the logical grammar) of the social sciences, and indeed of ordinary language about society. Lukács would not regard his ontology as falling within either of these two disciplines exclusively, because he rejects the sharp separation between them. For example, he says that Marx's economic works are works of science; but their scientific spirit is one that travelled through philosophy and never left it behind.[4] Lukács would doubtless say the same about his own *Ontology of Social Existence*, which is an attempt to develop Marxism and (as he puts it) to make it again a living force in philosophical development.[5] It will perhaps be asked how all this differs from dialectics, as Lukács understands the term. The answer is that there is no fundamental difference; the difference is simply one of emphasis. Lukács could have called his work 'The Dialectics of Social Existence'; but this would have failed to bring out the point that what is studied there is objective reality, that which *exists*.

Many Western philosophers would say that in so far as Lukács' ontology fails to distinguish between philosophy and science, it is seriously confused. But even if this is so, it does not follow that Lukács' ontology cannot contribute to philosophical development, as he hoped that it would do. We saw that, whatever Lukács' views about the nature of aesthetics may have been, *The Specific Nature of the Aesthetic* can be seen as a philosophical inquiry into the language of literary criticism; there is therefore no reason to suppose in advance that *The Ontology of Social Existence* will not contribute to the discussion of philosophical problems generated by the language used about society, both by scientists and non-scientists. Of these problems, perhaps the most pressing are those which spring from the fact that social processes are often described in terms of *laws,* and indeed of *necessary* laws, so giving rise to problems about human freedom. Such problems will form the main theme of our discussion of *The Ontology of Social Existence.*

II

The Ontology of Social Existence consists of two parts, each of four chapters. The first part is entitled 'The state of the problem at present'; in this, Lukács comments on the views of others. The order of his discussion may be called dialectical, in that he begins with views which are, in his opinion, most remote from the truth, and ends with those which are closest to it. His first chapter has as its subject existentialism and logical positivism; the second chapter is concerned with the ontology of Nicolai Hartmann (1882-1950), described in *The Destruction of Reason* as the only modern philosopher outside Marxism to have a positive attitude towards dialectics.[6] Chapter 3 is concerned with Hegel's ontology, and chapter 4 with the basic ontological principles of Marx. The second part of the work deals with problems rather than with individuals, and is entitled 'The most important problem-complexes'. Chapter 1 of this part is concerned with labour, chapter 2 with reproduction, chapter 3 with 'The ideal and ideology' and chapter 4 with alienation. At the time of writing, the complete work has not been published, but chapters 3 and 4 of part I and chapter 1 of part II have been issued as separate volumes. These are chapters that deal with the two men to whom Lukács owed most — Hegel and Marx — and with the concept of labour, Hegel's treatment of which Lukács regarded as an element of lasting value in his philosophy.[7] In discussing these chapters, then, we may be confident that we shall meet the central ideas of *The Ontology of Social Existence*.

The title of chapter 3 of part I is 'Hegel's true and false ontology'. By Hegel's 'true' ontology is meant, not that ontology which he really held (as opposed to one which he only appeared to hold), but that part of his ontology which contains elements of the truth. This, according to Lukács, is his view that reality is process, and that the fundamental principle of process or change is contradiction. Hegel's false ontology is his idealism, and in particular his theory of the identical subject-object. All this is familiar to us;[8] the only difference is that Lukács does not now base his views mainly on relatively early works, but concentrates instead on Hegel's logic, a product of his mature years.[9]

In discussing Hegel's false ontology, Lukács stresses what he regards as one aspect of the doctrine of the identical subject-object: namely, Hegel's tendency to confuse logical relations with real relations.[10] In Hegel's logic, the more concrete concepts are derived from the more abstract; identifying logical with real relations, Hegel says that there is a real transition from the less concrete to the more concrete — but he fails to explain how such a transition is made. In fact, says Lukács, the order is the reverse: the more complex and concrete is the ontological, the *real* starting point from which a variety of 'moments' or 'aspects' can be abstracted. This is what Lukács appears to have in mind when he speaks of 'the ontological priority of the complex'.[11] Such a doctrine is indeed the very reverse of philosophical idealism. Lukács is saying that in investigating reality we are discovering real connexions that are independent of us; we are not imposing on reality our own mental categories.

Another aspect of Lukács' ontology that is displayed in his chapter on Hegel is his view about the nature of the relations between physical nature and society. The problem is an important one. Briefly, it may be put in this way: are we to regard man and society in terms of the physical sciences, or are at least some of the concepts and laws of the social sciences of a special kind? Lukács' answer to this problem is roughly as follows. An ontology of social existence can be constructed only on the basis of an ontology of nature;[12] that is, one cannot explain social existence without a knowledge of the properties and laws of physical things. But this is not to say that social existence is *nothing but* nature. It would be wrong to treat the science of society as simply (say) a branch of physics, that happens to deal with matter of a very high degree of complexity. Hegel, says Lukács, saw this.[13] Hegel's view is that nature as it were prepares for the development of man, society and history; but though the dialectic of history is developed directly out of that of nature, it displays qualitatively new categories, connexions and laws. Perhaps the most important of these categories is that of teleology, i.e. that of purpose. Lukács says that this category must, as Hegel argues, be sharply distinguished from natural causality — that is, causality of the kind that holds between inanimate objects.[14] This theme is developed later in Lukács' chapter on labour.

In saying that social existence arises out of natural existence, Lukács is not going beyond the doctrines of classical Marxism. When the classical account of dialectical materialism was sketched in chapter 3, section II, it was seen that when Engels asserted the primacy of matter over mind, he meant that matter precedes mind, which is its highest product. Nor does Lukács go beyond classical

Marxism when he asserts that social existence is more than natural existence. Here he is in effect simply drawing the distinction which is usually drawn between mechanistic materialism and dialectical materialism. By 'mechanistic materialism' is meant the doctrine of the materialist philosophers of the Enlightenment; it also refers to what Engels calls the 'vulgar materialism' of such nineteenth-century scientists as Büchner, Vogt and Moleschott — a materialism which, he said, was essentially eighteenth century in character.[15] Such materialism, Engels argued, was defective in that it failed to do justice to the dialectical law of the transformation of quantity into quality.[16] It is, for example, wrong to apply the criteria of mechanics to processes of a chemical and organic nature. The laws of mechanics are indeed valid here, but they are pushed into the background by other, higher laws.[17]

III

In chapter 4 of part I, entitled 'Marx's basic ontological principles', Lukács gives his answer to some problems raised by historical materialism — namely, in what sense it is a determinism, and what are its relations to human freedom, understanding by this the capacity to do something other than what one actually does.

We will begin with questions about basis and superstructure, and see how Lukács interprets Marx's famous assertion that existence 'determines' consciousness.[18] Lukács says that 'vulgar Marxism' took this as asserting a direct causal relationship between economics and ideology.[19] But this was a misunderstanding. Marx did not bring the world of consciousness into an *immediate* relation with the economic basis, as something directly produced by it. Rather, he related it to the totality of social existence. To interpret correctly what Marx says about basis and superstructure, Lukács says, we have to grasp the 'decisive Marxist category' of 'the dominant moment' (*das übergreifende Moment*).[20]

To see what all this means, we may start from the thesis of classical Marxism, expounded in some of Engels' letters,[21] that the basis does not determine the superstructure in a one-sided way; there is interaction between the two. Now Lukács asserts that in the case of any interaction, however complex, there holds good what he calls 'the basic fact of the materialist dialectic', that 'there is no real interaction without a dominant moment'.[22] We may take this to mean that given that (say) A and B interact, one of the two will be the more powerful, and will influence the other more than the other influences it — the alternative is equilibrium, which contradicts the fact that there is constant change.[23] This explains the term 'dominant'; in speaking of 'moments' Lukács is in effect saying that A and B must not be regarded as independent entities; they are elements *of a totality,* and can be understood only in relation to it. Lukács gives as an example Marx's argument that production and consumption are moments of a totality which interact with each other, the dominant moment here being production. That was an example from the sphere of economics; in the case of the relation between the economic and the extra-economic there is again constant interaction, and here the economic is the dominant moment.[24] It is in this sense, then, that we are to understand what Marx says about the determination of consciousness by social existence.

This makes it clear that, although Lukács may call the concept of the dominant moment the decisive Marxist category, that category itself presupposes the category of totality,[25] whose importance for Marxism Lukács had stressed since *History and Class Consciousness.* But it is now time to see what bearing the concept of the dominant moment has on a major problem of historical materialism: the problem of human freedom. There is no doubt that Lukács, in *The Ontology of Social Existence,* thought that necessary laws govern social development; the very origin of human society, he says, is the unwilled and necessary product of the development of productive forces. But he adds that those of Marx's followers who turned economic necessity into a mechanistic fatalism were wrong, and Engels was right in opposing them.[26]

We saw in section II that Lukács, like Engels, rejected mechanistic materialism; the question remains, how Lukács understood social development to be determined. To say that social development occurs with dialectical necessity tells us nothing; we want to know what 'dialectical' means here. In giving his answer, Lukács goes beyond Marx's texts. He takes up another theme mentioned in section II, that of teleology. He begins by emphasising that when he speaks of teleology he is speaking only of 'individual acts of human, social activity, whose most pregnant form and model is labour'.[27] In other words, teleological or purposive activity is the activity of human beings, and of human beings only; physical things, plants and the lower animals do not act teleologically. Now, purposive acts involve choices, involve *alternatives*.[28] Man, Lukács says, is faced with questions to which he tries to find answers.[29] All this may seem trite, but according to Lukács it makes it possible to answer the question of the way in which the non-economic is determined by the economic. At a given stage of human development there arise concrete alternatives, to which men try to find concrete answers.[30] Lukács seems to mean that the fact that the alternatives are presented, that the questions arise, is unwilled and necessary; but the answers given are not necessary. This is put more clearly by Lukács in his conversations of 1966 with Holz, Kofler and Abendroth, in which he says:[31]

> Alternatives are possible within the concrete room for manoeuvre [*innerhalb des konkreten Spielraums*] that the great laws of development prescribe. There cannot therefore be freedom in the absolute sense .... Freedom exists, in the sense that life presents men with concrete alternatives .... A man is a being that gives answers [*ein antwortendes Wesen*], and his freedom consists in the fact that he has to make, and can make, a choice between the possibilities that lie within his room for manoeuvre.

This is Lukács' formulation of Marx's thesis that men make their own history, but not in circumstances that they themselves have chosen.[32] The view put forward here does not seem to differ fundamentally from one to be found in *History and Class Consciousness*. There (cf. chapter 3, section V) Lukács said that the destruction of capitalism is not inevitable; for it to be destroyed, the conscious will of the proletariat is required. In the language of *The Ontology of Social Existence,* social conditions under capitalism put a question to the proletariat. There is an answer to that question that will lead, not to the destruction of civilisation, but to continued human progress; but there is no guarantee that the proletariat will give that answer.

It is clear from all this that Lukács allows human freedom only a limited scope. Human choice is real, and is between real alternatives; nevertheless, it operates only within a given *Spielraum*, a limited room for manoeuvre. The economic moment is dominant in society, in that it poses the questions that human beings have to answer. Further, it must be borne in mind that the economic moment is not something abstract, but is a process whose main tendencies proceed in accordance with necessary laws. Human beings can accelerate or retard this necessary process, but this, it appears, is all that they can do.[33]

IV

We have seen already that Lukács regards Hegel's emphasis on labour as one of the most valuable parts of his philosophy, and in his own theoretical treatment of the ontology of social existence he takes labour as his first topic. He does so because he regards it as the basis of the specific nature of social existence, the source, not only of sociality, but also of speech and of the first division of labour.[34] Lukács stresses that in beginning with labour he is abstracting one element from a totality, and that labour can be understood adequately only in the context of social existence as a whole. Still, he says that the method that he follows — to begin with the abstract and work up to the concrete — is one described and recommended by Marx in the Introduction to the *Critique of Political Economy*.[35] Marx emphasised that the order one has to adopt in trying to understand political economy need not correspond to the temporal order of the stages described; similarly, Lukács says that his account is not in precise chronological order. Although sociality, the first division of labour, and speech all spring from labour, they do not do so in a clearly determinable time-sequence.[36]

The first section of Lukács' chapter on labour is in effect a long analysis of the concept of labour, and an account of the way in which it is fundamental to social existence. Lukács takes as his starting-point the account of the nature of labour with which Marx begins part 3 of the first volume of *Capital*. In trying to grasp the nature of labour, Marx argues, we must pay attention not only to what is produced, but also to how it is produced. Labour is something that is exclusively human; yet the bee, in building its cells, puts many a human architect to shame. What distinguishes the worst architect from the best bee is the fact that the former has built the cell in his head before he builds it in wax. He does not merely bring about a change of form in a natural object; 'at the same time he realises in the natural object his end, that he knows'.[37] It is clear from this that when Marx and Lukács speak of 'labour', they speak of the *making* of some *thing*. That labour is a making is also implied by a later passage in the *Ontology*, in which Lukács comments approvingly on what he calls Aristotle's account of labour in the *Metaphysics,* which is in fact an account of what would literally be translated as 'makings' (*poiēseis*).[38] In labour, then, some object is made; further, the making of the object is the conscious end or purpose of the maker.

According to Lukács, this passage from Marx states the central ontological category of labour. 'Through labour', Lukács says, 'a teleological project [*teleologische Setzung*] is made real within material existence as the origin of a new objectivity.'[39] More simply, he says in the same paragraph that labour is the realisation (*Verwirklichung*) of a teleological project. The term 'teleological project' is obscure, and it may be wondered what it adds to Marx's simpler term 'end' or 'purpose' (*Zweck*). The distinction does not, indeed, appear to be great. Marx had spoken of the cell 'in the head' of the architect: similarly, Lukács says that a teleological project is an act of consciousness.[40] For Lukács, labour is the realisation of the teleological project in the object, just as for Marx, labour is the realisation in the natural object of the end that the labourer has in mind. The only difference between Lukács' 'teleological project' and Marx's 'end' seems to be that the former includes, not only the thought of the end, but also the thought of the means of realising the end.[41]

Lukács says that he follows Marx in denying all teleological activity outside labour.[42] This implies that animals do not have any purposes in acting as they do, and that it is labour that constitutes the fundamental distinction between man and the animals. Lukács is well aware of the fact that scientists have studied the use of tools by animals; but, he says, such a use always occurs in an artificially produced environment.[43] Lukács distinguishes between man and animal in another, related way. He says that it is not consciousness that marks off man from the lower animals; the difference is that, with labour, consciousness ceases to be a mere epiphenomenon. The lower animals are indeed conscious, but they merely adapt themselves to their environment; human labour is consciousness making changes in the environment itself.[44] The consciousness involved in human labour also differs in that it involves choice, alternatives, the importance of which Lukács had stressed in his chapter on Marx.[45] When a primitive man chooses a stone for a certain task, he does so by an act of consciousness which is not purely biological in nature, as is the consciousness which accompanies an animal's eating of grass. If it is said that a lion, for example, may choose to pursue one beast rather than another, Lukács would reply that this is not a case of choice in the strict sense; animals do not think, do not employ concepts.[46]

Lukács concludes the first section of his chapter on labour by drawing attention to the fact that labour is intimately connected with the knowledge of natural processes. This becomes clear when we remember that labour involves, not only the positing of an end, but also the search for means, a search which presupposes a knowledge of the processes involved in the making of the object in question.[47] Such knowledge of the means has a further consequence. Marx observed that labour alters a man's own nature; this may be seen, Lukács says, in the fact that in grasping the means in their real nature a man has to master what is merely instinctive or emotional — for example, he may have to master tiredness, and in some cases fear.[48] Man, Lukács adds, has often been called the tool-making animal, and rightly so;[49] but it is important to note that the making and the use of tools necessarily carries with it man's self-mastery. Such mastery, according to Lukács, is the main problem of every morality; we have, then, a clear line running from labour to ethics. We shall also see, at the end of section VI of this chapter, that the concept of self-mastery plays an important part in Lukács' account of human freedom.

V

In the second section of his chapter on labour, Lukács defends the view that labour is the model of every social practice, by which he means that every social practice is a more complicated variant of labour, and has to be understood by reference to it.[50] The most interesting part of this discussion is Lukács' account of judgments of obligation (*Sollen*) and value (*Wert*). Obligation and value are, of course, important concepts of ethics; Lukács does not give a detailed account of their ethical sense here, reserving such an account[51] for a treatise on ethics that he did not live to write. However, what he says in this chapter may be regarded as preliminary to an ethical theory.

Lukács argues that the nature of obligation is to be understood from the fact that teleology is the essence of labour.[52] In labour, as we have seen, there is the realisation of a teleological project, which involves both an end and the means to it. Now, Lukács declares that[53] 'The immediate determining moment of every action that is intended as a realisation must ... be obligation, since every step of the realisation is determined by whether and how it furthers the achievement of the goal.' This seems to mean that, given that we try to realise some end — for example, to make an object — there are certain things which we ought, and others which we ought not to do. There is also a *necessity* involved here, which is why Lukács speaks of a *determining* moment; we must (or must not) act in certain specifiable ways in order to achieve our end. Lukács notes that this differs from causal determination.[54] There, the past determines the present; but in the case of an action for an end, every step is governed by the future, in the sense that it is governed by the end to be brought about.

The category of obligation is one expression of the leap from one level of existence to another that is taken when social existence emerges out of merely organic existence. Lukács stresses that such a leap[55] demands a very long time. The notion of a leap that may take centuries to occur may well seem contradictory; Lukács explains that the leap is made as soon as the new quality emerges in primitive and isolated acts, but that a long period of development is necessary for the new categories either to constitute a new level of existence which is distinct and self-dependent, or, as Lukács says elsewhere, to become the objects of reflexive consciousness.[56] The point of this stress on the long period involved in the leap to social existence is that idealism, according to Lukács, ignores this.[57] Instead, it concentrates on the most highly developed and the subtlest manifestations of the new categories, and so is led to construct a sphere of obligation without any roots in social existence. 'Vulgar' (i.e. non-dialectical) materialism, on the other hand, ignores the role of obligation in social existence, and tries to understand the whole of social existence on the model of natural necessity.

It is natural to ask how Lukács proceeds from the obligations that are related to labour — e.g. 'To make a knife, you ought to do such and such' — to moral obligation. But before he gives any indication of his answer, he turns to the topic of value. Obligation and value, he says,[58] are closely related, but whereas obligation is the regulator of the teleological process itself, value chiefly influences the projection of the end, and is the principle of judging the finished product. This presumably means that whereas we say that to make a knife, we ought *to do* such and such (i.e. the process undertaken ought to be such and such), we say that a *knife* (i.e. the finished product) is valuable for such and such reasons, e.g. because it can cut. In this chapter, Lukács is concerned with use-values; in this sense, a thing is valuable if it is *useful for* the life of man.[59] He argues that such values are objective, in that the usefulness of an object can be precisely determined.[60] It may be asked, 'Can the same be said of moral virtues? Is the goodness of a man precisely determinable, as the goodness of a knife is said to be? What is the relation between the goodness of a man and the goodness of a knife?' These are questions for moral philosophy, and, as mentioned just now, *The Ontology of Social Existence* is not primarily concerned with such questions. However, the chapter on labour gives a hint of Lukács' answer. He would say that the development of moral values is a long process, a process which involves 'sublation' (*Aufhebung*), i.e. the preservation of certain elements in a state or process and the cancellation of others.[61] In this context, Lukács remarks that the philosophers of the Enlightenment were wrong in trying to derive the highest virtues from mere utility; in other words, it is wrong to say that the moral virtues, and moral values, are *nothing but* utility. At the same time, Lukács adds, some element of utility is preserved.

It seems, then, that Lukács would deny that the goodness of a knife and the goodness of a man are the same.[62] Does he think, then, that there are any objective values, outside the use-values that are related to labour? The answer seems to be that he does. He says that the multiplicity and mutual contradictoriness of moral values might lead one to suppose, as Max Weber did, that they are merely relative, i.e. that there are no real, objective moral values. But this, says Lukács, is not so.[63] We have to see the values as moments of the total socio-historical process, a process which is a contradictory unity — that is, a dialectical process. To see more clearly what Lukács has in mind here, we have to return to his historical materialism. There is, he maintains, objective economic development, and this provides the backbone of real progress. The decisive values, those that maintain themselves, are related — consciously or unconsciously, immediately or mediately — to this economic development.[64] Not that this means that economic criteria are ultimate. Purely economic projects cannot be realised without producing and developing human capacities which go far beyond the purely economic.[65] There is no economic act, says Lukács, which does not have an immanent bearing on man's becoming man, in the widest sense of the term.[66]

Let us now try to place this sketch of Lukács' ethical theory within the context of the rest of his thought. Lukács is saying in effect that the supreme moral value is the full development of the human personality — for so we may interpret 'man's becoming man, in the widest sense of the term'. Such a doctrine can be traced back to what is said about 'estrangement' in *History and Class Consciousness* — namely, that socialism will overcome the estrangement or alienation of man and will make of man a whole, instead of the fragmented being that capitalism has made of him (cf. chapter 3, section VII). A similar view is to be found in what *The Specific Nature of the Aesthetic* says about the 'all-sided man' (chapter 7, section IV). What is distinctive about Lukács' ethical theory, however, is not so much his view about the nature of the supreme value — as he knew, the ideal of the full development of the human personality originated long before Marxism (cf. chapter 5, section IV) — but rather the way in which he tries to show that this supreme value is objective. Here, his argument involves his historical materialism. The full development of the human personality, Lukács says, is an objective value in that its general acceptance will be brought about by the course of human development. In terms of social class, it is the supreme value of the proletariat, towards whose triumph history is moving.

VI

By far the most important part of the third section of the chapter on labour, which is entitled 'The subject-object relation in labour and its consequences', is a long discussion of freedom.[67] Lukács has already said something about the freedom of man, in the sense of his capacity to do something other than what he actually does, in his chapter on Marx. In that sense of the word 'freedom', Lukács argued, man's freedom is very limited. The economic factor is dominant in human history, and the economic process is a necessary one; all that human beings can do is to accelerate or retard it. This being so, it may be wondered what Lukács can have to add to what he has already said about freedom, apart from filling in some details. The answer is that several philosophers, of whom Spinoza and Hegel are the most famous, had said that freedom and determinism are not mutually exclusive; although a man's actions are determined, he may yet be called 'free'. This tradition of thought survives in classical Marxism, and it is also to be found in the last section of Lukács' chapter on labour. In this section, Lukács is concerned only to establish the basis of a discussion of the problem of freedom. Labour, he says, is only the genesis of freedom; an adequate discussion of the problem of freedom belongs to ethics.[68] However, in the course of this section Lukács looks beyond freedom in the context of labour, and in the absence of his proposed book on ethics what he says about freedom here is a valuable indication of his wider views on the subject.

As a first approximation, Lukács argues,[69] it may be said that freedom is that act of consciousness as a result of which there arises a new existence that is projected by it. The basis of freedom is a concrete decision between concrete possibilities. At first sight, this may seem wholly unsatisfactory. Lukács seems simply to have defined free activity as labour; he has begged the important question of whether labour is free in the sense that a man who produces something could do other than what he does — whether the so-called possibilities between which he is said to decide really *are* possibilities. It soon becomes clear, however, that Lukács is not concerned here with freedom in this sense. Instead, he offers two other definitions of freedom. These are interrelated, in that each is concerned with power — power over things other than oneself, and power over oneself, i.e. self-mastery. The first of these concepts of freedom begins to emerge when Lukács says that the dominant moment of the freedom that is manifested by labour is 'free movement in the material'.[70] This may again seem unsatisfactory, in that the definition appears circular, defining freedom in terms of freedom. It soon becomes clear, however, that what Lukács means by 'freedom' here is power over physical nature based on knowledge. There are certain objective causal connexions that will bring about the end aimed at by a man who is making something. Now, the greater a man's knowledge of these causal chains, the greater is his 'free movement in the material', or, the more sure is his mastery of these causal chains, i.e. his freedom.[71] As an example of what Lukács means, one may consider a man who wants to make a sword. There are certain causal processes (depending on the properties of the materials) of which he must make use. Now, the greater his knowledge of these processes — the greater his knowledge of metals and how they behave — the more power he has over them, and the greater is his freedom. 'Free movement in the material', then, means having the knowledge to choose the right material for one's ends, and to fashion the required object out of it.

In giving this account of freedom, Lukács (as he knew) is very close to a classical Marxist concept of freedom, to be found in Engels' *Anti-Dühring*.[72] Freedom, Engels said, does not consist in being independent of natural laws — such independence would be a mere dream. Rather, freedom is the knowledge of these laws, and the possibility which this knowledge gives of making them work towards determinate ends. In short, freedom means the capacity to make decisions with genuine knowledge of the subject.[73] In this context, Engels referred approvingly to Hegel's view that freedom is the insight into necessity, quoting his remark that 'Necessity is blind only in so far as it is not understood'.[74] Lukács expresses approval of the fact that Engels' interpretation of Hegel here is firmly oriented towards labour, but he thinks that the traditional opposition between freedom and necessity cannot embrace the whole problem: one needs to consider possibility as well.[75] The properties of an object, he says, are for the most part latent, mere possibilities. The labour process is not the becoming-conscious of blind necessity; rather, a latent possibility is consciously raised by labour into the sphere of actuality. Similarly, if we consider the change that work produces in the worker himself, we see that this too is an awakening of possibilities that hitherto had only slumbered in him. One may be tempted to find in this an echo of the philosophy of Lukács' old friend Ernst Bloch, for whom possibility is a fundamental category. In his major work, *Das Prinzip Hoffnung* (*The Principle of Hope*), Bloch wrote:[76]

> Man is the real possibility of everything that has become of him in his history, and above all of what can, with unhindered progress, still become of him .... Matter is the real possibility of all the forms that are latent in its womb and are delivered by process.

Bloch, however — as this quotation indicates — is inclined to find teleology, striving towards an end, in matter itself, a view which Lukács firmly rejects.[77] For Lukács, the presence of labour is essential if the possibilities inherent in matter are to become actual.

Leaving Bloch aside, let us now ask how important are the differences between Lukács and Engels on this issue. In stressing the importance of possibility, and of labour in the actualisation of possibility, Lukács is in effect stressing the importance of consciousness in human history. But, as we have seen, Engels would have been the last to deny this. Lukács may have thought that by emphasising necessity at the expense of possibility, Engels was suggesting a fatalistic view of human history; but, as Lukács well knew, this was not Engels' view. In modifying Engels, then, Lukács is modifying the expression of Engels' thought rather than the thought itself. Philosophically, the important point is this: by saying[78] that the greater one's knowledge of causal chains, the greater one's freedom, Lukács is employing a concept of freedom that is consistent with total determinism, and therefore also with his own restricted determinism, which allows some small area within which human actions could be other than they in fact are.

So far, Lukács has been concerned only with labour, and more specifically with labour as productive of use-values, i.e. objects considered simply as having a use. He says that the situation changes radically as soon as the teleological project is no longer concerned exclusively with changing natural objects, but is concerned with changing man's own mode of behaviour, his own inwardness.[79] The difference is that in the latter case the object of the teleological project, and the means of its realisation, become increasingly social in character. It is true that social existence has its own laws, and in this respect it is as independent of our choices as is nature itself. However, in so far as man takes part in the social process, he cannot avoid taking up an affirmative or negative attitude to it. With this, there enters something new, which influences the nature of the freedom that is manifested here: namely, man's inner subjective attitude. This played almost no part in the production of useful objects; now, however, it becomes increasingly important, and freedom is based on such attitudes to the total social process, or at least to its partial aspects.[80] This might give the impression that freedom consists in a kind of contemplation of law-governed social process; but one would hardly expect Lukács to hold such a view, and indeed he has already spoken in this context of man as *taking part* in the social process. On the analogy with what was said about labour, and the connexion between freedom and knowledge, one may infer that what is meant here is that to be free is to know the direction in which society is moving, and to further this movement. This is a different sense of freedom from that which was met in Lukács' discussion of historical materialism in his chapter on Marx. There it was suggested that a man is free to accelerate or retard the process of social development, and his freedom is manifested whether he grasps the laws of this process or not. Now, however, freedom seems to go with knowledge. The free man is the man who grasps the laws of social development, and co-operates with them.

Towards the end of his chapter on labour Lukács introduces another concept of freedom when he considers again the effects that labour produces in the worker himself.[81] Labour, he had said previously, leads to self-mastery; it is in and through the struggle against his own natural endowments that man becomes man, and Lukács adds that man's higher development can only be reached by going further along this way. So it can be said, Lukács argues, that[82] 'The toilsome way of self-overcoming, that goes from being determined by the natural instincts to conscious self-mastery, is the only real way to genuine human freedom.' Here Lukács seems to suggest that self-mastery *is* genuine human freedom. This is a very old concept of freedom, now often called the concept of 'positive freedom',[83] which includes among its defenders Hegel, Spinoza and the Stoics. It is connected with the view that a man is free in so far as he is his own master, to which is added the thesis that he is his own master in so far as his real self — reason — exercises control over the passions, which are regarded as external to him. This was also Engels' view. Freedom, he said in the passage quoted earlier from *Anti-Dühring,* is the mastery (*Herrschaft*) over ourselves and over external nature. Once again, therefore, Lukács is following a view which belongs to classical Marxism. It is also a view of the nature of freedom which is consistent with complete determinism; for whether or not a certain man *could* do other than achieve self-mastery, *given that* he has achieved self-mastery then he is, by definition, free.

VII

It is too soon to try to make any definite judgment about *The Ontology of Social Existence,* both because the whole book is not yet available, and because the assimilation and evaluation of such a large work must take time. Nevertheless, some tentative observations can be made. It can hardly be denied that the *Ontology* is remarkable in its scope, its solidity and its detail — the more so when one considers its author's advanced years. Yet one may doubt whether the book will add much to Lukács' reputation. The chapters published are without exception diffuse and repetitive. Further, although the terminology may sometimes be new, the ideas seldom are, in that they remain for the most part within the orbit of classical Marxism. It is hard to see how such a work can make of Marxism (as its author hoped) a living force in philosophical development. It seems most likely that Lukács' reputation will chiefly be based, as it has been based hitherto, on *History and Class Consciousness* and his literary criticism; though one may venture the conjecture that *The Specific Nature of the Aesthetic* will add to his reputation as it becomes more widely known, and may eventually be recognised as his master-work.

Abbreviations

A	Lukács, *Die Arbeit* (*Labour*)
AD	Engels, *Anti-Dühring* (Eng. trans.)
DL	Lukács, *Deutsche Literatur in zwei Jahrhunderten*, *Werke*, vii (*German Literature in Two Centuries*)
EA	Lukács, *Die Eigenart des Ästhetischen* (*The Specific Nature of the Aesthetic*)
ER	Lukács, *Essays über Realismus*, etc., *Probleme des Realismus* I: *Werke*, iv (*Essays on Realism*)
ETM	Lukács, *Essays on Thomas Mann*
GA	Lukács, *Goethe and His Age*
GK	Lukács, *Geschichte und Klassenbewusstsein* (*History and Class Consciousness*)
HCC	Lukács, *History and Class Consciousness*
HN	Lukács, *The Historical Novel*
HO	Lukács, *Hegels falsche und echte Ontologie* (*Hegel's true and false ontology*)
HR	Lukács, *Der historische Roman*, etc., *Probleme des Realismus* III: *Werke*, vi (*The Historical Novel*)
JH	Lukács, *Der junge Hegel* (*The Young Hegel*)
LS	P. Ludz (ed.), *Georg Lukács: Schriften zur Literatursoziologie* (*Georg Lukács: Writings on the Sociology of Literature*)
Ludz, *Ideologie*	P. Ludz (ed.), *Georg Lukács: Schriften zur Ideologie und Politik* (*Georg Lukács: Writings on Ideology and Politics*)
MCR	Lukács, *The Meaning of Contemporary Realism*
MESC	Marx and Engels, *Selected Correspondence*
MESW	Marx and Engels, *Selected Works*
MEW	Marx and Engels, *Werke*

Abbreviations

MHL	E. San Juan (ed.), *Marxism and Human Liberation*
MO	Lukács, *Die ontologischen Grundprinzipien von Marx* (*Marx's Basic Ontological Principles*)
NDL	Lukács, *Skizze einer Geschichte der neueren deutschen Literatur* (*Sketch of a History of Modern German Literature*)
Raddatz	F.J. Raddatz (ed.), *Marxismus und Literatur* (*Marxism and Literature*)
RR	Lukács, *Der russische Realismus in der Weltliteratur, Probleme des Realismus* II: *Werke*, v (*Russian Realism in World Literature*)
S	Lukács, *Solzhenitsyn*
SER	Lukács, *Studies in European Realism*
SF	Lukács, *Die Seele und die Formen* (*Soul and Form*)
Soul	Lukács, *Soul and Form*
Szyn	Lukács, *Solschenizyn*
TN	Lukács, *The Theory of the Novel*
TR	Lukács, *Die Theorie des Romans* (*The Theory of the Novel*)
WC	Lukács, *Writer and Critic*
YH	Lukács, *The Young Hegel*
ZV	Lukács, *Die Zerstörung der Vernunft* (*The Destruction of Reason*)

Notes

Chapter 1 Lukács' Life and Times

1 For biographical data relating to sec. I (1885–1917) see: F. Erdei (ed.), *Information Hungary*, Oxford and London, 1965, pp. 254 ff., 260ff., 635, 687, 765 ff.

T. Hanak, *Lukács war anders (Lukács was different)*, Meisenheim, 1973, pp. 5 ff.

P. Ignotus, *Hungary*, London, 1972, pp. 107 ff.

A.C. Janos and W.B. Slottman (eds), *Revolution in Perspective*, Berkeley and London, 1971, pp. 1–60.

T. Klaniczay, J. Szauder and M. Szabolcsi, *History of Hungarian Literature*, Budapest and London, 1964, pp. 187 ff.

P. Ludz (ed.), *Georg Lukács: Schriften zur Ideologie und Politik (Georg Lukács-Writings on Ideology and Politics)*, Neuwied, 1967, pp. 323 ff.

Lukács, *Werke*, ii, pp. 11–13; *History and Class Consciousness*, pp. ix–xi. Lukács, *Die Theorie des Romans*, pp. 5–18; *The Theory of the Novel*, pp. 11–23.

I. Mézaros, *Lukács' Concept of Dialectic,* London, 1972, pp, 115ft

E. Pamlényi (ed.), *A History of Hungary*, Budapest and London, 1975, pp. 345 ff.

F. Tökei, 'Lukács and Hungarian Culture', in *New Hungarian Quarterly*, XIII, no. 47, 1972, pp. 108 ff.

I. Völgyes (ed.), *Hungary in Revolution. 1918–19*, Lincoln, Nebraska, 1971, pp. 1 ff., 25 ff.

2 *New Hungarian Quarterly,* XIII, 1972, no. 47,p. 4.

3 Ibid.

4 Lukács, quoted Tökei, op. cit., p. 109.

5 Tökei, op. cit., p. 111. Unhappily, English translations of the works of

Ady and Móricz are few and not always easily accessible.
Móricz's novel *Be Faithful unto Death* has been published in translation
by the Corvina Press, Budapest, 1962, whilst *Poems of Endre Ady*,
translated by A.N. Nyerges, has been published by the Hungarian
Cultural Foundation, Buffalo, New York, 1969.

6 On the Thalia, see *New Hungarian Quarterly*, VIII, no. 28, 1967, p. 208.

7 The book was published in Hungarian in 1911; a German translation
of the introductory chapter, which deals with the sociology of the
modern drama, appeared in 1914. See P. Ludz (ed.), *Georg Lukács:
Schriften zur Literatursoziologie (Georg Lukács: Writings on the Sociology of
Literature)*, Neuwied, 1961, pp. 261 ff.

8 Cf. Lukács, 'Art and Society', in *New Hungarian Quarterly*, XIII, no.
47, 1972, pp. 44-5.

9 The nature of this influence will be considered when the book is
discussed in the next chapter (sec. II).

10 As he himself noted later; 1962 Preface to *Die Theorie des Romans*, p. 6;
The Theory of the Novel, p. 12.

11 The so-called *Geisteswissenschaften* movement. On this, see below,
chap. 2, sec. VII.

12 *Die Theorie des Romans*, p. 5; *The Theory of the Novel*, p. 11. Personal
factors may well have contributed to Lukács' depression. *The Theory of
the Novel* is dedicated to Yelyena Andreyevna Grabenko, Lukács' first
wife. The marriage proved a failure, and Yelyena remained in
Heidelberg when Lukács returned to Budapest in 1915; the marriage
was dissolved at the end of the war.

13 Lukács, *Werke*, ii, p. 13; *History and Class Consciousness*, p. xi.

14 For biographical data covering sec. II (1918-23), see:
Y. Bourdet, *Figures de Lukács (Aspects of Lukács)*, Paris, 1972, pp. 175 ff.
(A conversation with Lukács about his stay in Austria.)
Erdei, op. cit., pp. 264 ff.
Hanak, op. cit., pp. 31 ff.
Ignotus, op. cit., pp. 128 ff.
D. Kettler, 'Culture and Revolution: Lukács in the Hungarian
Revolutions of 1918/19', in *Telos*, no. 10, 1971, pp. 35 ff.
Lukács, *Taktik und Ethik (Tactics and Ethics)*, Neuwied, 1975. A
collection of essays, many of them from the period of the Hungarian
revolution of 1919.
Mészáros, op. cit., pp. 126 ff.
Pamlényi, op. cit., pp. 421 ff.
R.L. Tökés, *Béla Kun and the Hungarian Soviet Republic*, New York and
London, 1967.
Völgyes, op. cit., pp. 31 ff., 61 ff.

15 The poet and novelist Anna Lesznai; quoted by D. Kettler, op. cit., p. 69.
16 It was not published until December 1918, i.e. after Lukács had joined the Communist Party. A German translation may be found in *Taktik und Ethik*, pp. 27 ff.
17 Lukács, *Werke*, ii, pp. 52-3; *Taktik und Ethik*, pp. 52-3; *Political Writings, 1919-29*, London, 1972, pp. 10-11.
18 Lukács, *Werke*, ii, p. 33; *History and Class Consciousness*, p. xxxi.
19 Lukács, *Werke*, ii, p. 110; *Political Writings, 1919-29*, p. 69.
20 Lukács, *Werke*, ii, p. 13; *History and Class Consciousness*, p. xi.
21 R. Köves and T. Erényi, *Kunfi Zsigmond életútja* (*The Career of Zsigmond Kunfi*), Budapest, 1974, p. 119.
22 Another event that occurred during Lukács' stay in Vienna deserves mention: this was his marriage in 1920 to Gertrud Bortstieber, widow of the mathematician Imre Janossy. Unlike Lukács' first marriage, his second was long and happy, and one of his major works, *The Specific Nature of the Aesthetic*, is dedicated to the memoory of his second wife.
23 Cf. Lukács, *Werke*, ii, pp. 15, 30; *History and Class Consciousness*, pp. xiii, xxvii.
24 Lukács, *Werke*, ii, pp. 95 ff.; *Political Writings, 1919-29*, pp. 53 ff.
25 Lukács, *Werke*, ii, pp. 18, 30; *History and Class Consciousness*, pp. xvi, xxvii.
26 For biographical data covering sec. III (1923-8) see:
Hanak, op. cit., pp. 46 ff.
Lukács, *Werke*, ii, pp. 17, 32-4, 38-40; *History and Class Consciousness*, pp. xv, xxix-xxxi, xxxv-vii.
Mészáros, op. cit., pp. 133 ff.
Völgyes, op. cit., pp. 170 ff.
27 Bloch published a review in *Der neue Merkur* (*The New Mercury*), VII, 1924, pp. 457 ff., entitled 'Aktualität und Utopie' ('Actuality and Utopia'); Révai published a review in the *Archiv für die Geschichte des Sozialismus und der Arbeiterbewegung* (*Archives for the History of Socialism and the Workers' Movement*), vol. XI, 1925.
28 Excerpts from Zinoviev's speech may be found in a German version in Ludz, *Ideologie*, pp. 719 ff. More will be said about 'revisionism' below, chap. 3, sec. I.
29 Lukács, *Werke*, ii, pp. 630, 652, 681; *Political Writings, 1919-29*, pp. 167, 190, 219.
30 A German translation of excerpts from the Blum theses may be found in Lukács, *Werke*, ii, pp. 698 ff.; *Political Writings, 1919-29*, pp. 227 ff.
31 Lukács, *Werke*, ii, p. 12; *History and Class Consciousness*, p. x.
32 From Lukács' 1969 preface to *Hungarian Literature, Hungarian Culture*

(pub. in Hungarian, Budapest, 1970); quoted Tökei, op. cit., p. 116.

33 For biographical data covering sec. IV (1919-45), see:

Helga Gallas, *Marxistische Literaturtheorie* (*Marxist Literary Theory*), Neuwied, 1971. (Deals in great detail with Lukács' activities in Berlin, 1931-2.)

Hanak, op. cit., pp. 52 ff.

Lukács, 'Mein Weg zu Marx' ('My Road to Marx'), in Ludz, *Ideologie*, pp. 323 ff.

Lukács, 'Postscriptum 1957 zu: Mein Weg zu Marx' ('1957 Postscript to "My Road to Marx"'), in Ludz, *Ideologie*, pp. 646 ff.

Lukács, *Werke*, ii, pp. 38-40; *History and Class Consciousness*, pp. xxxvi-vii.

Mészáros, op. cit., pp. 137 ff.

J. Rühle, *Literature and Revolution*, London, 1969, pp. 146., 199 ff. (An English version of *Literatur und Revolution*, Cologne, 1960.) These pages deal with Lukács' stay in Berlin, 1931-2, and with his controversy with Anna Seghers, 1938-9.

M. Watnick, 'Georg Lukács: an intellectual biography, part II', *Soviet Survey*, 1958, no. 24, pp. 51 ff. (Also in L. Labedz (ed.), *Revisionism*, London, 1962, pp. 142 ff.)

34 Excerpts in Watnick, op. cit., p. 54 (Labedz, op. cit., p. 148).

35 The controversy with Bloch was concerned with expressionism. It began with Lukács' essay '"Grösse und Verfall" des Expressionismus' ('The "Grandeur and Decline" of Expressionism') (1934) (*Werke*, iv, pp. 109 ff.), to which Bloch replied in his 'Diskussion über Expressionismus' ('A Discussion of Expressionism') (1938); reprinted in Bloch, *Erbschaft dieser Zeit* (*The Heritage of this Age*), Frankfurt, 1962, pp. 264 ff. This was answered by Lukács in 'Es geht um den Realismus' ('The Issue is Realism') (1938) (*Werke*, iv, pp. 313 ff.). (These works can conveniently be consulted in F.J. Raddatz (ed.), *Marxismus und Literatur*, Hamburg, 1969, ii, pp. 7 ff.) The correspondence with Anna Seghers (1938-9) concerned realism, and may be found in Lukács, *Werke*, iv, pp. 345 ff.; Raddatz, op. cit., ii, pp. 110 ff. Lukács does not appear to have sought any controversy with Russian critics, but this was forced upon him when his book, *A Contribution to the History of Realism*, which appeared in Russian in 1939, was attacked in the Soviet press in 1939-40. (Cf. Lukács' Preface to *Art and Society*, *New Hungarian Quarterly*, XIII, 1972, no. 47, pp. 51-2.) Some of the texts. written by Lukács in this connexion and previously unpublished have appeared in a French translation, *Georges Lukács: Écrits de Moscou* (*Georg Lukács: Moscow Writings*), ed by C. Prévost, Paris, 1974.

36 Between 1933 and 1945 Lukács contributed to *Internationale Literatur* (*International Literature*); from 1933 to 1939 to *Literaturnyi Kritik*

(*Literary Critic*); from 1936 to 1938 to *Das Wort* (*The Word*); and from 1938 to 1941 to the Hungarian language journal *Uj Hang* (*New Voice*).

37 Quoted by Walter Benjamin, 'Conversations with Brecht', 26 July 1938 (in *Understanding Brecht*, London, 1973, p. 119). Because of what he believed to be the strength of Lukács' position in Moscow, Brecht withheld from publication some articles against him which he had intended for *Das Wort*, and they were not published until after the war. (See Raddatz, op. cit., ii, pp. 87 ff. ; English translation, 'Against Georg Lukács', in *New Left Review*, no. 84, 1974, pp. 39 ff.) On Lukács and Brecht, see e.g., Gallas, op. cit., pp. 135 ff., and W. Mittenzwei, 'Marxismus und Realismus', in J. Matzner (ed.), *Lehrstück Lukács* (*A Lukács Study*), Frankfurt, 1974, pp. 125 ff.

38 For biographical data covering sec. V (1945–56), see:
Hanak, op. cit., pp. 69 ff.
Mészáros, op. cit., pp. 143 ff.
For Hungary under Rákosi, see:
Erdei, op. cit., pp. 289 ff.
Ignotus, op. cit., pp. 193 ff.
D. Nemes (ed.), *History of the Revolutionary Workers Movement in Hungary, 1944-62*, Budapest, 1973, pp. 76 ff. (A translation of the third volume of a work published in Hungarian by the Party History Institute of the Hungarian Communist Party.)
F.A. Váli, *Rift and Revolt in Hungary*, Cambridge (Mass.) and London, 1961, pp. 31 ff.
The 1956 revolution in Hungary has been the subject of a vast literature. A bibliography of works published in the ten years after 1956 is contained in:
T. Aczel (ed.), *Ten Years After*, London, 1966, pp. 209 ff.
Among more recent works may be cited:
Juluis Hay, *Born 1900*, London, 1974. (The memoirs, first published in German in 1971, of one of the protagonists of the 1956 revolution.)
M. Molnar, *Budapest 1956*, London, 1971. (A translation of a book published in Paris in 1968 as *Victoire d'une défaite.*)

39 Quoted by W. Shawcross, *Crime and Compromise: Janos Kadar and the Politics of Hungary since Revolution*, London, 1974, p. 56.

40 Cf. Nemes, op. cit., pp. 219–20; Pamlényi, op. cit., p. 554. Cardinal Mindszenty's account of his own trial may be found in his *Memoirs*, English trans., London, 1975.

41 Figures given in J. Berecz, *Ellenforradalom tollal és fegyverrel, 1956* (*Counter-revolution with Pen and Sword, 1956*), Budapest, 1969, p. 30. 30.

42 1957 Postcript to 'Mein Weg zu Marx' ('My Road to Marx'); Ludz, *Ideologie*, p. 651.

43 See, e.g. Nemes, op. cit., p. 220.

44 See Ludz, *Ideologie*, pp. 593 ff.

45 For biographical data covering sec. VI (1957-71), see:
Hanak, op. cit., pp. 130 ff.
Ignotus, op. cit., pp. 255 ff.
Mészáros, op. cit., pp. 149 ff.
Nemes, op. cit., pp. 281 ff.
W.F. Robinson, *The Pattern of Reform in Hungary*, New York, 1973.
W. Shawcross, op. cit., pp. 99 ff.

46 At the Party Congress in June 1957 membership had dropped to 350,000 — only a little more than a third of the pre-1956 membership of the Hungarian Working People's Party (Nemes, op. cit., p. 319).

47 In Hungary, he was attacked by the Deputy Minister of Culture, József Szigeti, and by the philosophers Béla Fogarasi and Elemér Balogh. (See *Georg Lukács und der Revisionismus* (*Georg Lukács and Revisionism*), Berlin, 1960, pp. 137 ff., 213 ff., 303 ff.) In the USSR, Lukács was criticised in the philosophical journal *The Problems of Philosophy*. (Excerpts in a German translation in Ludz, *Ideologie*, pp. 775 ff.)

48 See E. Laszlo, *Studies in Soviet Thought*, IV, 1964, pp. 240-1; V, 1965, p. 319; VI, 1966, p. 42.

49 I. Eörsi, 'The Story of a Posthumous Work: Lukács' Ontology', *New Hungarian Quarterly*, XVI, no. 58, 1975, p. 107.

Chapter 2 Pre-Marxist Literary Criticism: *The Soul and the Forms* (1911) and *The Theory of the Novel* (1916)

1 References to *Die Seele und die Formen* are to the pagination of the 1911 edition, which is reproduced in the edition of 1971 (Neuwied), and also to the English translation, London, 1974. It should be added that this translation renders the title of the book as *Soul and Form*; however, I have followed what appears to be the more usual practice of translating the title as *The Soul and the Forms*.

2 *SF*, pp. 7, 22, 24 ff.; *Soul*, pp. 3, 10, 11-12.

3 *SF*, pp. 24-5; *Soul*, p. 11.

4 *SF*, pp. 36-7; *Soul*, pp. 16-17.

5 *Die Zerstörung der Vernunft* (*The Destruction of Reason*), Neuwied, 1962, p. 351.

6 *SF*, pp. 7, 223, 249; *Soul*, 3, 103-4, 116.

7 *SF*, p. 20; *Soul*, p. 9.

8 *SF*, pp. 17-18; *Soul*, p. 8.

9 *SF*, p. 308; *Soul*, p. 144.

10 *SF*, pp. 12, 17, 20, 369-70; *Soul*, pp. 5, 8, 9, 172-3.

11 *SF*, p. 32; *Soul*, p. 15. Cf. *SF*, pp. 20, 29; *Soul*, pp. 9, 13.

12 *SF*, pp. 63, 88; *Soul*, pp. 28, 40.

13 Preface to *Die Theorie des Romans*, Neuwied, 1963, p. 10; English trans., *The Theory of the Novel*, London, 1971, p. 16. On Rickert, cf. chap. 1, sec. I.

14 *SF*, p. 34; *Soul*, p. 16.

15 *SF*, p. 331; *Soul*, p. 154.

16 *SF*, pp. 328-9; *Soul*, p. 153.

17 See *SF*, p. 245; *Soul*, p. 114, on the Viennese poet and dramatist Richard Beer-Hofmann.

18 *SF*, pp. 258, 335-6; *Soul*, pp. 120, 156.

19 *SF*, p. 340; *Soul*, p. 158.

20 *SF*, p. 343; *Soul*, p. 159.

21 *SF*, pp. 345-6; *Soul*, pp. 160-1.

22 See especially Lucien Goldmann, 'Georg Lukács: L'Essayiste', in *Recherches Dialectiques* (*Dialectical Inquiries*), Paris, 1959, pp. 247ff.; 'Introduction aux premiers écrits de Georges Lukács' ('Introduction to the early writings of Georg Lukács'), *Les Temps Modernes*, XVIII, 1962-3, pp. 256 ff.; Introduction to the Italian translation of *The Theory of the Novel* (*Teoria del Romanzo*, Milan, 1962), pp. 13ff. Goldmann stressed the relation between Lukács' thought and Heidegger's, and planned to write a book on the theme: see his posthumously published *Lukács et Heidegger*, ed by Y. Ishaghpour, Paris, 1973, which is based on material that he left. One of the undoubted forerunners of existentialism was Kierkegaard, and the influence of Kierkegaard on *The Soul and the Forms* is stressed by T. Perlini, *Utopia e prospettiva in György Lukács* (*Utopia and Perspective in Georg Lukács*), Bari, 1968, pp. 103ff. See also Goldmann, in *Kierkegaard vivant* (*The Living Kierkegaard*), Paris, 1966, pp. 125ff.

23 Mary Warnock, *Existentialism*, Oxford, 1970, p. 59.

24 *Die Theorie des Romans*, p. 10; *The Theory of the Novel*, p. 15.

25 'Epopöe', *TR*, p. 53; *TN*, p. 56. Sometimes the term 'das Epos' is used in the same sense, e.g. *TR*, p. 23; *TN*, p. 30.

26 *TR*, p. 23; *TN*, p. 30.

27 *TR*, p. 27; *TN*, p. 34.

28 *TR*, p. 35; *TN*, p. 41.

29 On the drama, see *TR*, pp. 35, 41; *TN*, pp. 41, 46.

30 'Die Gesinnung zur Totalität', *TR*, p. 53; *TN*, p. 56.

31 Hegel, *Ästhetik* (*Aesthetics*), ii. ed. by F. Bassenge, Frankfurt, 1965, p. 406.

32 On the hero of the novel, see *TR*, pp. 57-8, 64, 66, 76, 79; *TN*, pp. 60, 66, 67, 78, 80.

33 *TR*, p. 79; *TN*, p. 80.

34 *TR*, p. 90; *TN*, p. 90. The concept of 'learned ignorance', '*docta ignorantia*', is to be found in the mediaeval philosopher Nicholas of Cusa. On the novel's irony, see also *TR*, pp. 73, 87; *TN*, pp. 74, 88.
35 *TR*, p. 100; *TN*, p. 100. On the 'narrow soul', see also *TR*, pp. 96, 98; *TN*, pp. 97, 99.
36 *TR*, pp. 100ff.; *TN*, pp. 101ff.
37 Lukács speaks (*TR*, p. 103; *TN*, p. 103) of 'die Idee', literally 'the idea'. Earlier, he distinguishes between 'Idee' and 'Ideal' (*TR*, p. 96; *TN*, p. 97); however, as he is thinking in the present context of an 'Idee' as something which refers to what *ought* to exist, 'ideal' seems the less misleading translation, and is used in the rest of this section.
38 *TR*, p. 107; *TN*, p. 107.
39 *TR*, p. 114; *TN*, p. 112.
40 1962 Preface to *The Theory of the Novel*, *TR*, p. 9; *TN*, p. 14. The relevant passages in *The Theory of the Novel* are *TR*, pp. 123ff.; *TN*, pp. 120ff. Many years later, in an essay first published in 1948 and included in his *Essays on Thomas Mann* (*Werke*, vii, p. 563-4; English trans., London, 1964, pp. 79-80) Lukács was to return to the theme of time in the novel of disillusionment.
41 He could have referred here to his discussion of tragedy in *The Soul and the Forms*, but instead he refers to his earlier book, *A History of the Development of Modern Drama* (*TR*, p. 124n.; *TN*, p. 121n.).
42 'Das gestaltende Gefühl des Sinnerfassens', *TR*, p. 127; *TN*, p. 124.
43 *TR*, p. 132; *TN*, p. 128.
44 Preface to *The Theory of the Novel*, *TR*, p. 9; *TN*, p. 14.
45 See especially Bloch's *Das Prinzip Hoffnung* (*The Principle of Hope*), Berlin, 1954-9. It is not suggested that Bloch derived the idea from Lukács — merely that the idea was 'in the air'.
46 On Goethe and Tolstoy, see especially *TR*, pp. 138, 154, 156-7; *TN*, pp. 135, 149, 151-2.
47 'Die Epoche der vollendeten Sündhaftigkeit'. The reference is to Fichte's *Grundzüge des gegenwärtigen Zeitalters* (*Characteristics of the Present Age*, lectures given in 1804-5), Fichte, *Werke*, ed. F. Medicus, Leipzig, 1908, vol. 4, p. 405. Fichte here divided history into five epochs, of which the present, the third, is the epoch of complete sinfulness.
48 Preface to *The Theory of the Novel*, *TR*, p. 15; *TN*, p. 20.
49 One could easily add to these: for example, Lukács' view that the novel is the form that the epic takes in a God-forsaken world (*TR*, p. 87; *TN*, p. 88) is expressed by Hegel more prosaically in the form of the assertion that the novel is the modern bourgeois epic (*Ästhetik*, p. 452).
50 The word for 'sublation', '*Aufhebung*', was quoted in sec. IV, where it was said that in the novel there is a '*Selbstaufhebung*' of subjectivity

(TR, p. 73; TN, p. 74). But the word does not always have the technical sense that Hegel gives to it, and in the passage in question it was rendered as 'self-transcendence'.

51 TR, p. 132; TN, p. 128. Again, although it is true that Goethe's *Wilhelm Meister* is presented by Lukács as an attempted synthesis, the attempt is regarded as a failure (TR, p. 147; TN, p. 142).

52 Cf. H.A. Hodges, *Wilhelm Dilthey: An Introduction*, London, 1944, p. 157.

53 Preface to *The Theory of the Novel*, TR, p. 7; TN, p. 13.

54 For a fuller account of Dilthey's philosophy, see the work by H.A. Hodges cited in n. 52. Dilthey and Lukács are discussed by the same author in G.H.R. Parkinson (ed.), *Georg Lukács: The Man, his Work and his Ideas*, London, 1970, pp. 86ff.

55 TR, pp. 7-8; TN, pp. 13-14.

Chapter 3 Marxism and Hegelianism: *History and Class Consciousness* (1923)

1 *Capital*, in Marx and Engels, *Werke*, vol. 23, Dietz Verlag, Berlin, 1956-8, p. 27 (abbreviated MEW 23.27); E. and C. Paul trans., London, 1930, p. 873.

2 Neo-Kantians of this kind are referred to when Lukács speaks of 'criticism'. Max Adler and Otto Bauer, criticised in *History and Class Consciousness* were leading neo-Kantian Marxists. See *Geschichte und Klassenbewusstsein*, pp. 16, 23-4, 43-4; English trans., *History and Class Consciousness*, London, 1971, pp. 4, 10-11, 31. References to GK are to the pagination of the original 1923 edition, which is reproduced in the edition of the work in Lukács, *Werke*, ii.

3 There is some doubt as to whether Bernstein can properly be called a Kantian, but there is no doubt that he appealed to the authority of Kant (Karl Vorländer, *Kant und Marx*, Tübingen, 1926, p. 183).

   Vorländer's book, the standard work on Marxism and neo-Kantianism, is written from a neo-Kantian point of view. G. Lichtheim (*Marxism*, 2nd edn, London, 1964, pp. 290ff.) discusses the neo-Kantians from a more Hegelian standpoint.

4 *Capital*, p. 27.

5 A reader in 1923 would have had access to the scattered references to dialectic in *Capital* and in Marx's correspondence (cf. GK, p. 8; HCC, p. xliv). He could also have known of the Introduction to the *Critique of Political Economy* (MEW, 13; Eng. trans., Moscow and London, 1971), written in 1857 but first published in 1903, in which Marx discusses the 'method of political economy', but in effect gives an account of dialectics.

6 See *Anti-Dühring*, ME*W*, 20.20ff.; English trans., London, 1934, pp. 26ff.

7 *Anti-Dühring*, ME*W*, 20.131-2; *AD*, p. 158.

8 On the laws of dialectics, see *Anti-Dühring*, ME*W*, 20.13, 21, 42, 61, 116-17, 126, 129; *AD*, pp. 17, 28, 54, 77, 140-1, 152, 155: *Dialectics of Nature*, ME*W*, 20.348; English trans., Moscow and London, 1964, p. 63.

9 *Dialectics of Nature*, 20.348.

10 ME*W*, 21.275, 277; Marx and Engels, *Selected Works*, ii, Moscow and London, 1949, pp. 335, 337.

11 On the transformation of quantity into quality, see *GK*, pp. 183-4; *HCC*, pp. 166-7: there are also some brief references in *GK*, pp. 188, 256, 283; *HCC*, pp. 171, 250, 280. It is not certain that Lukács always understood the law as Engels did, for he speaks of it as asserting that quantification is a 'reifying and reified cloak' spread over the true essence of objects (*GK*, p. 183; *HCC*, p. 166), which is not suggested by Engels. (On reification, cf. sec. VII below.) On the unity of opposites in *History and Class Consciousness*, see *GK*, p. 282; *HCC*, p. 278.

12 *GK*, p. 13; *HCC*, p. 1.

13 Engels, ME*W*, 21.268, ME*SW*, ii, p. 329; Vorländer, op. cit., p. 113; Lenin, *Collected Works*, vol. 14, Moscow and London, 1962, p. 143.

14 1967 Preface to *History and Class Consciousness*, *Werke*, ii, p. 28; *HCC*, p. xxv.

15 *GK*, pp. 23, 39; *HCC*, pp. 10, 27.

16 *GK*, p. 40; *HCC*, p. 28.

17 *GK*, pp. 40, 51; *HCC*, pp. 28, 39.

18 E.g. *GK*, p. 32; *HCC*, p. 18.

19 Engels, *Ludwig Feuerbach*, ME*W*, 21.267; ME*SW*, ii, p. 328. A philosopher such as Leibniz would be regarded as belonging, not to the classical period, but to the Enlightenment. (For this contrast, cf. Lukács, *Der junge Hegel*, p. 35; English trans., *The Young Hegel*, p. 3.)

20 *GK*, p. 125; *HCC*, p. 113.

21 *GK*, p. 123; *HCC*, p. 112. The reference to Kant is to the *Critique of Pure Reason*, 2nd edn, (B), p. xvi.

22 Cf. *GK*, p. 129; *HCC*, p. 117.

23 Vico, *The New Science*, Bk I, trans. T.G. Bergin and M.H. Fisch, Ithaca, N.Y., 1948, par. 349. Lukács notes that there is a glancing reference to this passage in Marx, *Capital*, ME*W*, 23.393n., trans. E. and C. Paul, p. 392n.

24 *GK*, p. 126; *HCC*, p. 114.

25 *GK*, p. 128; *HCC*, p. 116.

26 *GK*, p. 130; *HCC*, p. 118. Lukács adds that the second alternative was suggested, but not clearly stated, by Emil Lask, the neo-Kantian

philosopher whose friend and pupil he had been during his Heidelberg years (cf. chap. 1, sec. I). Lask attacked Kant's theory of categories, those very general concepts by means of which the understanding gives form or structure to our knowledge of the world. He argued that Kant's separation of form from content — the latter being provided by our sensations — was too sharp, and that if we are to distinguish the categories from one another we must say that they are not just pure form, but also have content. See the notes relating to Lask in *GK*, pp. 128, 130; *HCC*, pp. 211-12, and Lukács' obituary of Lask in *Kant-Studien*, XXII, 1917-18, pp. 349ff.; also P. Ludz, Introduction to *Georg Lukács: Schriften zur Ideologie und Politik* (*Lukács: Writings on Ideology and Politics*), Neuwied, 1967, pp. xxii-iii, and H. Rosshoff, *Emil Lask als Lehrer von Georg Lukács* (*Emil Lask as a teacher of Georg Lukács*), Bonn, 1975.

27 *GK*, pp. 132-4; *HCC*, pp. 119-21.

28 *GK*, pp. 135-7; *HCC*, pp. 122-4.

29 *GK*, pp. 157-60; *HCC*, pp. 142-5.

30 *GK*, p. 162; *HCC*, p. 147.

31 *GK*, p. 216; *HCC*, p. 197. Cf. *GK*, pp. 14-15; *HCC*, pp. 2-3.

32 *GK*, pp. 218, 224; *HCC*, pp. 199, 205. See also Engels, *Ludwig Feuerbach*, MEW, 21.293; MESW, ii, p. 350; Lenin, *Collected Works*, vol. 14, pp. 105, 129, 178, 190, 262, 302, 326, 346.

33 *GK*, p. 51; *HCC*, p. 39. Cf. *GK*, p. 211; *HCC*, p. 193.

34 *GK*, pp. 164-5; *HCC*, p. 149. The reference to Marx is to MEW, 1.391; English trans. in Marx and Engels, *Collected Works*, vol. 3, Moscow and London, 1975, p. 187.

35 *GK*, p. 81; *HCC*, p. 69. Cf. *GK*, p. 78; *HCC*, pp. 65-6.

36 *GK*, pp. 185, 218; *HCC*, pp. 168-9, 199.

37 *GK*, pp. 51, 53, 207; *HCC*, pp. 39, 41, 189.

38 Stalin, *Foundations of Leninism* (1924), in *Problems of Leninism*, Moscow, 1953, p. 31. Quoted by G. Wetter, *Dialectical Materialism*, London, 1958, p. 259. The notion is also to be found in the Soviet philosophy of the post-Stalin era: e.g. G. Kursanov (ed.) *Fundamentals of Dialectical Materialism*, Moscow, 1967, pp. 297ff.

39 *GK*, p. 215; *HCC*, p. 197. Cf. *GK*, p. 179; *HCC*, p. 163.

40 *History and Class Consciousness* has a little to say about art, but only in the context of the history of German aesthetics in the eighteenth century (*GK*, pp. 151ff.; *HCC*, pp. 137ff.).

41 *GK*, pp. 7, 17n.; *HCC*, pp. xlii, 24.

42 *GK*, p. 18; *HCC*, p. xvi.

43 E.g. *GK*, pp. 32, 37, 207; *HCC*, pp. 18, 23, 189.

44 MEW, 13.8-9; English trans., *Critique of Political Economy*, pp. 20-1.

45 *GK*, p. 256; *HCC*, p. 249. Cf. *GK*, p. 32; *HCC*, p. 18.

46 *GK*, pp. 35, 80, 230; *HCC*, pp. 20-1, 68, 224.

47 *GK*, pp. 254, 258; *HCC*, pp. 247, 251. For the 'realm of freedom', see *Anti-Dühring*, ME*W*, 20.264; *AD*, p. 312, and the end of vol. III of *Capital*.

48 *GK*, p. 260; *HCC*, p. 253.

49 Engels, letter to Franz Mehring, 14 July 1893, quoted in *GK*, p. 61; *HCC*, p. 50 (ME*W*, 39.97; Marx and Engels, *Selected Correspondence*, Moscow and London, n.d., p. 541.)

50 *GK*, p. 234; *HCC*, p. 228.

51 Cf. H.B. Acton, *The Illusion of the Epoch*, London, 1955, pp. 125ff.

52 *GK*, p. 234; *HCC*, p. 228. Cf. Acton, op. cit., p. 131.

53 *GK*, pp. 234-5, 244-5; *HCC*, pp. 228-9, 238-9.

54 *GK*, pp. 204ff.; *HCC*, pp. 187ff.

55 ME*W*, 23.12, 28, 791; Paul trans., pp. 863, 874, 846.

56 *GK*, p. 189; *HCC*, p. 173.

57 *GK*, p. 228; *HCC*, p. 209.

58 *GK*, pp. 55, 214, 228; *HCC*, pp. 43, 196, 208.

59 GK, pp. 82, 286, 316; *HCC*, pp. 70, 282, 313.

60 *GK*, p. 216; *HCC*, pp. 197-8. Cf. *GK*, p. 78; *HCC*, p. 65, it is not only in the interests of the bourgeoisie, but also *unavoidably necessary* for it to become aware of class interests in every particular question.

61 *GK*, p. 194; *HCC*, p. 177.

62 *GK*, p. 62; *HCC*, p. 51.

63 *GK*, p. 57; *HCC*, p. 46.

64 *GK*, p. 62; *HCC*, p. 51.

65 *GK*, p. 88; *HCC*, pp. 75-6.

66 As Lukács himself noted, *GK*, p. 62n.1; *HCC*, p. 81. A clear account of Weber's doctrine may be found in W.G. Runciman, *A Critique of Max Weber's Philosophy of Social Science*, Cambridge, 1972, pp. 33ff.

67 *GK*, pp. 318, 329, 339; *HCC*, pp. 315-16, 326, 336-7.

68 *GK*, p. 329; *HCC*, p. 326.

69 Lukács, *Werke*, ii, p. 536; Eng. trans., *Lenin*, London, 1970, p. 27.

70 For these views on the Communist Party, see *GK*, pp. 324, 330-1, 334, 339; *HCC*, pp. 321, 327-9, 331, 336.

71 Lukács, *Werke*, ii, p. 545; Eng. trans., *Lenin*, pp. 37-8.

72 Cf. Engels' account of the way in which 'metaphysical' thinking breaks down because of its inner contradictions; also his account of the relations between primitive materialism, idealism and modern materialism (chap. 3, sec. II).

73 Cf. Engels on eighteenth-century philosophy, which he declares to be 'in essence only the philosophical expression of thoughts corresponding to the development of the small and middle bourgeoisie into the great bourgeoisie': *Ludwig Feuerbach*, ME*W*, 21.302-3; ME*SW*, ii, pp. 359-60.

74 GK, pp. 112, 122; HCC, pp. 100, 110.
75 Capital, vol. I, chap. 1, sec. 4: MEW, 23.86; Paul trans., p. 45.
76 GK, p. 97; HCC, p. 86.
77 Capital, MEW, 23.89-90; Paul trans., pp. 49-50. Cf. Introduction to the Critique of Political Economy, MEW, 13.618-9; English trans., p. 192.
78 GK, pp. 97-8, 105-6; HCC, pp. 86-7, 93-5.
79 GK, p. 141; HCC, p. 128.
80 MEW, Ergänzungsband 1, pp. 514-15; English trans., Economic and Philosophic Manuscripts of 1844, in Marx and Engels, Collected Works, vol. 3, pp. 274-5.
81 On the relations between Simmel and Lukács, see above, chap. 1, sec. I. The influence of The Philosophy of Money on Lukács is stressed by A. Arato, 'Lukács' path to Marxism (1910-1923)', Telos, no. 7, 1971, pp. 128ff. See also H. Becker, 'On Simmel's Philosophy of Money', in K.H. Wolff (ed.), Georg Simmel, 1858-1918, Ohio, 1959, pp. 216ff.
82 Simmel, The Philosophy of Money, 3rd edn, Munich and Leipzig, 1920, pp. 502ff.
83 Simmel, op. cit., pp. 516, 519.
84 GK, p. 106; HCC, p. 95.
85 Lukács, Werke, ii, p. 24; HCC, p. xxii.
86 Lukács, Werke, ii, p. 41; HCC, p. xxxviii.

Chapter 4 Marxism and the History of Philosophy: The Young Hegel (1948) and The Destruction of Reason (1954)

1 Preface to History and Class Consciousness: Werke, ii, p. 38; HCC, p. xxxv.
2 Ibid.
3 Der junge Hegel (abbreviated, JH), Werke, viii, p. 30; English trans., The Young Hegel (abbreviated YH), London, 1975, p. xxviii.
4 JH, pp. 22, 29-30; YH, pp. xxi-ii, xxviii.
5 JH, p. 29; YH, p. xxvii.
6 JH, p. 669; YH, p. 548.
7 On Aufhebung ('sublation') cf. chap. 2, sec. VII: also JH, pp. 165, 252, 493, 533, 675, 677-8; YH, pp. 118, 188, 398, 432, 553, 555.
8 MEW Ergänzungsband 1 pp. 570, 574; English trans., Marx and Collected Works, vol. 3, pp. 329, 332-3. Cf. JH, p. 29; YH, p. xxvii.
9 JH, pp. 399-400; YH, pp. 320-1. Cf. chap. 3, sec. IV.
10 JH, p. 406; YH, p. 325. Cf. JH, p. 401; YH, p. 321, where Lukács quotes again the second of the passages from Marx's 1844 Manuscripts cited earlier (note 8).

11 *JH*, pp. 406 ff; *YH*, pp. 325 ff. The reference to the *Phenomenology* is primarily to the section on 'Master and Slave'; the lectures in question are those given by Hegel in Jena in the years immediately preceding the publication of the *Phenomenology* and published long after his death as the *Jenenser Realphilosophie* (*Jena Philosophy of Reality*), Leipzig, 1931-2.

12 *JH*, pp. 659 ff.; *YH*, pp. 539 ff.

13 *JH*, p. 659; *YH*, p. 539. Cf. chap. 3, sec. IV, and *GK*, pp. 123, 160; *HCC*, pp. 112, 145.

14 *JH*, pp. 659-60; *YH*, pp. 540-1: cf. *JH*, p. 671; *YH*, p. 549.

15 *JH*, pp. 411 ff.; *YH*, pp. 329 ff. Lukács quotes from the *Jenenser Realphilosophie*; some relevant excerpts from this work are translated by S. Avineri, *Hegel's Theory of the Modern State*, Cambridge, 1972, pp. 93 ff.

16 Hegel, *Phänomenologie des Geistes*, ed by J. Hoffmeister, 6th edn, Hamburg, 1952, e.g. pp. 21, 32; trans. J.B. Baillie, *The Phenomenology of Mind*, London and New York, 1967, pp. 82-3, 96.

17 *Werke*, ii, pp. 26-7; *HCC*, pp. xxiii-iv.

18 *JH*, p. 14; *YH*, p. xv.

19 *JH*, p. 689; *YH*, p. 564.

20 The importance of the concept of mediation in Hegel's philosophy had already been stressed by Lukács in his essay *Moses Hess und die Probleme der idealistischen Dialektik* (*Moses Hess and the Problems of Idealist Dialectics*) (1926); *Werke*, ii, p. 665; *Georg Lukács: Political Writings 1919-29*, London, 1972, pp. 202-3.

21 *JH*, p. 626; *YH*, p. 510.

22 *JH*, p. 26; *YH*, p. xxv.

23 *JH*, pp. 25, 139; *YH*, pp. xxiv, 96. Cf. *JH*, pp. 555 ff.; *YH*, pp. 451 ff., on the attitudes of Hegel and Goethe towards Napoleon.

24 *JH*, p. 140; *YH*, p. 97. Cf. *JH*, pp. 150, 349; *YH*, pp. 105, 276.

25 *Wissenschaft der Logik*, ed. by Lasson, Leipzig, 1923, ii, p. 58; trans. A.V. Miller, *Hegel's Science of Logic*, London, 1969, p. 439.

26 ME*W*, 20.112-3; *AD*, pp. 135-6.

27 *JH*, p. 160; *YH*, p. 114.

28 *JH*, pp. 454, 670, 674, 687; *YH*, pp. 366-7, 548, 552, 562.

29 Lenin, *Philosophical Notebooks*, in *Collected Works*, vol. 38, Moscow and London, 1962, p. 363: quoted in *JH*, p. 246; *YH*, p. 184.

30 See especially *JH*, pp. 18, 61, 303, 336-7, 637, 647-8; *YH*, pp. xviii, 24, 233, 266-7, 519, 526-7.

31 Cf. chap. 1, sec. IV; Ludz, *Ideologie*, p. 648.

32 *JH*, p. 458; *YH*, p. 369. Cf. *JH*, pp. 114, 364, 457, 487, 568; *YH*, pp. 72, 289, 369, 392, 461.

33 *Die Zerstörung der Vernunft*, *Werke*, ix, p. 10.

34 *ZV*, p. 18.

35 *ZV*, p. 10.
36 *ZV*, pp. 11, 14, 16: cf. *JH*, p. 14; *YH*, p. xv.
37 Engels, to C. Schmidt, 27 Oct. 1890, ME*W*. 37.493; Marx and Engels, *Selected Correspondence*, Moscow and London, n.d., p. 507. Cf. op. cit., ME*W*, 37.490, 492; ME*SC*, pp. 503, 505: to J. Bloch, 21-2 Sept. 1890, ME*W*, 37.463.465, ME*SC*, pp. 498, 500; to F. Methring, 14 July 1893, ME*W*, 39.98, ME*SC*, p. 542; to 'H. Starkenburg' (W. Borgius), 25 Jan. 1894, ME*W*, 39.206, ME*SC*, p. 549.
38 *ZV*, p. 10. For a recent Soviet statement of this view, cf. D.I. Chesnokov, *Historical Materialism*, Moscow, 1969, p. 280.
39 *ZV*, pp. 34-5, 82-3.
40 *ZV*, p. 9.
41 Cf. T. Adorno, 'Erpresste Versöhnung' ('Enforced Reconciliation') in Adorno, *Noten zur Literatur* (*Notes on Literature*), vol. II, Frankfurt, 1961, pp. 152 ff.
42 *ZV*, pp. 277, 309. Nietzsche's criticism of the capitalist division of labour is briefly described as a manifestation of 'romantic anti-capitalism' (*ZV*, p. 300).
43 *ZV*, p. 87.
44 *ZV*, p. 86.
45 Cf. sec. III above, and notes 24-6.
46 *JH*, pp. 341-2; *YH*, pp. 269-70. Cf. *ZV*, pp. 162, 222, where Lukács states that the doctrine of the identical subject-object is a weak part of Hegel's philosophy.
47 *ZV*, p. 223. Contrast *History and Class Consciousness*: chap. 3, sec. IV above.
48 *ZV*, p. 282. Engels does not say in so many words that dialectics is a summary of the results of the sciences; however, this was the orthodox Soviet view when Lukács wrote. See, e.g., V. Svetlov and T. Oizerman, 'The rise of Marxism — a revolutionary upheaval in philosophy', *Bolshevik*, 1948: dialectical materialism is 'a total world-outlook which generalises the findings of all the sciences'. (Quoted by G.A. Wetter, *Dialectical Materialism*, London, 1958, p. 251.)
49 *ZV*, p. 15.
50 *GK*, p. 125; *HCC*, p. 113; cf. chap. 3, sec. IV. The distinguishing feature of modern rationalism is that its systems are complete, whereas earlier versions of rationalism present only partial systems.
51 *ZV*, pp. 93, 99.
52 *ZV*, pp. 101 ff.
53 Mainly, but not exclusively. In the course of this chapter Lukács sometimes anticipates his later argument, and shows how irrationalism itself contributed to the rise of Nazism (e.g. pp. 77, 79). But these are exceptions.

54 *ZV*, p. 37. Cf. Engels, *The Peasant War in Germany*, MEW, 7.534, MESW, i, p. 582.

55 *ZV*, pp. 38 ff.

56 *ZV*, pp. 41 ff.

57 *ZV*, p. 54. The reference to Engels is to *The Peasant War in Germany*, MEW, 7.538; MESW, i, p. 587.

58 *ZV*, pp. 63 ff. For the date, cf. Lukács, *Skizze einer Geschichte der neueren deutschen Literatur* (*A Sketch of a History of Modern German Literature*), 2nd edn, Neuwied, 1963, p. 138.

59 *ZV*, pp. 71 ff.

60 Lenin, *Imperialism, the Last Stage of Capitalism, Collected Works*, vol. 22 (1964), p. 298.

61 Lukács, *Werke*, ii, p. 11; *HCC*, p. ix. Cf. chap. 2, sec. II and note 17; also *ZV*, pp. 220, 264.

62 *ZV*, pp. 270-2; cf. *ZV*, p. 12.

63 *ZV*, pp. 119 ff.: cf. *JH*, pp. 308 ff; *YH*, pp. 241 ff.

64 *ZV*, pp. 121-2.

65 *ZV*, pp. 131, 136, 138, 141-2.

66 *ZV*, pp. 147, 152.

67 *ZV*, pp. 162-4.

68 *ZV*, p. 172.

69 *ZV*, p. 173.

70 'Die Fähigkeit gedanklicher Hellhörigkeit': *ZV*, p. 177. Lukács says elsewhere ('Es geht um den Realismus' ('The Issue is Realism'): *Werke*, iv, p. 331) that Marxism has always recognised the 'anticipatory function' of ideology. He quotes a statement of Marx, recorded by his son-in-law Paul Lafargue, to the effect that Balzac was not only the historian of his own epoch, but also the creator of prophetic figures, which existed only in embryonic form in his own day. (See M. Kliem (ed.), *Marx und Engels über Kunst und Literatur*, i, Berlin, 1967-8, p. 21.)

71 *ZV*, p. 181.

72 *ZV*, pp. 182-3, 216.

73 *ZV*, p. 184.

74 *ZV*, p. 208.

75 *ZV*, pp. 191-2. Cf. *ZV*, pp. 261, 266, 316-17, 392-3, 452, 535, 700.

76 *ZV*, p. 219.

77 *ZV*, p. 221.

78 *ZV*, pp. 231-2, 235.

79 *ZV*, p. 259.

80 *ZV*, pp. 256, 260.

81 *ZV*, pp. 261-2; cf. *ZV*, p. 391.

82 *ZV*, p. 11. Cf. *JH*, p. 626, cited in no. 21 above.

83 *ZV*, p. 391.

84 Compare what was said earlier (sec. II) about 'alienation' in Heidegger. Lukács argues (*ZV*, p. 452) that Heidegger aimed at the creation of a philosophy of history for religious atheism.

85 'Scheinaktivität': *ZV*, p. 264.

86 *ZV*; p. 264; cf. *ZV*, p. 452.

87 *ZV*, p. 275.

88 *ZV*, pp. 273 ff.

89 *ZV*, pp. 275, 278-9.

90 *ZV*, p. 282. Cf. R.J. Hollingdale, *Nietzsche*, London, 1973, p. 176.

91 *ZV*, pp. 279-80.

92 *ZV*, p. 305.

93 *ZV*, p. 312.

94 *ZV*, p. 313.

95 *Die fröhliche Wissenschaft* (*The Joyful Wisdom*), par. 125, Nietzsche, *Werke*, ed. by G. Colli and M. Montinari; sec. V, vol. 2, Berlin and New York, 1973, p. 159. Cf. *ZV*, p. 317, and Hollingdale, op. cit., pp. 65 ff.

96 *ZV*, pp. 302, 318.

97 *ZV*, p. 324; cf. p. 321.

98 *ZV*, p. 269.

99 *ZV*, p. 354.

100 *ZV*, p. 355.

101 *ZV*, p. 392.

102 *ZV*, pp. 359, 361.

103 *ZV*, p. 429.

104 *ZV*, p. 441.

105 *ZV*, p. 362.

106 *ZV*, pp. 77, 363.

107 E.g. *Encyclopaedia*, Part I (Logic) par. 209 (Eng. trans. by W. Wallace, *The Logic of Hegel*, Oxford, 1892, p. 305). Cf. S. Avineri, 'Consciousness and History: *List der Vernunft* in Hegel and Marx', in W.E. Steinkraus (ed.), *New Studies in Hegel's Philosophy*, New York, 1971, pp. 108 ff.

108 *ZV*, p. 363.

109 *ZV*, pp. 457-8.

Chapter 5 Marxism and Literary Criticism: (1) The Literature of the West

1 Vols iv-vii, and part of vol. iii.

2 On Lifschitz, cf. chap. 1, sec. IV. Lifschitz originally published (with F. Schiller) a book of selections in a Russian translation, *Marks i Engels ob iskusstve* (*Marx and Engels on Art*), Moscow, 1933. Lifschitz alone edited

some more extensive selections published in Moscow and Leningrad in 1937, *K. Marx i F. Engels: ob iskusstve* (*K. Marx and F. Engels: on Art*); this went through six editions between 1948 and 1953. The most complete edition of the relevant works now available is the two-volume work edited by M. Kliem, *Marx und Engels über Kunst und Literatur* (*Marx and Engels on Art and Literature*), Berlin, 1967-8.

3 For a fuller account of this theory, see P. Demetz, *Marx, Engels and the Poets*, Chicago and London, 2nd edn, 1967.

4 On this work, cf. chap. 3, sec. II, n 5. Marx and Engels also discuss the way in which art is socially conditioned in *The German Ideology*, MEW, 3.377-8; Eng. trans., Moscow 1964, p. 430. This work was first published in full in Moscow in 1932; it is not clear whether Lukács was able to consult it when in Moscow in 1930 (cf. chap. 1, sec. IV).

5 MEW, 13.640-42; Eng. trans., *Critique of Political Economy*, Moscow and London, 1971, pp. 216-7.

6 The letter to Frau Kautsky is to be found in MEW, 36.392-4: MESC, pp. 466 ff. For the letter to Miss Harkness, see MEW, 37.42-4 (a German translation of the English original); MESC, pp. 478 ff. This letter was first published in *Die Linkskurve*, March 1932 (Helga Gallas, *Marxistische Literaturtheorie* (*Marxist Literary Theory*) Neuwied, 1971, p. 39).

7 Gorky's speech may be found in *Maxim Gorky on Literature*, Moscow, n.d., pp. 228 ff.; a German translation of Zhdanov's speech is in F.J. Raddatz (ed.), *Marxismus und Literatur*, i, Hamburg, 1969, pp. 347 ff.

8 Zhdanov, in Raddatz, p. 351.

9 Gorky, op. cit., p. 244; Raddatz, p. 352.

10 Cf. *ER*, p. 62; *LS*, p. 150; also Helga Gallas, op. cit., pp. 75 ff., 210-11. Gallas argues that much of Lukács' *Linkskurve* work was directed against the influence of 'Proletkult' views.

11 Gorky, op. cit., p. 242; Raddatz, p. 352.

12 E.g. in *A History of Realism* (English trans., Moscow, 1973, pp. 121-2, 155, 185, 199) Boris Suchkov gives as examples of critical realists Balzac, Tolstoy, Flaubert, Ibsen, Kingsley, Dickens, Charlotte Brontë, Mrs Gaskell, Shaw and Heinrich Mann.

13 *HR*, p. 376; *HN*, p. 307: *HR*, p. 468; *SER*, p. 43: *DL*, p. 556; *ETM*, p. 71: *WC*, p. 12: *Die Eigenart des Ästhetischen* (*The Specific Nature of the Aesthetic*), i, Neuwied, 1963, pp. 592-3, 851. The lines are the epigraph of Goethe's *Marienbad Elegy* (1823).

14 As Lukács puts it: 'Self-knowledge and world-knowledge are not to be separated' ('Marx and the Problem of Ideological Decline', *ER*, p. 274).

15 *RR*, p. 116; *SER*, p. 117: *ER*, pp. 33, 42; *LS*, pp. 119-20, 129-30: *ER*, pp. 156, 160; *WC*, pp. 154, 158.

16 *ER*, p. 40: *LS*, p. 127: *ER*, p. 588; *MCR*, p. 122.

17 *HR*, p. 496; *SER*, p. 71: *ER*, p. 588; *MCR*, p. 122.

18 *HR*, p. 436; *SER*, p. 6: *ER*, pp. 42-3; *LS*, p. 130: *RR*, p. 116; *SER*, p. 117.

19 *ER*, p. 501; *MCR*, p. 48: *RR*, p. 27; *WC*, p. 231.

20 *Werke*, x, p. 222; *LS*, p. 231; *WC*, pp. 78-9. On Hoffmann, cf. *ER*, p. p. 506; *MCR*, p. 52: *NDL*, p. 86.

21 *HR*, p. 444; *SER*, p. 19. Cf. *HR*, pp. 421, 427; *HN*, pp. 344, 349: *ER*, p. 646.

22 *HR*, p. 409; *HN*, pp. 333-4.

23 *ER*, p. 508; *MCR*, p. 54.

24 *ER*, p. 43 n.4; *LS*, p. 130 n.2.

25 Cf. chap. 4, sec. VII; also *HR*, pp. 207, 209; *HN*, pp. 171, 173; *HR*, p. 510; *SER*, p. 85.

26 *DL*, p. 85; *GA*, p. 64

27 *DL*, p. 57; *GA*, p. 39: *NDL*, p. 42: *HR*, p. 25; *HN*, p. 20.

28 *NDL*, pp. 43, 53. Cf. Engels, *MEW*, 20.17; *AD*, p. 24.

29 The first two chapters of *GA* are devoted to Lessing's *Minna von Barnhelm* (1767) and Goethe's *Werther* (1774).

30 *DL*, p. 123; *GA*, p. 99. It should be added that Lukács does not say that no Enlightenment writer had any concept of dialectics; Diderot (*Le Neveu de Rameau*: *NDL*, p. 37: *HR*, pp. 472, 487; *SER*, pp. 47, 62) and Rousseau (*DL*, p. 57; *GA*, p. 38) both had some notion of thought.

31 *DL*, pp. 53 ff.; *GA*, pp. 35 ff.

32 *DL*, pp. 58, 64, 72 ff., 80 ff.; *GA*, pp. 39-40, 45, 52 ff., 60 ff.

33 *HR*, p. 435; *SER*, p. 5.

34 Cf. *DL*, pp. 21, 92; *GA*, pp. 19, 71.

35 *HR*, p. 544; *GA*, p. 176. On *Faust* and Hegel's *Phenomenology* see, besides *HR*, pp. 544 ff., *JH*, pp. 691 ff.; *YH*, pp. 566-7.

36 *HR*, pp. 549, 561, 568, 582; *GA*, pp. 180-1, 193, 200, 215.

37 *DL*, pp. 80, 95; *GA*, pp. 60-1, 74: *HR*, p. 612; *GA*, p. 245.

38 *DL*, pp. 51-52; *GA*, p. 17.

39 'Report on the Novel' and 'The Novel as the bourgeois epic'; see *Écrits de Moscou*, Paris, 1974, pp. 19, 71-2, 108 ff.

40 *Écrits de Moscou*, p. 65; Hegel, *Ästhetik*, ii, ed. by Bassenge, 2nd ed. Frankfurt, 1965, p. 452. Cf. chap. 2 n.49 above and *HR*, p. 160; *HN*, p. 133.

41 *DL*, p. 85; *GA*, p. 65: *HR*, p. 605; *GA*, p. 238.

42 *HR*, p. 36; *HN*, p. 30. In fact Lukács does sometimes note the influence of one writer on another — e.g. the influence of Goethe's *Götz* on Scott (*HR*, p. 26; *HN*, p. 22: *HR*, p. 444, *SER*, p. 19). But he clearly regards this as only a secondary concern of the critic.

43 *HR*, pp. 525, 605-6; *GA*, pp. 157, 238: *NDL*, p. 90.

44 *HR*, pp. 525-6; *GA*, pp. 157-8.

45 *NDL*, p. 44: *HR*, pp. 608-9; *GA*, p. 241: *RR*, pp. 26, 33, 42; *WC*, pp. 230, 238, 247. See also S. Mitchell, 'Lukács' concept of "the beautiful"' in G.H.R. Parkinson (ed.), *Georg Lukács: The Man, his Work and his Ideas*, London, 1970, pp. 219 ff.

46 Some critics express surprise that Lukács, a Hungarian, should have devoted much attention to the works of Scott. In fact, however, Scott's novels were very popular in Hungarian middle-class society in the nineteenth century, and have indeed retained their popularity in the twentieth. (Géza Hegedüs, Intro. to Eng. trans. of Mór Jókai, *The Dark Diamonds*, Budapest, 1968,pp. viii-ix.)

47 *HR*, p. 23; *HN*, p. 19.

48 *HR*, pp. 27 ff.; *HN*, pp. 23 ff.

49 *HR*, p. 185; *HN*, p. 152.

50 *HR*, p. 280; *HN*, pp. 230-31.

51 *HR*, p. 65; *HN*, p. 54.

52 *HR*, p. 66; *HN*, p. 54.

53 *HR*, p. 64; *HN*, p. 53.

54 *HR*, p. 42; *HN*, p. 35.

55 *HR*, pp. 38-9, 44-5; *HN*, pp. 32-3, 36-7; cf. *ER*, pp. 226-7; *WC*, pp. 140-1.

56 *HR*, pp. 57-8; *HN*, pp. 47-8.

57 *HR*, p. 68; *HN*, p. 56; cf. *HR*, p. 345; *HN*, pp. 282-3.

58 *HR*, pp. 58 ff.; *HN*, pp. 48 ff. Cf. 'Gottfried Keller', *DL*, p. 415.

59 *HR*, pp. 106, 184-5; *HN*, pp. 89, 152. On the importance of a Marxist theory of genres, cf. *ER*, pp. 635, 396 ff.; *WC*, pp. 54, 210 ff.

60 *HR*, p. 108; *HN*, pp. 90-91.

61 The case of comedy, Lukács says, is somewhat different (*HR*, p. 109; *HN*, p. 91). Lukács returns briefly to the topic of comedy in *HR*, p. 293; *HN*, p. 241, but does not explain what differentiates it; see, however, his essay on Lessing's comedy *Minna von Barnhelm*, *DL*, pp. 26 ff.; *GA*, pp. 24 ff. Briefly, Lukács sees this comedy as portraying the conflict between abstract morality based on universal principles, such as Stoic morality, and concrete ethics. This conflict, he says, is the foundation of all great drama (*DL*, p. 25; *GA*, p. 22); what distinguishes comedy is that there, an excess of virtue becomes the target of laughter, which thus becomes a new cathartic principle (*DL*, p. 26; *GA*, p. 24).

62 *HR*, pp. 110-11; *HN*, pp. 92-3. In relating the epic to a totality of things or objects, Lukács is taking up an idea to be found in Hegel's *Ästhetikü,* ii, p. 438.

63 *HR*, pp. 112-13; *HN*, pp. 93-4. Cf. *ER*, p. 214; *WC*, p. 127, in which

Lukács remarks that drama is more abstract than (great) epic.

64 *HR*, p. 128; *HN*, p. 107. Lukács goes into this in greater detail in part 4 of chapter 2 (*HR*, pp. 167 ff.; *HN*, pp. 138 ff.)

65 *HR*, p. 143; *HN*, p. 119. Cf. *HR*, pp. 141, 153; *HN*, 117-18, 127.

66 *HR*, p. 185; *HN*, p. 153.

67 *HR*, p. 205; *HN*, pp. 169-70; cf. *HR*, p. 293; *HN*, p. 241.

68 *HR*, pp. 110-11, 167; *HN*, pp. 92-3, 139.

69 *HR*, pp. 175, 206, 293; *HN*, pp. 145, 170, 241: *DL*, p. 114; *GA*, p. 91.

70 Major representatives of the classical historical novel are (besides Scott) Fenimore Cooper and Manzoni: *HR*, pp. 77 ff., 83-4; *HN* pp. 64 ff., 69-70.

71 *HR*, pp. 205, 290 ff.; *HN*, pp. 170, 239 ff.

72 *HR*, pp. 97-8; *HN*, p. 81.

73 *HR*, pp. 99, 101; *HN*, pp. 83, 84.

74 *HR*, p. 443; *SER*, pp. 12-13. Cf. *HR*, pp. 441, 447-8, 466; *SER*, pp. 10, 22, 40: *Werke*, x, pp. 226 ff.,; *LS*, pp. 236 ff.; *WC*, pp. 83 ff.: *ER*, p. 44; *LS*, p. 131.

75 See his essay on the tragedies of Heinrich von Kleist, in his *German Realists of the 19th Century*, *DL*, pp. 229-30; also *Werke*, x, pp. 226 ff., and *ER*, pp. 268 ff.

76 *ER*, pp. 160-1, 630-61; *WC*, pp. 159, 49. Cf. *HR*, pp. 485-6, 513; *SER*, pp. 60, 88.

77 *HR*, pp. 492, 502; *SER*, pp. 67, 77: *DL*, pp. 78, 177; *GA*, pp. 58, 149.

78 *HR*, p. 529; *GA*, p. 161: *NDL*, pp. 67, 81. Cf. sec. IV on the relations between Goethe and romanticism.

79 *HR*, p. 492; *SER*, p. 68.

80 See especially *HR*, pp. 493, 503, 506 ff.; *SER*, pp. 68, 77, 80 ff.

81 *RR*, p. 192; *SER*, p. 140.

82 *HR*, pp. 442, 514; *SER*, pp. 11-12, 89: *RR*, pp. 111-12, 192, 201; *SER*, pp. 112-13, 140, 148: *ER*, p. 205; *WC*, pp. 118-19. Zola may seem to provide an obvious exception to this thesis, but Lukács argues that Zola's involvement in the Dreyfus affair came too late to influence his artistic methods (*HR*, p. 515; *SER*, p. 90).

83 *HR*, p. 514; *SER*, p. 89: *ER*, p. 517; *MCR*, p. 61.

84 *Werke*, x, p. 219; *LS*, p. 227; *WC*, p. 75. Cf. *WC*, p. 14.

85 *HR*, p. 261; *HN*, p. 215: *ER*, p. 583; *MCR*, p. 119.

86 *HR*, pp. 511, 514; *SER*, pp. 86, 89: *RR*, p. 112; *SER*, pp. 113-14.

87 *HR*, p. 516; *SER*, p. 91: *RR*, pp. 222-3, 230; *SER*, pp. 169, 176.

88 *ER*, p. 590; *MCR*, pp. 124-5: *HR*, pp. 517 ff.; *SER*, pp. 92 ff.

89 *NDL*, p. 121: *HR*, p. 517; *SER*, p. 92.

90 *ER*, p. 486; *MCR*, p. 34.

91 *NDL*, pp. 160-1: *ER*, p. 321; Raddatz, ii, p. 67.

92 *NDL*, p. 161: *ER*, p. 336; Raddatz, ii, p. 80.

93 Bloch made this point in a reply to Lukács, 'A Discussion of Expressionism', Raddatz, ii, p. 52.

94 *ER*, pp. 138, 141, 321-2, 325-6, 336; Raddatz, ii, pp. 32, 35, 67-8, 71, 80.

95 *ER*, pp. 130, 136, 139; Raddatz, ii, pp. 26, 30, 33.

96 *ER*, pp. 121, 126-7, 146; Raddatz, ii, pp. 17, 22-3, 40.

97 *ER*, p. 486; *MCR*, p. 34. On 'new objectivity' (*die neue Sachlichkeit*) cf. *ER*, p. 148; Raddatz, ii, p. 41; *NDL*, p. 205; *ER*, p. 583; *MCR*, p. 119; *HR*, p. 306; *HN*, p. 251.

98 *ER*, p. 486; *MCR*, p. 34; *ER*, p. 319; Raddatz, ii, p. 65.

99 *ER*, pp. 467-8; *MCR*, pp. 17-18.

100 This is the title given in *Werke*, iv. The first German edition (1958) had the title *Wider den missverstandenen Realismus* (*Against Misunderstandings of Realism*). It should be added that the English translation, *The Meaning of Contemporary Realism*, London 1963, is unreliable. In trying to find an acceptable English version of Lukács' often complex German, the translators are often led to offer a rough and shortened paraphrase.

101 *ER*, pp. 505, 534; *MCR*, pp. 51-2, 77.

102 *ER*, p. 489; *MCR*, p. 36. Cf. *ER*, pp. 533-4, 538; *MCR*, pp. 76-7, 80.

103 *ER*, pp. 534-5; *MCR*, pp. 77-8.

104 *ER*, p. 497; *MCR*, p. 44. Cf. chap. 4, sec. VII, and *ZV*, pp. 452, 680, 700.

105 *ER*, pp. 493-4, 496 ff., 507, 535; *MCR*, pp. 40-1, 43 ff., 53, 78. On allegory, compare chap. 7, sec. VI.

106 E.g. *ER*, pp. 465, 489.

107 Critical realism, Lukács says, begins before Scott (*ER*, p. 554; *MCR*, 96). In a short essay on Don Quixote (1952) he instances as critical realists Swift, Fielding, Sterne, Diderot, Scott and Balzac (*HR*, pp. 623, 629).

108 *ER*, pp. 466, 517, 554, 559; *MCR*, pp. 16, 61, 96, 100.

109 *DL*, p. 501; *ETM*, p. 10.

110 *DL*, p. 567; *ETM*, p. 83; cf. *DL*, p. 590; *ETM*, p. 105 and *ER*, p. 504; *MCR*, p. 51. In connexion with *The Magic Mountain*, it may be mentioned here that it is generally agreed that the character of the Jesuit Naphta in this book is modelled on Lukács. See, e.g., Y. Bourdet, *Figures de Lukács*, Paris, 1972, pp. 95 ff.

111 *ER*, p. 536; *MCR*, pp. 78-9.

112 *HR*, pp. 419-20; *HN*, pp. 343-4.

113 See 'Das Problem der Perspektive' ('The Problem of Perspective'), a lecture given in Jan. 1956, *ER*, p. 651.

114 *DL*, p. 581; *ETM*, p. 97. On Mann's perspective, cf. *DL*, pp. 589-90, 609; *ETM*, pp. 105, 125.

115 *ER*, p. 551; *MCR*, p. 93.

116 *ER*, pp. 554, 560; *MCR*, pp. 96, 100.

117 *ER*, p. 555; *MCR*, p. 97.

118 *ER*, p. 564; *MCR*, p. 104.

119 *ER*, p. 545; *MCR*, p. 87.

120 *ER*, p. 546; *MCR*, p. 88. For Lukács' views on Brecht, see also 'Über einen Aspekt der Aktualität Shakespeares' (English version, 'Theatre and Environment', *Times Literary Supplement*, 23 April 1964, p. 347), *HR*, p. 634.

121 *NDL*, p. 6.

Chapter 6 Marxism and Literary Criticism: (2) Russian Literature

1 *RR*, p. 25; *WC*, p. 229.

2 *RR*, pp. 178, 188-9, 191; *SER*, pp. 126, 136, 138.

3 *RR*, p. 25; *WC*, p. 229.

4 *RR*, p. 16.

5 An essay on Kazakievich was omitted from the 1964 edition of *Russian Realism* (*RR*, p. 5).

6 Ehrenburg was briefly criticised by Lukács during his *Linkskurve* period (*ER*, pp. 35, 46, 67; *LS*, pp. 122, 133, 155) and again in 'Die intellektuelle Physiognomie des künstlerischen Gestaltens' ('The Intellectual Physiognomy of Characterisation'), 1936 (*ER*, pp. 194-5; *WC*, pp. 186-7).

7 *HR*, p. 22; *HN*, p. 17.

8 *RR*, p. 16.

9 *RR*, p. 9.

10 *RR*, p. 11.

11 *RR*, p. 11.

12 *Die Eigenart des Ästhetischen* (*The Specific Nature of the Aesthetic*), ii, Neuwied, 1963, p. 59. In 1936, in an article on Gorky written just after that novelist's death ('Der Befreier': 'The Liberator'), Lukács repeated with apparent approval Gorky's verdict on Dostoevsky, contained in his address to the Congress of Soviet Writers in 1934. This was, that Dostoevsky justified the brutal and animal instincts of man, and (as Lukács put it) preached a spiritualised form of barbarism (*RR*, p. 289; cf. *Maxim Gorky on Literature*, Moscow, n.d., p. 246). In view of the praise that Lukács later gave to Dostoevsky, it may be assumed that his 1943 article represents his real, or at any rate an altered view.

13 'Dostojewskij', *RR*, p. 161; English translation, 'Dostoevsky', in E. San Juan (ed.), *Marxism and Human Liberation*, New York, 1973, p. 180.

14 *RR*, p. 162; *MHL*, p. 181.

15 *RR*, p. 169; *MHL*, p. 189.
16 *RR*, pp. 164, 174; *MHL*, pp. 183, 194.
17 *RR*, pp. 172 ff.; *MHL*, pp. 193 ff.
18 *RR*, pp. 172, 175; *MHL*, pp. 193, 195. *ZV*, pp. 262, 392; *Die Eigenart des Ästhetischen*, ii, p. 824.
19 *RR*, p. 14. Cf. *RR*, p. 174; *MHL*, p. 192.
20 First published in 1938. In vol. 5 of the *Werke*, the title is given as 'Tolstoy and the Problems of Realism'. Lukács also wrote an essay on 'Leo Tolstoy and Western European Literature', *RR*, pp. 262 ff.; *SER*, pp. 242 ff.
21 *RR*, pp. 192, 200-1; *SER*, pp. 140, 148.
22 *RR*, pp. 177, 189, 198; *SER*, pp. 126, 136, 145. Cf. Lenin, 'Leo Tolstoy as the Mirror of the Russian Revolution' (1908): Lenin, *Collected Works*, vol. 15 (1963), pp. 202 ff.
23 *RR*, pp. 250, 254; *SER*, pp. 194, 198.
24 *RR*, p. 191; *SER*, p. 139.
25 *RR*, pp. 215-16; *SER*, p. 162.
26 *RR*, pp. 213 ff.; *SER*, pp. 160-1.
27 *RR*, p. 246; *SER*, p. 190.
28 *RR*, p. 247; *SER*, p. 191.
29 *RR*, p. 213; *SER*, p. 159.
30 Chap. 5, secs VII-VIII. Cf. *RR*, p. 222; *SER*, p. 168.
31 *RR*, p. 224; *SER*, p. 170.
32 *RR*, pp. 225-6, 230; *SER*, pp. 171-2, 176.
33 *RR*, pp. 228-9, 232-3; *SER*, pp. 174-5, 178-9.
34 *RR*, pp. 227, 234; *SER*, pp. 173, 179.
35 *RR*, p. 16. On Tolstoy, cf. *RR*, p. 260; *SER*, p. 203.
36 This was written in 1936, and first published in 1937. Reference has already been made (n. 12) to a short article on Gorky, 'The Liberator', first published in 1936.
37 *RR*, p. 299; *SER*, p. 207.
38 *RR*, p. 14.
39 *RR*, pp. 305, 330; *SER*, pp. 212, 236.
40 *RR*, p. 303; *SER*, p. 210.
41 *RR*, p. 325; *SER*, p. 231.
42 *RR*, p. 326; *SER*, p. 232.
43 *RR*, p. 329; *SER*, p. 234.
44 *RR*, pp. 330 ff.; *SER*, pp. 236 ff.
45 *RR*, p. 332; *SER*, p. 238.
46 *RR*, p. 403.
47 *RR*, pp. 404 ff.
48 *RR*, p. 411.
49 *RR*, p. 384.

50 *RR*, p. 387.
51 *RR*, p. 386.
52 *RR*, p. 401.
53 *RR*, p. 387. Lukács discussed this novel in an essay written in 1951: *RR*, pp. 337 ff.
54 *RR*, p. 18.
55 *RR*, p. 5 (1964).
56 *RR*, p. 494.
57 *RR*, p. 496.
58 *RR*, pp. 509 ff.
59 *RR*, p. 512.
60 Ludz, *Ideologie*, pp. 658 ff. There is an abbreviated English translation in *MHL*, pp. 61 ff.
61 Ludz, *Ideologie*, p. 661; *MHL*, p. 63.
62 Ludz, *Ideologie*, p. 663; *MHL*, p. 65.
63 Lukács, 'On the Debate between China and the Soviet Union', Ludz, *Ideologie*, p. 682; *MHL*, p. 74.
64 Ludz, *Ideologie*, p. 659; *MHL*, p. 62. Cf. Ludz, *Ideologie*, p. 664.
65 Ludz, *Ideologie*, p. 664; *MHL*, p. 66. Cf. *ER*, p. 582; *MCR*, p. 118.
66 Ludz, *Ideologie*, p. 667.
67 Ludz, *Ideologie*, p. 670; *MHL*, p. 69. Cf. *ER*, p. 584; *MCR*, p. 119.
68 Ludz, *Ideologie*, p. 668. Cf. *ER*, p. 580; *MCR*, p. 117.
69 *ER*, pp. 581 ff.; *MCR*, pp. 118 ff.
70 *ER*, pp. 592 ff.; *MCR*, pp. 126 ff. See also chap. 5, sec. II.
71 *Solschenizyn*, Neuwied, 1970, p. 15; English trans., *Solzhenitsyn*, London, 1970, p. 17.
72 The essay on *One Day in the Life of Ivan Denisovich* also appears in *RR*, pp. 545 ff. References here are to the separate German edition of 1970 and to the English translation of this edition.
73 'Short story': *WC*, p. 54; *ER*, p. 635: *SER*, p. 227; *RR*, p. 320: *HN*, p. 241; *HR*, pp. 293-4. 'Novella': *S*, p. 7; *Szyn*, p. 5.
74 *HR*, p. 293; *HN*, p. 241.
75 *Szyn*, p. 6; *S*, p. 8.
76 *Szyn*, p. 6; *S*, p. 8.
77 *DL*, p. 375.
78 *Szyn*, p. 14; *S*, pp. 16-17. Cf. *Szyn*, p. 20; *S*, p. 22.
79 *Szyn*, p. 14; *S*, p. 17. Cf. *HR*, p. 262; *HN*, p. 215.
80 *Szyn*, p. 8; *S*, p. 10.
81 *Szyn*, pp. 33, 60-1, 78-9; *S*, pp. 35, 63-4, 81 ff.
82 *Szyn*, pp. 82-3; *S*, p. 86.
83 *Szyn*, p. 83; *S*, p. 87.

Notes

Chapter 7 A Marxist Philosophy of Art: *The Specific Nature of the Aesthetic* (1963)

1 Two vols, Neuwied, 1963 (*Werke*, vols xi–xii).
2 *EA*, i, p. 13.
3 A useful survey is provided by Bela Kiralyfalvi, *The Aesthetics of György Lukács*, Princeton, 1975.
4 *EA*, i, p. 20; ii, pp. 673–4.
5 *EA*, i, p. 566.
6 *EA*, ii, p. 193.
7 This is shown by the titles of such works as J. Casey, *The Language of Criticism*, London, 1966.
8 *EA*, i, pp. 17–18.
9 *EA*, i, p. 18.
10 *EA*, i, p. 14.
11 *EA*, i, pp. 25, 80, 251; ii, p. 675.
12 Lukács, 'Hegels Ästhetik' ('Hegel's Aesthetics'), *Werke*, x, p. 117. (Also in Hegel, *Ästhetik*, ii, ed. by Bassenge, Frankfurt, 1965, p. 599.)
13 On 'Absolute Mind', and Lukács' views on this, cf. chap. 3, sec. IV.
14 *EA*, i, pp. 20–2.
15 E.g. *EA*, i, pp. 352, 382–3.
16 *EA*, i, p. 352.
17 *EA*, i, pp. 22, 35, 103ff., 136.
18 Engels, on Marx's *Critique of Political Economy* (MEW, 13.475; MESW, i, pp. 338–9); *Ludwig Feuerbach* (MEW, 21.292–3; MESW, ii, p. 350). Lenin, *Materialism and Empirio-Criticism*, *Collected Works*, vol. 14, p. 302; *Philosophical Notebooks*, *Collected Works*, vol. 38, p. 372.
19 *EA*, ii, pp. 347–8; cf. *EA*, i, pp. 35, 355ff., 379; ii, p. 289.
20 *EA*, i, p. 105; cf. i, p. 377. Lukács adds later (*EA*, i, p. 439) that science did not develop directly out of magic; it developed out of handicrafts.
21 *EA*, i, p. 253; cf. i, pp. 79–80.
22 *EA*, i, pp. 219ff.
23 *EA*, i, p. 25.
24 *EA*, i, pp. 140, 182.
25 *EA*, i, p. 382.
26 *EA*, i, p. 26. Cf. i, pp. 248, 285.
27 *EA*, i, p. 26.
28 *EA*, i, p. 611; cf. i, pp. 281, 529.
29 *EA*, i, p. 529.
30 *EA*, i, pp. 26, 529, 620. Lukács also uses the phrase 'Tua res agitur': *EA*, i, p. 396; ii, p. 298.
31 *EA*, i, p. 529; ii, p. 297.
32 *EA*, i, pp. 281, 283, 298–9, 370, 430, 688–9.
33 Cf. *EA*, i, p. 411, on the 'evocative effects of thought'.

34 *EA*, i, pp. 408, 417, 678ff.
35 *EA*, ii, p. 603. Lukács quotes from a letter of Marx to his wife (21 June 1856) about her portrait.
36 *EA*, i, pp. 438, 510, 803-4.
37 *EA*, i, p. 511; ii, pp. 326-7. Cf. *Werke*, iv, p. 274, quoted in chap. 5, n. 14.
38 *EA*, i, p. 477; cf. i, p. 510.
39 *EA*, i, p. 564.
40 *EA*, i, pp. 248, 655.
41 *EA*, i, p. 248.
42 *EA*, i, p. 649.
43 *EA*, i, pp. 640, 642.
44 *EA*, i, pp. 650-51, 654ff. The topic of the 'disinterestedness' of aesthetic experience is also discussed by Lukács in *EA*, i, pp. 295ff. and ii, pp. 524ff.
45 *EA*, i, p. 784; ii, pp. 237, 241, 570, 582.
46 *EA*, i, p. 812; cf. i, p. 778.
47 *EA*, i, p. 811. The reference to Lessing is to his *Hamburgische Dramaturgie*, no. 78 (not 82, as Lukács says). On Lessing's theory of catharsis, cf. H.B. Garland, *Lessing*, 2nd edn, London, 1962, p. 71; J.G. Robertson, *Lessing's Dramatic Theory*, Cambridge, 1939, pp. 374-5.
48 *EA*, i, p. 698.
49 *EA*, i, p. 814; cf. i, p. 845.
50 *EA*, i, p. 818.
51 *EA*, i, p. 818. Cf. i, p. 825.
52 *EA*, i, p. 842.
53 *EA*, i, pp. 846, 848.
54 I have discussed this category in greater detail in my paper 'Lukács on the Central Category of Aesthetics', in G.H.R. Parkinson (ed.), *Georg Lukács: The Man, his Work and his Ideas*, London, 1970, pp. 109ff.
55 *Werke*, x, pp. 787ff.
56 *Werke*, x, p. 669; cf. *EA*, ii, pp. 206, 302, 307.
57 *Werke*, x, p. 597.
58 ME*W*, 13.631. (English trans., *Critique of Political Economy*, Moscow and London, 1971, pp. 205-6.) Lukács cites this passage in *EA*, ii, p. 201.
59 *EA*, ii, p. 205.
60 *EA*, ii, p. 206.
61 *EA*, ii, p. 244; cf. ii, pp. 302, 328.
62 *EA*, ii, p. 245.
63 *EA*, ii, p. 247. Cf. ii, pp. 197-8, in which Lukács refers to Hegel's discussion of 'sense-certainty' in the *Phenomenology* (J. Hoffmeister

(ed.), pp. 79ff.). With the point that relations are discovered, not invented, compare what is said in the next chapter (sec. II) about the 'ontological priority of the complex'.

64 *EA*, ii, p. 247.
65 Cf. *EA*, i, p. 690; ii, p. 305.
66 *EA*, ii, pp. 240-1; cf. *EA*, i, pp. 690-1.
67 *EA*, i, pp. 100, 103.
68 *EA*, i, pp. 281, 378, 382.
69 *EA*, i, pp. 132, 382.
70 *EA*, i, pp. 136-7; cf. ii, pp. 743-4.
71 *EA*, i, pp. 137-8.
72 *EA*, ii, pp. 778, 833.
73 *EA*, ii, p. 803.
74 *EA*, ii, p. 846.
75 *EA*, ii, pp. 777, 834.
76 *EA*, ii, pp. 778, 794, 834, 838.
77 *EA*, ii, pp. 816, 856, 872.
78 *EA*, i, p. 137.
79 *EA*, i, p. 382; ii, p. 703. Compare the distinction that Lukács often draws in his literary criticism (e.g. chap. 5, sec. VII) between the views that an artist presents in his work and his consciously held views.
80 *EA*, ii, p. 721. On Rembrandt, cf. ii, p. 719.
81 The relations between allegory and religious transcendence have already been mentioned in chap. 5, sec. IX, which discussed Lukács' views about Kafka.
82 *EA*, i, p. 333.
83 *EA*, i, p. 312.
84 *EA*, ii, pp. 737-8.
85 Compare Lukács' discussion of Worringer's view that art has abstraction as its end, *EA*, i, pp. 345ff.; also i, p. 477.
86 *EA*, ii, pp. 331, 339, 346.
87 *EA*, ii, pp. 330, 366, 401.
88 *EA*, ii, pp. 363-4.
89 *EA*, ii, p. 339; cf. ii, p. 340.
90 *EA*, ii, pp. 355, 363, 366-7, 378.
91 *EA*, ii, pp. 366-7.
92 *EA*, ii, pp. 360, 378.
93 *EA*, ii, pp. 367-8; cf. ii, pp. 254-5.
94 *EA*, ii, p. 368.
95 *EA*, ii, p. 395. This passage occurs in the context of a discussion of realism in music, but the connexion between realism and the type has already been noted.

Chapter 8 The Ontology of Social Existence

1 References here will be to the three chapters of the work so far published in book form:
Hegels falsche und echte Ontologie (*Hegel's True and False Ontology*), Neuwied, 1971.
Die ontologischen Grundprinzipien von Marx (*Marx's Basic Ontological Principles*), Neuwied, 1972.
Die Arbeit (*Labour*), Neuwied, 1973.

2 *MO*, pp. 11, 14.

3 Cf. chap. 4, sec. V; chap. 7, sec. II.

4 *MO*, pp. 17-19.

5 *MO*, pp. 30-1.

6 *ZV*, p. 498.

7 Cf. chap. 4, sec. II.

8 Cf. chap. 4, secs I-III, V; compare *HO*, p. 34.

9 He follows Engels in finding the second part of Hegel's logic, the doctrine of 'essence' (*Wesen*), of most value: *HO*, pp. 90 ff. Cf. Engels, to C. Schmidt, 1 Nov. 1891, ME*W*, 38.203; MESC, p. 519.

10 *HO*, pp. 58, 74, 84, 90-3.

11 *HO*, pp. 95-6, 125; cf. *A*, p. 63. Lukács states that in modern times this doctrine was first propounded by Nicolai Hartmann; see T. Pinkus (ed.), *Gespräche mit Georg Lukács* (*Conversations with Georg Lukács*), Hamburg, 1967, p. 12.

12 *HO*, p. 11.

13 *HO*, p. 13.

14 *HO*, pp. 61 ff.

15 ME*W*, 20.332, *Dialectics of Nature*, p. 46; *Ludwig Feuerbach*, ME*W*, 21.278, MES*W*, ii, p. 338.

16 See chap. 3, sec. II; cf. *HO*, p. 11, where Lukács says that the philosophers of the Enlightenment failed to grasp the principle of qualitative difference within ultimate unity.

17 *Ludwig Feuerbach*, loc. cit. Cf. ME*W*, 20.479, 483; *Dialectics of Nature*, pp. 212, 217.

18 Cf. chap. 3, sec. V.

19 *MO*, p. 39; cf. *MO*, p. 176.

20 *MO*, p. 39; cf. *MO*, p. 73. The phrase is taken by Lukács from the Introduction to Marx's *Critique of Political Economy*, ME*W*, 13.625; English trans. p. 199. This also appears as the Introduction to Marx's *Grundrisse der Kritik der politischen Ökonomie* (*Outlines of the Critique of Political Economy*), and Lukács quotes the phrase from this work (Berlin, 1953, p. 15). 'Moment' is a technical term of Hegel's logic: see his *Wissenschaft der Logik*, ed. by Lasson, Leipzig, 1923, i, pp. 93-4; trans. A.V. Miller, *Hegel's Science of Logic*, London, 1969, p. 107.

21 Cf. chap. 4, sec. IV.

22 *MO*, p. 73.

23 Cf. *HO*, pp. 105-6: if interaction is not to result in equilibrium, one 'moment' must be dominant.

24 *MO*, pp. 42, 70, 72.

25 On totality, cf. *MO*, pp. 33-4.

26 *MO*, pp. 164, 170.

27 *MO*, p. 85.

28 *MO*, pp. 85-6, 170, 172, 183. Lukács asserts (pp. 183-4) that this view was put forward by Marx, e.g. in *The Communist Manifesto*, ME*W*, 4.462; ME*SW*, i, p. 33.

29 *MO*, p. 176.

30 Ibid.

31 *Gespräche mit Georg Lukács*, p. 103.

32 *Gespräche mit Georg Lukács*, p. 105 (cf. *MO*, p. 88); Marx, *The Eighteenth Brumaire of Louis Bonaparte*, ME*W*, 8.115, ME*SW*, i, p. 225.

33 *MO*, pp. 183, 187, 189.

34 *A*, pp. 8-9, 32. On language, see also *A*, pp. 64-5.

35 *A*, p. 5; Marx, ME*W*, 13.631 ff., English trans., *Critique of Political Economy*, pp. 205 ff. Cf. chap. 7, sec. V.

36 *A*, pp. 8-9.

37 *A*, pp. 12-13; *Capital*, ME*W*, 23.193, E. and C. Paul trans., pp. 169-70.

38 *A*, p. 20; Aristotle, *Metaphysics* Z 7, 1032 a26.

39 *A*, p. 13.

40 *A*, p. 34.

41 Ibid. Compare the account (*A*, p. 20) of Aristotle's distinction between 'thinking' (noēsis) and 'making' (poiēsis) in *Metaphysics* Z 7, 1032 b15 ff.

42 *A*, p. 19. Cf. *MO*, p. 85, quoted in n.27 above.

43 *A*, p. 34; cf. *A*, p. 7.

44 *A*, pp. 33-4.

45 *A*, pp. 47, 54; cf. notes 28-31 above.

46 *A*, pp. 37, 44. Cf. *Gespräche mit Georg Lukács*, p. 105: 'If a lion mauls an antelope, that is a purely biological process, in which no alternative is present.'

47 *A*, pp. 22-3.

48 *A*, pp. 55, 59; Marx, *Capital*, ME*W*, 23.192, Paul trans., p. 169.

49 *A*, p. 59.

50 *A*, pp. 13, 61, 89. On models in relation to explanation, cf. *A*, p. 85.

51 E.g. *A*, p. 113.

52 *A*, p. 89.

53 *A*, p. 82.

54 *A*, p. 83.
55 *A*, p. 84; cf. *A*, pp. 11–12. On qualitative leaps, cf. chap. 3, sec. II.
56 *A*, pp. 65, 98.
57 *A*, p. 85.
58 *A*, pp. 92–3.
59 *A*, p. 93.
60 *A*, p. 95.
61 *A*, pp. 98–9. Cf. chap. 4, sec. I.
62 To be exact, he would probably say that the relation is one of identity and non-identity: cf. *A*, p. 89.
63 *A*, pp. 112, 117.
64 *A*, pp. 104–5, 118.
65 *A*, p. 109. Lukács is probably referring to man's mastery over himself (cf. sec. IV).
66 *A*, p. 106.
67 *A*, pp. 133–59.
68 *A*, pp. 133–4.
69 *A*, p. 135.
70 *A*, p. 139. Cf. pp. 138, 140, 147, 153.
71 *A*, p. 138.
72 ME*W*, 20.106; *AD*, p. 128. Cf. D.I. Chesnokov, *Historical Materialism*, Moscow, 1969, p. 61.
73 *Sachkenntnis*. This passage is quoted by Lukács, *A*, p. 148.
74 *Encyclopaedia*, Part I (Logic), par. 147, Addition. (English trans. by W. Wallace, *The Logic of Hegel*, Oxford, 1892, p. 269).
75 *A*, pp. 144–6. Cf. *HO*, pp. 112–13.
76 *Das Prinzip Hoffnung*, Frankfurt-am-Main, 1959, p. 271.
77 Cf. sec. III above, quoting *MO*, p. 85; also *HO*, p. 61; *A*, pp. 20, 141.
78 *A*, p. 138.
79 *A*, pp. 151, 154.
80 *A*, p. 153.
81 *A*, pp. 157–8. Cf. *A*, pp. 55, 59, discussed in sec. IV.
82 *A*, p. 158.
83 Cf. Isaiah Berlin, 'Two Concepts of Liberty' (1958), in his *Four Essays on Liberty*, Oxford, 1969, p. 131.

Bibliography

I LUKÁCS' WRITINGS

A The Collected Works Lukács' collected works (*Lukács: Werke*) are published by the Luchterhand Verlag, Neuwied. The series comprises the following volumes (volumes without dates had not been published at the time that this bibliography was compiled):

1 *Frühschriften I* (*Early Writings I*). Includes *Die Seele und die Formen* (*The Soul and the Forms*) and *Die Theorie des Romans* (*The Theory of the Novel*).
2 *Frühschriften II* (*Early Writings II*) (1968). Includes *Geschichte und Klassenbewusstsein* (*History and Class Consciousness*) and *Lenin*.
3 *Kleine Schriften* (*Shorter Works*). Includes *Skizze einer Geschichte der neueren deutschen Literatur* (*Sketch of a History of Modern German Literature*) and *Existenzialismus oder Marxismus* (*Existentialism or Marxism*).
4 *Probleme des Realismus I. Essays über Realismus* (*Problems of Realism I. Essays on Realism*) (1971). Includes essays from the *Linkskurve* (*Left Curve*) and *Wider den missverstandenen Realismus* (*The Meaning of Contemporary Realism*).
5 *Probleme des Realismus II. Der russische Realismus in der Weltliteratur* (*Problems of Realism II. Russian Realism in World Literature*) (1964).
6 *Probleme des Realismus III. Der historische Roman.* (*Problems of Realism III. The Historical Novel*) (1965). Also includes *Balzac und der französische Realismus* (*Balzac and French Realism*) and *Fauststudien* (*Faust Studies*).
7 *Deutsche Literatur in zwei Jahrhunderten* (*Two Centuries of German Literature*) (1964). Includes *Goethe und seine Zeit* (*Goethe and his Age*),

Deutsche Realisten des 19. Jahrhunderts (German Realists of the 19th Century) and Thomas Mann.

8 Der junge Hegel (The Young Hegel) (1967).

9 Die Zerstörung der Vernunft (The Destruction of Reason) (1962).

10 Probleme der Ästhetik (Problems of Aesthetics) (1969). Includes essays on the history of aesthetics, and Über die Besonderheit als Kategorie der Ästhetik (On Speciality as a Category of Aesthetics).

11-12 Die Eigenart des Ästhetischen (The Specific Nature of the Aesthetic) (1963).

13-14 Zur Ontologie des gesellschaftlichen Seins (The Ontology of Social Existence).

15 Prolegomena zur Ontologie des gesellschaftlichen Seins (Prolegomena to an Ontology of Social Existence).

16 Frühe Schriften zur Ästhetik I. Heidelberger Philosophie der Kunst, 1912-14 (Early Writings on Aesthetics I. The Heidelberg Philosophy of Art, 1912-14) (1974).

17 Frühe Schriften zur Ästhetik II. Heidelberger Ästhetik, 1916-18 (Early Writings on Aesthetics II. The Heidelberg Aesthetics, 1916-18) (1975).

B Separate Editions   The following works of Lukács have been published separately in forms that are more convenient, and less expensive, than that of the collected works. The publisher is in each case Luchterhand, Neuwied; many of the volumes appear in the series 'Sammlung Luchterhand' (abbreviated, SL).

Ästhetik I-IV (Aesthetics I-IV) (1972) (SL, 63-4, 70-71). (An abridged version of Die Eigenart des Ästhetischen).

Geschichte und Klassenbewusstsein (1970) (SL, 11).

Lenin (1967).

Zur Ontologie des gesellschaftlichen Seins (excerpts):

Hegels falsche und echte Ontologie (Hegel's true and false Ontology) (1971) (SL, 49).

Die ontologischen Grundprinzipien von Marx (Marx's basic ontological principles) (1972) (SL, 86).

Die Arbeit (Labour) (1973) (SL, 92).

Die Seele und die Formen (1971) (SL, 21).

Skizze einer Geschichte der neueren deutschen Literatur (1965).

Solschenizyn (Solzhenitsyn) (1970) (SL, 28).

Taktik und Ethik (Tactics and Ethics) (1975) (SL, 39).

Die Theorie des Romans (3rd edn, 1965). (Also published as SL, 36, 1971.)

Über die Besonderheit als Kategorie der Ästhetik (1967).

Mention may also be made of the following useful collections:

P. Ludz (ed.), Georg Lukács: Schriften zur Literatursoziologie (Georg Lukács: Writings on the Sociology of Literature), Luchterhand, Neuwied, 1961.

Bibliography

P. Ludz (ed.), *Georg Lukács: Schriften zur Ideologie und Politik* (*Georg Lukács: Writings on Ideology and Politics*), Luchterhand, Neuwied, 1967.
The following volume is outside the framework of Lukács' collected works:
T. Pinkus (ed.), *Gespräche mit Georg Lukács* (*Conversations with Georg Lukács*), Rowohlt, Hamburg, 1967.
The most extensive bibliography of Lukács' works is that by Jürgen Hartmann, in F. Benseler (ed.), *Festschrift zum achtzigsten Geburtstag von Georg Lukács* (*A Festschrift for Georg Lukács' 80th Birthday*), Luchterhand, Neuwied, 1965, pp. 625-96.

C *English Translations* *Essays on Thomas Mann*, trans. by S. Mitchell, Merlin Press, London, 1964.
Georg Lukács: Political Writings 1919-29, trans. by M. McColgan, New Left Books, London, 1972. (Includes not only political writings, such as 'Tactics and Ethics', but also works of a more philosophical kind, such as Lukács' essay on Moses Hess.)
Goethe and his Age, trans. by R. Anchor, Merlin Press, London, 1968.
The Historical Novel, trans. by H. and S. Mitchell, Merlin Press, London, 1962.
History and Class Consciousness, trans. by R. Livingstone, Merlin Press, London, 1971.
Lenin, trans. by N. Jacobs, New Left Books, London, 1970.
Marxism and Human Liberation, ed. by E. San Juan, Dell, New York, 1973. (A collection of previously published translations, by various writers, of articles and chapters by Lukács.)
The Meaning of Contemporary Realism, trans. by J. and N. Mander, Merlin Press, London, 1963.
Solzhenitsyn, trans. by W.D. Graf, Merlin Press, London, 1970.
Soul and Form, trans. by A. Bostock, Merlin Press, London, 1974.
Studies in European Realism, trans. by E. Bone, Grosset and Dunlap, New York, 1964; Merlin Press, London, 1972. (A translation of *Balzac und der französische Realismus* and parts of *Der russische Realismus in der Weltliteratur*.)
The Theory of the Novel, trans. by A. Bostock, Merlin Press, London, 1971.
Writer and Critic, trans. by A. Kahn, Merlin Press, London, 1970. (Selections from Lukács' literary criticism, chiefly from *Werke*, vol. 4.)
The Young Hegel, trans. by R. Livingstone, Merlin Press, London, 1975.

II WORKS ON LUKÁCS

The literature on Lukács is very considerable. Useful bibliographies are to be found in P. Ludz, *Georg Lukács: Schriften zur Literatursoziologie* (cf. part IB of

Bibliography

this bibliography) and in the works by Hanak and Mészáros cited below. The list that follows covers all books by Lukács published in English, and a few of those published in French or German.

Bourdet, Y., *Figures de Lukács (Aspects of Lukács)*, Éditions Anthropos, Paris, 1972. Includes essays on Lukács' exile in Vienna, and on Lukács in relation to Mann's *The Magic Mountain*.

Goldmann, L., *Lukács et Heidegger*, Éditions Denoël, Paris, 1973. Fragments on the relations between Lukács and Heidegger, edited after the author's death by Y. Ishaghpour.

Hanak, T., *Lukács war anders (Lukács was Different)*, Anton Hain, Meisenheim, 1973. A well-documented biography, which argues that Lukács' career was not the unity that it is often thought to be.

Kiralyfalvi, B., *The Aesthetics of György Lukács*, Princeton University Press, 1975. An elementary introduction to Lukács' Marxist aesthetics; its value to the average student is lessened by the fact that references are given, not to the German text of Lukács' works, but to Hungarian translations.

Lichtheim, G., *Lukács* (Fontana Modern Masters), Fontana/Collins, London, 1970. The author had a high reputation as a historian of Marxist thought, but this little book on Lukács gives the impression of being a perfunctory piece of work.

Matzner, J. (ed.), *Lehrstück Lukács (A Lukács Study)*, Suhrkamp, Frankfurt, 1974. Includes essays by L. Goldmann on Lukács as an essayist and on *The Theory of the Novel*, and by W. Mittenzwei on the Brecht-Lukács controversy.

Mészáros, I., *Lukács' Concept of Dialectic*, Merlin Press, London, 1972. A reissue of a paper contained in Parkinson (see below), with some supplementary material, including valuable biographical data.

Parkinson, G.H.R. (ed.), *Georg Lukács: The Man, his Work and his Ideas*, Weidenfeld & Nicolson, London, 1970. Contains papers by I. Mészáros, H.A. Hodges and G.H.R. Parkinson on Lukács' philosophy, and by R. Pascal, A.G. Lehmann, D. Craig and S. Mitchell on his literary criticism.

Raddatz, F.J., *Georg Lukács in Selbstzeugnissen und Bilddokumenten (Georg Lukács: A Pictorial Biography)*, Rowohlt, Hamburg, 1972.

Zitta, V., *Georg Lukács' Marxism: Alienation, Dialectics, Revolution*, Nijhoff, The Hague, 1964. A fiercely polemical work, contributing little or nothing to an understanding of Lukács' thought.

A number of journals have produced Lukács issues, of which the following may be mentioned:

Cambridge Review, 28 January 1972, pp. 85ff. *Georg Lukács: A Symposium*.
New Hungarian Quarterly, XIII, no. 47, Autumn 1972.
The Philosophical Forum (Boston, Mass.), vol. III, 3-4, 1972.

Bibliography

Revue Internationale de Philosophie (Brussels), 1973, no. 106.

Telos (St Louis, Missouri), no. 10, 1971. Includes a long essay by D. Kettler, 'Culture and Revolution: Lukács in the Hungarian Revolutions of 1918/19', which is a revised version of a work first published in German as *Marxismus und Kultur*, Neuwied, 1967.

Telos, no. 11, 1972.

Index

Index

Index